The Emergence of Entrepreneurship Policy

Governance, Start-ups, and Growth in the U.S. Knowledge Economy

Edited by

DAVID M. HART

Harvard University

CAMBRIDGE
UNIVERSITY PRESS

CAMBRIDGE UNIVERSITY PRESS
Cambridge, New York, Melbourne, Madrid, Cape Town, Singapore,
São Paulo, Delhi, Dubai, Tokyo

Cambridge University Press
32 Avenue of the Americas, New York, NY 10013-2473, USA

www.cambridge.org
Information on this title: www.cambridge.org/9780521124188

© David M. Hart 2003

First published 2003
Reprinted 2007
This digitally printed version 2009

A catalog record for this publication is available from the British Library

Library of Congress Cataloging in Publication data

The emergence of entrepreneurship policy : governance, start-ups, and growth in the
US knowledge economy / edited by David M. Hart.
p. cm.
"This project originated in a conference co-sponsored by the National Commission on
Entrepreneurship and the Kennedy School's Center for Business and Government,
which was held at the Kennedy School on April 10–11, 2001" –Editor's note.
Includes bibliographical references and index.
ISBN 0-521-82677-2
1. High technology industries – Government policy – United States – Congresses.
2. Entrepreneurship – Government policy – United States – Congresses.
3. Knowledge management – United States – Congresses. I. Hart, David M., 1961–
HC110.H53E45 2003
338'.04'0973–dc21 2002041554

ISBN 978-0-521-82677-8 Hardback
ISBN 978-0-521-12418-8 Paperback

of Entre

This volume seeks to catalyze the emergence of a new field of policy studies: entrepreneurship policy. Practical experience and academic research both point to the central role of entrepreneurs in the process of economic growth and to the importance of public policy in creating the conditions under which entrepreneurial companies can flourish. The contributors, who hail from the disciplines of economics, geography, history, law, management, and political science, seek to crystallize key findings and to stimulate debate about future opportunities for policy-makers and researchers in this area. The chapters include surveys of the economic, social, and cultural contexts for U.S. entrepreneurship policy; assessments of regional efforts to link knowledge producers to new enterprises; explorations of policies that aim to foster entrepreneurship in under-represented communities; detailed analyses of three key industries (biotechnology, e-commerce, and telecommunications); and considerations of challenges in policy implementation.

David M. Hart is Associate Professor of Public Policy at the John F. Kennedy School of Government, Harvard University, and author of *Forged Consensus: Science, Technology, and Economic Policy in the U.S., 1921–1953* (1998). He is currently at work on a book about the role of the high-technology industry in American politics since 1970. Professor Hart has published widely in the fields of science and technology policy and political science. His recent publications include contributions to the 2002 edition of Allen Cigler and Burdette Loomis' *Interest Group Politics* and to *Constructing Corporate America* (Kenneth Lipartito and David Sicilia, editors) and single-authored articles in *Science and Public Policy, Research Policy,* and *Journal of Politics.* Professor Hart serves on the Whitehead Institute's task force on genetics and public policy, the U.S.–China seminar on science and technology policy, and the academic advisory board of the Center for Science, Policy, and Outcomes.

Contents

Editor's Acknowledgments

This project originated in a conference cosponsored by the National Commission on Entrepreneurship and the Kennedy School's Center for Business and Government (CBG), which was held at the Kennedy School on April 10 and 11, 2001. I am particularly grateful to Ira Jackson, then director of the CBG, for offering me the opportunity to take on the project, and I wish him well in his new life in a different rat race. I would also like to thank the staff at the National Commission for their unfailing good humor and effort, the Ewing Marion Kauffman Foundation for its financial support, and Scott Parris at Cambridge University Press for his responsiveness and good counsel. The contributors to this volume have been a source of assistance and advice as well as scholarship. Finally, Lois Frankel and Eleanor Frankel Hart (who arrived while the conference was being planned) get loads of credit for being there when I needed them.

Contributors

David B. Audretsch holds the Ameritech Chair of Economic Development and is the director of the Institute for Development Strategies at Indiana University.

Philip E. Auerswald is Assistant Professor of Public Policy at George Mason University.

Timothy Bates is Distinguished Professor of Labor and Urban Affairs at Wayne State University.

Lewis M. Branscomb is Aetna Professor Emeritus of Public Management at the Kennedy School of Government, Harvard University.

Candida G. Brush is Associate Professor of Strategy and Policy, director of the Council for Women's Entrepreneurship and Leadership, and research director for the Entrepreneurial Management Institute at Boston University.

Nancy M. Carter holds the Richard M. Schulze Chair in Entrepreneurship at the University of St. Thomas.

Maryann P. Feldman is Associate Professor of Business Economics, Rotman School of Management, University of Toronto.

Richard Florida is the Heinz Professor of Regional Economic Development and codirector of the Software Industry Center, Carnegie Mellon University.

Doris Freedman is director of the National Commission on Entrepreneurship.

Elizabeth Gatewood holds the Jack M. Gill Chair of Entrepreneurship and is director of the Johnson Center for Entrepreneurship and Innovation at Indiana University.

Patricia G. Greene holds the Ewing Marion Kauffman/Missouri Chair in Entrepreneurial Leadership at the University of Missouri and is executive director of the Entrepreneurial Growth Resource Center.

David M. Hart is Associate Professor of Public Policy at the Kennedy School of Government, Harvard University.

Myra M. Hart is MBA Class of 1961 Professor of Management Practice at Harvard Business School, Harvard University.

Viktor Mayer-Schönberger is Assistant Professor of Public Policy at the Kennedy School of Government, Harvard University.

Eli M. Noam is Professor of Economics and director of the Institute of Tele-Information at Columbia University.

Erik R. Pages, formerly a policy director for the National Commission on Entrepreneurship, is President of Entre Works Consulting.

Michael E. Porter is University Professor at Harvard University and directs the Institute for Strategy and Competitiveness at Harvard Business School.

Nathan Rosenberg is Professor of Economics at Stanford University.

Andrew A. Toole is Assistant Professor of Economics at Illinois State University.

Patrick Von Bargen, formerly executive director of the National Commission on Entrepreneurship, is Managing Executive for Policy and Staff at the Securities and Exchange Commission.

PART ONE

THE ENTREPRENEURIAL SOCIETY

What's Governance Got to Do with It?

1

Entrepreneurship Policy

What It Is and Where It Came from

David M. Hart

Entrepreneurship was in vogue in the 1990s. Best-selling books and feature-length movies documented the trials and tribulations of trendy start-up companies, complete with foosball tables and macaws-in-residence. Twenty-somethings worth billions on paper partied with Hollywood stars and were feted by Washington pols. After the dotcom bubble burst in 2000, turning a lot of that paper into confetti, the cultural fascination with entrepreneurship faded. The old brand names of corporate America, by and large, regained their places in the consciousness of consumers and investors. As 2001 closed, the autobiography of General Electric CEO Jack Welch topped business book buyers' Christmas lists; one can be confident that neither "foosball" nor "macaw" appears in the index of *Jack: Straight from the Gut.*

But appearances can be deceptive. The entrepreneurship fad rested on a foundation of fact. New companies have made significant contributions to economic growth in the past decade, both directly and by stimulating their more established competitors, as they indeed had in the decades before that. If the fad exaggerated these contributions, its fading should not obscure them entirely. Entrepreneurship is an economic phenomenon worthy of attention from those who worry about

Thanks to Maryann Feldman, Erik Pages, and Candy Brush for their comments on this chapter and to the Center for Business and Government (especially its director, Ira Jackson) and the National Commission on Entrepreneurship for their support of this project.

economic growth and particularly from those charged with sustaining that growth.

Such, in any case, is the premise of this volume. The contributors collectively assert that the level and quality of entrepreneurship make a difference in the economic vitality of communities, regions, industries, and the nation as a whole. We argue that policymakers may be able to enhance the economy by enhancing entrepreneurship, although we are hardly uniform in our assessment of how to go about trying. What matters most at this point is that the policy community not toss out the entrepreneurship baby with the dot-com bathwater. Entrepreneurship ought to be an explicit focus of policy design, choice, and implementation. Analysts can and should do a much better job of assisting policymakers in making it so.

The term "entrepreneurship policy" is intended to capture this concept.[1] The domain of entrepreneurship policy is large. It encompasses activities at several levels of government, from local to national (and perhaps beyond). It bears on low-technology economic activity as well as high-technology (although the latter is emphasized here). It includes governance capacities more familiar under other headings, ranging from regulatory policy to economic development partnerships to poverty alleviation, along with some capacities that are new.

A modest volume like this one cannot comprehensively survey the myriad facets of this sprawling domain. Nor, given the inchoate state of scholarship, does it make much sense to attempt to establish a consensus about what entrepreneurship policy ought to be. We aspire merely to crystallize the idea of entrepreneurship policy and to illustrate its significance. If a lively national conversation about the interaction between public policy and entrepreneurship ensues (and even if we receive some brickbats in the process), we will have accomplished our main objective.

We have good reason to believe that the ground for such a discussion remains fertile, the boom and bust of the 1990s notwithstanding. U.S. policymakers, particularly at the state and local levels, have been groping toward an explicit entrepreneurship policy for at least a couple of

---

[1] "Entrepreneurship policy" is a concept and a phrase whose time seems to have come. Although rarely used in the past, it has begun to achieve modest prominence, particularly in Europe. See Lundstrom and Stevenson (2001); European Commission (2003).

decades. Their experiments have typically been pragmatic, inspired by immediate needs and pressures and by one another's examples, rather than by a grand theoretical design. Scholars have come to the subject more recently (with the exception of a few pioneers, some of whom are contributors to this volume, who have been exploring this terrain for many years). A number of disciplines, each with its own distinctive history, style, and language, have now converged on it, and their interaction promises to add momentum to all.

In the rest of this introductory chapter, I sketch out the domain of entrepreneurship policy more fully, defining crucial terms and situating the contents of this volume in a variety of contexts, including the international comparative context. I also lay out one version of what might ultimately be called the "prehistory" of entrepreneurship policy in the United States. I conclude by mapping out the rest of the volume.

ENTREPRENEURSHIP: A NARROW DEFINITION

"Entrepreneur," "entrepreneurial," and the like have become highly desirable labels in recent years, so much so that the definition of entrepreneurship has blurred nearly beyond recognition. Public agencies are urged by advocates of reinventing government to become more entrepreneurial. The founders of nonprofit service delivery and advocacy groups call themselves "social entrepreneurs." "Intrapreneurs" challenge large corporations to adopt new ways of doing things.

None of these neologisms is relevant to "entrepreneurship policy" as the phrase is employed in this volume. As will be seen, we adopt a dangerously broad definition of "policy," but by "entrepreneurship" we mean (with the inevitable few exceptions) the processes of starting and continuing to expand new businesses. Our vision of these processes derives from Joseph A. Schumpeter, who conceived of the entrepreneurial venture as "the fundamental engine that sets and keeps the capitalist engine in motion" by creating new goods, inventing new methods of production, devising new business models, and opening new markets (Schumpeter 1942, 83). Entrepreneurship policy aims to foster a socially optimal level of such venturing. Usually (although this need not necessarily be the case), policymakers seek to raise the level of entrepreneurship; entrepreneurship policy thus bears not only on actual entrepreneurs but also on "nascent" entrepreneurs, who are seriously considering starting a firm (Reynolds et al. 2000).

Entrepreneurial ventures are not the same as small businesses, and entrepreneurship policy is therefore distinct from small business policy. Although many entrepreneurial ventures are small, they can be quite large in lines of business like airlines and telephony where the minimum efficient scale of operation is large. On the other hand, the well-established neighborhood restaurant or dry cleaner, although small, falls outside the definition. The distinguishing elements of entrepreneurship are novelty and dynamism. The phrase "continuing to expand" is essential to the definition, even though it creates serious difficulties for measurement and analysis.[2]

As Schumpeter suggests, technological innovation is a particularly important mechanism through which entrepreneurial ventures express their novelty and dynamism. Its importance stems in large part from the contribution that new technologies make to economic growth. Whether by saving capital, labor, or natural resources or by creating new capabilities, technological innovation expands the potential output of the economy, rather than simply shifting economic activity from one enterprise to another. Writing in 1940, Schumpeter predicted that the innovation process would be routinized in large, stable enterprises, but this prediction has not been fully realized. New entrants seem to be important catalysts of technological innovation, even when they prove to be business failures, as they often do (Scherer 1992; Utterback 1994). Older firms are forced to adapt under the pressure of innovative rivals, lest they be replaced. The current interactions between traditional retailers and electronic commerce start-ups and between large pharmaceutical firms and biotechnology start-ups illustrate some of the potential patterns.

Economic globalization heightens the importance of technology-based entrepreneurship for the contemporary United States, as David Audretsch points out in his chapter and elsewhere (Audretsch and

---

[2] Some researchers, following the lead of David Birch, address this difficulty by focusing on "gazelles," publicly traded companies that have grown at an annual average compound rate of 20 percent or more for the previous four years.

Thurik 2001). The country cannot and should not compete internationally on the basis of labor costs. Huge pools of low-cost labor in developing countries are becoming available for export production, and they are likely to continue to grow in the coming years. U.S. competitive advantage lies in the creation and rapid exploitation of new ideas, whether for products, services, or productivity improvements. The term "knowledge economy" in this volume's title signals this emphasis in the selection of contributions.

The knowledge economy, let me be clear, is only an emphasis and not an exclusive focus of this volume and of the field of entrepreneurship policy that we hope it will help to spawn. Entrepreneurship policy strategies that target lower-technology entrepreneurial ventures may well be appropriate for particular jurisdictions. Analyses using aggregate data on entrepreneurship may shed light particularly on such strategies and ventures, since they vastly outnumber their high-tech brethren. The definition of entrepreneurship offered here embraces all businesses that are new and dynamic, regardless of size or line of business, while excluding businesses that are neither new nor dynamic as well as all nonbusiness organizations.

PUBLIC POLICY AND GOVERNANCE WITHIN THE CONTEXT FOR ENTREPRENEURSHIP

The determinants of entrepreneurship, entrepreneurial success, and the impacts of entrepreneurship on society are the subjects of a growing body of research, primarily in the disciplines of economics, geography, management, psychology, and sociology.[3] Early work in the field concentrated on the qualities of entrepreneurs as individuals and the business strategies that they employed. Recent work has sought to integrate this understanding of the "supply" of entrepreneurs and entrepreneurial strategies with an analysis of the "demand" for entrepreneurial ventures or, more broadly, the "opportunity structure" or "context" for entrepreneurship (Aldrich and Wiedenmayer 1993; Thornton 1999).

---

[3] My own field of political science is notably absent from this area of social science research.

The context for entrepreneurship includes a wide range of economic, social, and cultural factors. General economic conditions and the availability of such resources as financial capital, intellectual property protection, and specialized skills are clearly important. So too are the density and intensity of competition within the nascent entrepreneur's chosen market. The legitimacy of the potential venture – whether it conforms to well-understood and well-accepted social and cultural norms – may influence its viability, success, and impact as well. The availability of specialized information may determine whether entrepreneurs are able to recognize and act on potential opportunities (Aldrich and Fiol 1994; Shane and Venkataraman 2000).[4]

Public policy and governance can shape virtually all the contextual determinants of the demand for entrepreneurship and, over a longer time scale, the supply of entrepreneurs as well. Public policy and governance, as these terms are employed in this volume, refer to intertwined but distinct processes. Public policy means the intentional use of the powers of government to effect a societal outcome, like a change in the number of entrepreneurial ventures. Governance refers to conscious collective action that extends beyond government, deploying, for instance, the capacities of businesses, community groups, and academic institutions to bring about such an outcome. Entrepreneurship policy often aims to catalyze better governance, for instance, by fostering networks of potential customers and service providers, the presence of which reduces the uncertainty facing nascent entrepreneurs.

Not all public policy that shapes the context for entrepreneurship and the supply of potential entrepreneurs is entrepreneurship policy, as we use the term here. Education policy, for instance, may influence the legitimacy of entrepreneurial ventures and the knowledge, skills, and networks possessed by individuals and social groups. Macroeconomic policy, to take another example, affects short-term capital availability and the conditions of international trade. All these policy outcomes contribute to the context for entrepreneurship. This volume, however, concentrates on policy that can have an impact within a period

---

[4] This paragraph illustrates, rather than exhausts, the list of contextual factors that may affect entrepreneurship.

of years on what the 2001 *Global Entrepreneurship Monitor* (*GEM*) labels "intermediate conditions" for entrepreneurship, rather than education policy and the like, which influence "background conditions" over a decade or more, or macroeconomic and associated policies that shape "short-term conditions" on a monthly basis (Reynolds et al. 2001).[5]

The reader should not draw the conclusion that areas of public policy and governance omitted from our definition of entrepreneurship policy are unimportant. Indeed, a growing body of research suggests that background conditions are especially important in explaining differences in levels of entrepreneurship and economic development across countries over long periods of time. Systems of property rights, for instance, which provide the fundamental legal underpinnings of markets, profoundly structure investment and risk-taking behavior. There are complex feedbacks between legal systems, cultures, institutional development, and economic change that warrant further attention from scholars and practitioners alike. U.S. institutions, viewed at this high level of abstraction, are quite supportive of entrepreneurship (Rosenberg and Birdzell 1986; North 1994).

Our limitation of the scope of entrepreneurship policy by reference to intermediate conditions is largely pragmatic. Since the contributions to this volume are confined to a single country, background conditions do not vary very much. More important, the time scale on which intermediate conditions can change allows policymakers the possibility of perceiving (and perhaps taking credit for) the consequences of their efforts. This definition also permits us to take for granted some well-established boundaries among policy domains, like education and macroeconomic policy, for which entrepreneurship is not generally a driving consideration. Without such boundaries, there is a danger that entrepreneurship policy will simply encompass all of public policy and thus lose its meaning. As *GEM* puts it, "the more careful the analysis, the more complex the entrepreneurial process appears to be"; the same could be said of the linkages between entrepreneurial and policy processes (Reynolds et al. 2001, 23).

---

[5] One of the inevitable exceptions to this statement that merits note is the discussion of entrepreneurial education programs in the chapter by Pages, Freedman, and Von Bargen.

ENTREPRENEURSHIP POLICY BY OTHER NAMES: A BRIEF HISTORICAL OUTLINE

Entrepreneurship policy and related processes of governance for our purposes, then, are not unlimited in scope, but they nonetheless encompass quite a bit. They are carried out at the local, regional, state, and national levels within the United States. The specific capacities of government and its partners in governance that are deployed to foster entrepreneurship vary as substantially as the communities and economic activities they seek to influence. Some of these capacities are quite old, whereas others have risen afresh in just the past few years. We hope to knit these diverse threads together conceptually to form the fabric of entrepreneurship policy.

The Federal Level

Perhaps the most obvious place to begin a survey of what we hope our new rubric will embrace is the Sherman Antitrust Act, which was passed by the U.S. Congress in 1890. It is this legislation more than any other single entrepreneurship policy measure that distinguishes the United States from other industrial countries historically. The Sherman Act was the culmination of years of popular agitation sparked by the perception that large firms were becoming dominant in the economy. It restricted the behavior of these firms in part to preserve opportunities for entrepreneurship, although it is important to acknowledge other motives behind the antitrust movement, including protectionism (with respect to existing small town businesses) and moral outrage (at the power wielded by the captains of industry). Over more than a century of development of antitrust law and policy, the entrepreneurship motivation has endured, and the analysis of barriers to entry and how they are maintained remain at its center (Hart 2001a).

Federal regulatory policy also intersects significantly with entrepreneurship. Economic regulation, such as that imposed on the energy, communications, transportation, and financial sectors, was initially oriented toward stability, reliability, and coordination, virtues thought to inhere in monopolistic or oligopolistic industrial structures. Regulatory policy as it was implemented through most of the twentieth century thus discouraged entrepreneurship. On the other hand, the architects of "deregulation" over the past quarter century (which might, as Viktor Mayer-Schönberger describes in his chapter, more appropriately be labeled "regulatory restructuring") have sometimes explicitly sought to expand entrepreneurial opportunities in regulated sectors. Eli Noam's chapter on entrepreneurship in telecommunications describes one particularly vivid chapter in this story.

The constraints imposed on established firms by antitrust and regulatory policy have been paralleled by a set of federal policies intended, at least by some accounts, to support entrepreneurial ventures. The intellectual property rights regime, for instance, has been tightened steadily since the 1970s, so that rights-holders have become more likely to win protection and to prevail in court. New sorts of products and processes, ranging from life forms to business methods, have become patentable, and software and other new digital forms of expression can be copyrighted. Universities and other recipients of federal research and development (R&D) funding have been encouraged to seek intellectual property protection for findings made with federal support and permitted to offer exclusive licenses to exploit them. These protections have provided the asset base for many recent entrepreneurial ventures.

Financial incentives for entrepreneurship have also been forthcoming from federal policymakers. Modest direct subsidies for entrepreneurial ventures have been made available through, for instance, the government-wide Small Business Innovation Research (SBIR) program and the Commerce Department's Advanced Technology Program. More significant are preferential procurement programs that have channeled money from federal projects to small businesses and to businesses owned by women, minorities, and other groups historically underrepresented in the entrepreneurial community (although not all the recipients necessarily meet our definition of an entrepreneurial venture). Federal loan guarantee programs encourage private lenders to do business with such firms as well. Changes in the U.S. tax code, such as fluctuations in the treatment of capital gains, have affected the availability of equity financing for entrepreneurial ventures. Federal rules governing investment also have such effects on occasion; a 1979 rule change that permitted pension funds to place a small portion of their assets in high-risk investments, for example, contributed significantly to the expansion of the venture capital industry, which in turn has fueled entrepreneurship.

Relatively few federal entrepreneurship policy measures have had impacts as unambiguous as this rule change. More often, the consequences for entrepreneurship continue to be debated, sometimes hotly. Early antitrust policy, for instance, probably facilitated rather than slowed the concentration of industry. Stronger intellectual property laws may have provided more new avenues for incumbents to entrench themselves than opportunities for start-ups to create defensible positions. Subsidies like SBIR may provide life support to firms that are not viable (Wallsten 1998). Moreover, the various areas of policy-making touched on here are typically not coordinated, and the resulting policies may even pull in opposite directions. All the more reason, then, to try to conceptualize and analyze entrepreneurship policy as a whole and perhaps to move toward making it in the same fashion.

State, Regional, and Local Initiatives

If one dates federal entrepreneurship policy from the passage of the Sherman Act, it has been in force for more than a century. Comparable activities at other levels of government have a more recent provenance, but they have often been more explicitly oriented toward fostering entrepreneurship than federal policy. The "entrepreneurial state," to use Peter K. Eisinger's characterization, arose in the 1980s as a response to the perception that established state, regional, and local economic development models, especially "smokestack-chasing" (that is, offering incentives for firms from outside the jurisdiction to locate facilities there), were no longer effective in an age of rapid technological innovation, global economic integration, and federal downsizing (Eisinger 1988). States, regions, and localities, advocates for new forms of economic development policy argued, would have to "grow their own" economic base. The example of Silicon Valley, with its knowledge-based economy powered by research universities, start-up companies, and supporting services, loomed large in many of these discussions. Several streams of policy experimentation emerged from this conversation that continue today.[6]

---

[6] For further details and a contrasting perspective on state and local development policy efforts, the reader need look no further than the chapter by Pages, Freedman, and Von Bargen.

The challenges facing subnational economies in the United States vary substantially; entrepreneurship policy naturally reflects this variation. Strategies for nurturing knowledge creation, for instance, range from "making the peaks higher"[7] where centers of academic excellence already exist to starting from scratch where they are absent. California, for instance, is making substantial investments in university-based institutes in such fields as biotechnology, information technology, and telecommunications that will supplement the substantial federal R&D funding that nourishes the state's world-leading centers of high-technology entrepreneurship. Georgia, by contrast, has made extensive efforts to build a competitive university system from a very weak foundation. An important element of the state's program is the Georgia Research Alliance, a public-private partnership that spent $242 million in state funds and $65 million in private funds during the 1990s, in an effort "to foster economic development . . . by developing and leveraging the research capabilities of the research universities" (Georgia Research Alliance 1999).

As the term "leveraging" in the Georgia Research Alliance's mission statement highlights, knowledge creation alone does not necessarily lead to entrepreneurship. Subnational governments in the United States use a variety of policy instruments to facilitate the movement of knowledge out of academia and into start-up and growth businesses. Some sponsor facilities such as incubators and science parks in which these firms can locate their offices and operations. University technology transfer offices, many of which are entities of state government, oversee the licensing of intellectual property rights from campus research; increasingly, they are willing to exchange these rights for equity stakes in entrepreneurial ventures. A number of states have created venture capital funds (often with investments from state university endowments), the most successful of which specialize in seed funding, a stage at which private venture funds are typically reluctant to invest (Plosila 2001).

Another set of initiatives at the state, regional, and local levels aims to provide business services and networking opportunities to

---

[7] This quotation, attributed to Wickliffe Rose, summarized the early investment strategy of the Rockefeller Foundation, which seeded American research universities in the first half of the twentieth century, before the advent of large-scale federal R&D funding.

entrepreneurs, whether affiliated with universities or not. The federal-state Manufacturing Extension Partnership, for instance, has outposts in all fifty states that disseminate best practices among small manufacturing firms (although these firms are not exclusively entrepreneurial ventures) and link them to a range of service providers (Shapira 1998). Subnational governments commonly seek as well to identify emerging clusters of industrial activity and to catalyze the development of industry-wide institutions that foster connections within the cluster and articulate its needs; these processes often clarify and enhance opportunities for entrepreneurship (Porter 1990; 1997). Broader strategies for attracting and retaining talented people by enhancing the quality of life, like the investment in its creative community of Austin, Texas, may also have important consequences for entrepreneurship (Watson 2001).

Finally, policymakers concerned about distressed communities have sometimes sought to rely on entrepreneurship as a tool for alleviating poverty. Michael E. Porter of the Harvard Business School, for example, stirred significant controversy with a 1995 article articulating "The Competitive Advantages of the Inner City," and his Initiative for a Competitive Inner City is working with city officials around the United States to implement entrepreneurship-oriented strategies (Porter 1995). Some programs (for instance, in the welfare-to-work and microenterprise areas) even seek to make entrepreneurs out of the nation's most disadvantaged citizens, although whether entrepreneurship motivated by necessity (as opposed to entrepreneurship motivated by opportunity (see Reynolds 2001)) ought to be conceived of as a mechanism of economic growth is unclear.

DOES ENTREPRENEURSHIP POLICY PRODUCE ENTREPRENEURSHIP?

Entrepreneurship policy is the sum of all the often uncoordinated and sometimes poorly designed activities illustrated in the previous section. The nascent entrepreneur faces a series of discrete choices on the path to organizing a functioning firm, and so totals the impact of assistance flowing from government and governance on a single bottom line, whether that assistance appears in the form of a loan or subsidy, a contribution to social or intellectual capital, or a constraint on a future competitor. She may not even recognize public policy as the ultimate source of some forms of assistance, such as ideas developed by academic scientists with the support of government research funds or government guarantees that facilitate loans made by private financial institutions.

In any event, it is possible that the entry on her ledger for entrepreneurship policy – even if accounted for accurately – is but a pittance (Bhide 2000). The context for entrepreneurship is complex and encompasses far more than public policy and governance. Background conditions, such as the educational and demographic profile of a jurisdiction and its institutional endowment, may be strongly self-reinforcing, whether in the direction of spurring entrepreneurship (as in the case of well-known high-technology regions) or not (as some declining areas know all too well). Short-term conditions, like interest rates and capital availability, can also be powerful influences on entrepreneurial decision-making, although over the course of an economic cycle, the immediate stimuli and deterrents to entrepreneurship ought to roughly balance out. Even within the intermediate time frame on which we focus our attention, there are many forces immune from manipulation by entrepreneurship policymakers. Industries rise and decline; potential key customers display strategic brilliance or blunder; new technologies take off or peter out. Natural disasters and acts of war happen.

The impact of entrepreneurship policy on entrepreneurship surely is swamped sometimes by other factors, perhaps even much of the time and in many places and sectors. A certain skepticism for the concept is warranted. But the skeptics ought to be open-minded. One can just as surely identify instances in which public policy and governance were the key determinants of the level and quality of entrepreneurship. Biotechnology entrepreneurship, as the chapters in this volume by Nathan Rosenberg and Andrew Toole show, is one such instance. The rise of the Washington, D.C. area as a hotbed of high-technology entrepreneurship is a regional example (Feldman 2001). Cases lie in between these extremes often enough to merit attention, we believe; entrepreneurship policy in these instances is one evident set of forces among many shaping the context for entrepreneurship. The impact of entrepreneurship policy, in any case, need not be static. Well-designed and carefully implemented policy initiatives may enhance its impact, just as poorly thought through and badly managed efforts may reduce it or produce negative effects.

Most of the time, though, policy analysts do not know enough about the interaction between entrepreneurship and public policy to identify these opportunities and risks (see Bartik 1991; Isserman 1994; Dewar 1998).[8] Policymakers are no better informed than scholars and may not even necessarily be aware that such opportunities and risks exist. Policymakers and their partners in governance need to acquire more knowledge and to give entrepreneurship more attention if they are to govern the economy – especially the knowledge economy – well. Although entrepreneurship is a booming area of study in business schools, it has been ignored almost completely by schools of public policy and government. This volume is an effort to highlight our ignorance and to begin to diminish it. Entrepreneurship policy will never by itself determine what entrepreneurs do and how they affect society, nor should it aim to do so. But where public policy and governance can and do shape entrepreneurial behavior, we ought to be conscious of their consequences and improve them to the extent possible. Where we can learn enough to take action, we ought to do so.

AN INTRODUCTION TO THE VOLUME

The twelve chapters of this volume (not counting this introduction) are divided into five sections. The first section takes the broadest view of entrepreneurship policy, asking the question, "The Entrepreneurial Society: What's Governance Got to Do with It?" David B. Audretsch of Indiana University argues that entrepreneurship policy ought to be seen as a key element in the "strategic management of places." In a world in which firms can migrate easily, regional decisionmakers need to cultivate more permanent sources of competitive advantage, namely, the capacities to create new firms and to innovate. As Audretsch shows, this shift in thinking represents a marked break from the past. The chapter by Richard Florida of Carnegie Mellon University picks up on this theme, connecting entrepreneurial vitality to broader strains in the culture and life-style of particular places. He shows the importance of

---

[8] There is a growing literature on the impact of the "entrepreneurial state," but it is still inconclusive.

diversity and openness in attracting talented and well-educated people who are likely to become entrepreneurs. Regional development outcomes will be shaped much more by the distribution of people, he argues, than by the distribution of firms.

The next section focuses on the impact of public policy on the internal process of two of the key institutions of the knowledge economy: technology-based entrepreneurial ventures and research universities. Philip E. Auerswald of George Mason University and Lewis M. Branscomb of Harvard University's John F. Kennedy School of Government analyze the often arduous process that is entailed in bringing newly invented technologies to the point of commercial viability. Their model of the path "from invention to innovation" leads them to highlight actors, particularly "angel" investors, corporate venture funds, and federal programs, that have been overlooked in previous work. Auerswald and Branscomb highlight opportunities for governance processes to break bottlenecks that otherwise cause good ideas to lie fallow. Maryann P. Feldman of the University of Toronto takes the reader one step up the chain of knowledge creation and entrepreneurship in her chapter on university-based entrepreneurship and technology transfer offices. The institution of the technology transfer office has diffused throughout the United States in the past twenty years; few self-respecting research universities are without one these days. Feldman analyzes the instruments they use to channel technologies from the lab to the market and points to both strengths and weaknesses in their contribution to the governance of entrepreneurship. Stanford University's Nathan Rosenberg takes us the rest of the way up the chain into the core activities of research universities in his chapter. He shows that universities in the United States are highly responsive to their environment, and particularly responsive to the emergence of entrepreneurial ventures that demand that new knowledge be created or diffused. Strongly influenced by federal and state policies, universities alter their curricula, initiate research, and participate in collaborations that serve these ventures, thereby allowing them to be more competitive with larger and better financed competitors.

The third section explores equity issues in entrepreneurship policy, emphasizing opportunities for policymakers to support the participation of women and minorities in the knowledge economy. Science policy analysts have long been concerned with the "pipeline" of women and minorities with training in science and engineering; we extend that discussion here into the realm of entrepreneurship. Candida G. Brush of Boston University and her colleagues in the "Diana Project" analyze why women-led businesses receive a disproportionately low share of venture capital investments. They argue that the most likely cause of this maldistribution lies in the network structure of the venture capital industry, rather than in the aspirations or capabilities of women entrepreneurs. Innovative, but modest, policies might help to rectify the situation. Timothy Bates of Wayne State University reviews what he sees as the failed history of federal and state programs to support minority entrepreneurship. Most of these programs, he argues, are designed to fail, since they target individuals who do not have the requisites for entrepreneurial success. A few programs, however, have escaped this trap, focusing their attention on well-educated and experienced people who might become successful "opportunity" rather than "necessity" entrepreneurs. Bates recommends that the principles of these exemplars be adopted more widely.

Like the particular communities highlighted in the third section, particular economic sectors have unique attributes as objects of entrepreneurship policy, which are explored in the volume's fourth section. The biotechnology industry, which is intimately entwined with public policy, is the subject of the chapter by Andrew Toole of Illinois State University. Toole sketches the influence of public research funding, intellectual property law, regulation, and ethical controversies on biotechnology entrepreneurship. He then looks in detail at the determinants of success in building this industry up at the regional level, providing findings that link tightly to the chapters on research universities. Viktor Mayer-Schönberger's (Kennedy School of Government, Harvard University) chapter on e-commerce moves in quite a different direction, reflecting the very different features of this industry; he dissents from the commonly held view among Internet entrepreneurs that the law can only be a drag on their endeavors. To the contrary, he claims that entrepreneurs need legal structures to minimize the few risks that they can control. Using a transactional analytic approach, Mayer-Schönberger maps out a legislative agenda to improve law's utility for e-commerce entrepreneurs and suggests that legislators tackle it via "legal entrepreneurship." A chapter on telecommunications entrepreneurship by Eli Noam of Columbia University closes the section. Policy initiatives over the past several decades have gradually opened the telecommunications system to new entrants, peaking with the 1996 Telecommunications Act, which unleashed a frenzy of entrepreneurship. This trend, Noam shows, has now reversed, reflecting the cyclicality injected into this previously stable industry in the presence of large economies of scale and considerable regulation. Policymakers will need to take affirmative steps to aid new entrants in the future if further entrepreneurship in this industry is to occur.

The final section of the volume broadens the perspective once again, looking at questions related to the enactment and implementation of entrepreneurship policy. My own chapter explores how entrepreneurs, who are intrinsically resistant to engagement in public policy and governance, may nonetheless be induced to take part in making entrepreneurship policy. New institutions that overcome the barriers to participation by entrepreneurs in the policy process are required for them to make this leap at the same time as they are taking the leap in business. Erik R. Pages, Doris Freedman, and Patrick Von Bargen of the National Commission on Entrepreneurship dig into the nitty-gritty of state and local economic development strategies that focus on entrepreneurship. They assess earlier efforts that they view as largely unsuccessful and contrast these with promising new approaches aimed at building an entrepreneurial climate. The Pages, Freedman, and Von Bargen chapter returns us full circle to the issues raised by Audretsch and Florida in the opening section of the book.

This volume is more *tapas* than *smorgasbord*. As I noted at the outset of this chapter, we do not claim to have digested the whole domain of entrepreneurship policy, much less to have resolved all the academic controversies and given guidance on all the burning policy choices within it. We encourage the reader whose appetite has been whetted to forage further, to keep her eyes peeled for further developments that are sure to follow, and to take part in the debates among academics and practitioners who form the entrepreneurship policy community.

2

Entrepreneurship Policy and the Strategic Management of Places

David B. Audretsch

The role of entrepreneurship in society has changed drastically over the last half-century. During the immediate post-World War II period the importance of entrepreneurship seemed to be fading away. When Jean Jacques Servan-Schreiber (1968: 159) warned Europeans of the *American Challenge* in 1968, it was not from small entrepreneurial firms, but exactly the opposite – from the "dynamism, organisation, innovation, and boldness that characterize the giant American corporations." By that time, a generation of scholars had systematically documented and supported the conclusion of Joseph A. Schumpeter (1942: 106): "What we have got to accept is that the large-scale establishment or unit of control has come to be the most powerful engine of progress and in particular of the long-run expansion of output." John Kenneth Galbraith (1956: 86) put it this way: "There is no more pleasant fiction than that technological change is the product of the matchless ingenuity of the small man forced by competition to employ his wits to better his neighbor." Servan-Schreiber (1968: 159) thus prescribed that Europeans create "large industrial units which are able both in size and management to compete with the American giants."

An earlier version of this paper was presented at the April 2001 conference on entrepreneurship and public policy at the Kennedy School of Government, Harvard University. I am grateful for the suggestions of David Hart, Maryann P. Feldman, and Charles Wessner.

Public policy toward business in this period revolved around find-ing solutions to the perceived trade-off between scale and efficiency on the one hand, and decentralization and inefficiency on the other hand. The three main policy mechanisms deployed to achieve the re-quired balance in the industrialized countries were antitrust (or com-petition policy, as it was called in Europe), regulation, and public own-ership of business. A heated debate emerged about which approach best promoted large-scale production while simultaneously constrain-ing the ability of large corporations to exert market power, but there was much less debate about public policy toward small business and entrepreneurship. The only issue was whether public policymakers should simply allow small firms to disappear as a result of their ineffi-ciency or intervene to preserve them on social and political grounds. Those who perceived small firms to be contributing significantly to growth, employment generation, and competitiveness were few and far between.

This situation has been reversed completely in recent years. En-trepreneurship has come to be perceived as an engine of economic and social development throughout the world. For example, Romano Prodi, president of the European Commission, proclaimed recently that the promotion of entrepreneurship was a central thrust of European economic strategy. The rationale: "Our lacunae in the field of entrepreneurship need to be taken seriously because there is mounting evidence that the key to economic growth and productivity improvements lies in the entrepreneurial capacity of an economy" (Prodi 2002: 1).

The purpose of this chapter is to explain how and why the role of entrepreneurship policy has changed. The next section explains why public policy toward business after World War II focused on constrain-ing the freedom of large corporations to contract, while small firms were treated as relics to be preserved. In section three I explain how this traditional policy approach changed as a result of globalization, producing what I call the "strategic management of places." I then ex-plore the role that entrepreneurship plays in the strategic management of places and analyze a range of approaches to entrepreneurship policy. The chapter reaches the conclusion that a new mandate for governance has emerged that is (1) enabling rather than constraining, (2) more local and less centralized, and (3) focused on knowledge inputs rather than on targeting outputs or specific firms.

PUBLIC POLICY TOWARD BUSINESS AFTER WORLD WAR II

The pervasive fear of the Soviet Union that emerged as the Cold War succeeded World War II went beyond concerns about military competition and the space race. Many in the West worried that the launching of *Sputnik* demonstrated the superior organization of Soviet industry. Facilitated by centralized planning, the Soviet economy apparently generated rates of growth higher than those of Western economies, threatening, ultimately, to "bury" (as Soviet Premier Nikita Khruschev famously put it) the free market competition. After all, the nations of Eastern Europe, and the Soviet Union in particular, had a "luxury" inherent in their systems of centralized planning – a concentration of economic assets on a scale beyond anything imaginable in the West, where the commitment to democracy seemingly imposed a concomitant commitment to economic decentralization.

Western economists and policymakers of the day were nearly unanimous in their acclaim for large-scale enterprises. It is an irony of history that this consensus mirrored a remarkably similar giantism embedded in Soviet doctrine, fueled by the writings of Marx and ultimately implemented by the iron fist of Stalin. This was the era of mass production when economies of scale seemed to be the decisive factor in determining efficiency. This was the world so colorfully described by John Kenneth Galbraith (1956) in his theory of countervailing power, in which big business was held in check by big labor and by big government. This was the era of the man in the gray flannel suit (Riesman 1950) and the organization man (Whyte 1960), when virtually every major social and economic institution acted to reinforce the stability and predictability needed for mass production (Piore and Sabel 1984; Chandler 1977).

Scholars spanning a broad spectrum of academic fields and disciplines generated a massive literature that attempted to sort out the perceived trade-off between economic efficiency on the one hand and political and economic decentralization on the other. The large corporation was thought not only to have superior productive efficiency, but was also assumed to be the engine of technological innovation.

Ironically, the literature's obsession with oligopoly was combined with an analysis that was essentially static. There was considerable concern about what to do about the existing industrial structure, but little attention paid to where it came from and where it was going. Oliver Williamson's classic 1968 article, "Economies as an Antitrust Defense: The Welfare Tradeoffs," became something of a final statement demonstrating that gains in productive efficiency could be obtained through increased concentration and that gains in terms of competition, and implicitly democracy, could be achieved through decentralizing policies. But it did not seem possible to have both, certainly not in Williamson's completely static model.

The key public policy question of the day was "How can society reap the benefits of the large corporation in an oligopolistic setting while avoiding or at least minimizing the costs imposed by a concentration of economic power?" The answer centered on constraining the freedom of large firms to contract through public ownership, regulation, and antitrust. Different countries blended these three policy instruments in very different proportions. France and Sweden were in the vanguard of government ownership of business. The Netherlands and Germany, by contrast, emphasized regulation. The United States placed more weight on antitrust. Although these differences loomed large to scholars at the time, at this remove they are better seen as manifestations of a common policy approach that aimed to restrict the power of the large corporation.

Even advocates of small business agreed that small firms were less efficient than big companies. These advocates were willing to sacrifice a modicum of efficiency, however, because of other contributions – moral, political, and otherwise – made by small business to society. Small business policy was thus "preservationist" in character. The passage of the Robinson-Patman Act in 1936, for instance, was widely interpreted as one effort to protect small firms such as independent retailers that would otherwise have been too inefficient to survive in open competition with large corporations.[1] According to

---

[1] According to the Robinson-Patman Act, "It shall be unlawful for any person engaged in commerce, in the course of such commerce, either directly or indirectly, to discriminate in price between different purchasers of commodities of like grade and quality." The A&P super market chain, for instance, was found in violation of the Robinson-Patman Act for direct purchases from suppliers and for performing its own wholesale

Richard Posner (1976: 57), "The Robinson-Patman Act . . . is almost uniformly condemned by professional and academic opinion, legal and economic." Similarly, Robert Bork (1978: 382) observed, "One often hears of the baseball player who, although a weak hitter, was also a poor fielder. Robinson-Patman is a little like that. Although it does not prevent much price discrimination, at least it has stifled a great deal of competition."

Preservationist sentiments were also at work in the passage of the Small Business Act of 1953. Congress authorized the creation of the Small Business Administration with an explicit mandate to "aid, counsel, assist and protect . . . the interests of small business concerns."[2] This legislation was clearly an attempt by the Congress to halt the continued disappearance of small businesses and to preserve their role in the U.S. economy. Thus, in the traditional, managed economies of the postwar era, small firms and entrepreneurship were viewed as a luxury, perhaps needed by the West to ensure that decision-making remained decentralized, but in any case obtained only at a cost to efficiency. Despite the preservationist policy, however, the role of small business continued to diminish subsequent to World War II. The employment share of small firms in all industries declined from 55.1 percent in 1958 to 52.5 percent in 1977. Declines in the small business employment share reached double digits for minerals, retail, and wholesale, and single digits for construction, manufacturing, and services.

GLOBALIZATION AND THE STRATEGIC MANAGEMENT OF PLACES

A half-century later, this consensus has been shattered by the complex of forces captured in the term "globalization." The shift in economic activity from a local or national sphere to an international or global orientation ranks among the most profound trends of the recent period. Paradoxically, though, larger markets have weakened large firms. Unraveling this paradox requires some explanation.

---

functions. Although these activities resulted in lower distribution costs, the gains in efficiency were seen as being irrelevant because small business was threatened.

[2] U.S. Small Business Administration, "47 Years Of Service To America's Small Business," *http://www.sba.gov/aboutsba/sbahistory.html.*

One driving force underlying globalization has been technology. Observing the speed at virtually no cost with which information can be transmitted across geographic space via the internet, fax machines, and electronic "superhighways," *The Economist* recently proclaimed on its cover "The Death of Distance." The advent of the microprocessor combined with its application in telecommunications has altered the economic meaning of national borders and transformed the geography of production.

Globalization would not have occurred to the degree that it has, however, if the fundamental changes were restricted to technology. It took political revolutions in many parts of the world to reap the benefits of technological change. Throughout the Cold War, military and ideological antagonism combined with internal political instability to render potential investments in Eastern Europe and much of the developing world risky and impractical. International trade and investment were therefore generally confined to Europe and North America, and later a few of the Asian countries, principally Japan and the "four tigers" of South Korea, Taiwan, Singapore, and Hong Kong. Trade with countries behind the Iron Curtain was restricted and in some cases prohibited. Even trade with Asia was highly regulated and restricted. Investments in Latin America and the Middle East were undermined by episodes of nationalization in which foreign investors were expropriated.

The fall of the Berlin Wall and subsequent downfall of communism in Eastern Europe and the former Soviet Union changed the outlook radically. Within just a few years it became possible not just to trade with but also to invest in countries such as Hungary, the Czech Republic, Poland, and Slovenia as well as China, Vietnam, and Indonesia. India, too, became accessible as a trading and investment partner after economic reforms in the early 1990s. The opening of these areas to the world economy brought the long post-World War II equilibrium to a sudden end. The gaping wage differentials that existed while the Berlin Wall stood were suddenly exposed. Massive populations craving to enjoy the high levels of consumption that had become the norm in Western Europe and North America were willing to work for much less than their Western counterparts. Of course, the productivity of labor is vastly greater in the developed world, which compensates to a significant degree for such large wage differentials. Still, the magnitude of the differences caused trade and investment flows to swell hugely. Traditional measures of trade (exports and imports), foreign direct investment (inward and outward), international capital flows, and intercountry labor mobility have all trended strongly positive.

Many companies have responded to the opportunities made possible by the events of 1989. Confronted with low-cost competition in foreign locations, producers in the high-cost countries had three options as they sought to retain their leading positions: (1) reduce wages and other production costs sufficiently to compete with the low-cost foreign producers, (2) substitute equipment and technology for labor to increase productivity, and (3) shift production out of high-cost locations and into low-cost locations.

Many of the European and American firms that have successfully restructured resorted to the last two alternatives. Substituting capital and technology for labor along with shifting production to low-cost locations has resulted in waves of corporate downsizing throughout Europe and North America. For example, between 1979 and 1995 more than 43 million jobs were lost in the United States as a result of corporate downsizing. This figure includes 24.8 million blue-collar jobs and 18.7 million white-collar jobs. The 500 largest U.S. manufacturing corporations cut 4.7 million jobs between 1980 and 1993, or one quarter of their work force (Audretsch 1995). Perhaps most disconcerting, the rate of corporate downsizing has apparently increased over time in the United States, even as the unemployment rate has fallen. During most of the 1980s, about one in twenty-five workers lost a job. In the 1990s the share rose to one in twenty workers. Companies have shed labor to preserve their viability; many have thrived as a result.

The experience has not been different in Europe. Pressed to maintain competitiveness in traditional industries, where economic activity can be easily transferred across geographic space to access lower production costs, the largest and most prominent German companies have been downsizing their domestic employment. For example, Siemens decreased employment in Germany by 12 percent between 1985 and 1995, even as it increased the amount of employment outside Germany by 50 percent. The numbers for Volkswagen, Hoechst, and BASF are variations on the same theme.

The result of this wave of downsizing in Germany in the 1990s has been levels of unemployment – four million – not seen since the 1940s.

The impact was not confined to individual firms, but spread across entire industries and geographical regions. Stuttgart, which is home to Daimler-Chrysler (formerly Daimler-Benz), experienced an increase in manufacturing employment throughout the 1970s, 1980s, and into the 1990s. After reaching a peak of around 480,000 in 1991, manufacturing employment fell by more than one-third, to around 350,000 by the mid-1990s. The resulting unemployment triggered cries of betrayal from the critics of large corporations.[3] But this is a mistake. Corporations were simply trying to survive in global competition made fierce by easy access to low-cost inputs.

Much of the policy debate responding to globalization revolved around a perceived trade-off between maintaining higher wages but suffering greater unemployment on the one hand, and attaining higher levels of employment at the cost of lower wage rates on the other. There is, however, another alternative. It does not require sacrificing wages to create new jobs, nor does it require fewer jobs to maintain wage levels and the social safety net. This alternative involves shifting economic activity out of the traditional industries where the high-cost countries of Europe and North America have lost their comparative advantage and into those industries where comparative advantage is compatible with both high wages and high levels of employment – knowledge-based and innovative economic activity.

The locus of action in this strategy is not firms, but places. As long as corporations were inextricably linked to their regional location by substantial sunk costs, such as capital investment, the competitiveness of a region was identical to the competitiveness of the corporations located in that region. "What is good for General Motors is good for America" may have been controversial even a half-century ago, but few would have disagreed that "What is good for General Motors is good for Detroit." And so it was with U.S. Steel in Pittsburgh and Volkswagen in Wolfsburg. As long as the corporation thrived, so would the region. That world is gone. At the heart of the strategic management of places is the development and enhancement of factors of

---

[3] As the German newspaper *Die Zeit* (2 February, 1996: p. 1) pointed out in a front page article, "When Profits Lead to Ruin – More Profits and More Unemployment: Where is the Social Responsibility of the Firms?", the German public has responded to the recent waves of corporate downsizing with accusations that corporate Germany is no longer fulfilling its share of the social contract.

production that cannot be transferred across geographic space at low cost – principally, although not exclusively, knowledge and ideas.

THE SPATIAL BASIS OF THE KNOWLEDGE ECONOMY

Knowledge spills over from its initial producers to many secondary users. This fact is barely disputed. The big question is whether these spillovers have geographic limits such that locally produced knowledge can be retained and exploited locally. In a world of e-mail, fax machines, and cyberspace, the claim that geographic location is important to the process linking knowledge spillovers to innovative activity may seem surprising and even paradoxical. The resolution to the paradox posed lies in a distinction between knowledge and information. *Information*, such as the price of gold in New York, or the value of the yen in London, can be easily codified and has a singular meaning and interpretation. By contrast, *knowledge* is vague, difficult to codify, and often only serendipitously recognized. Whereas the marginal cost of transmitting information across geographic space has been rendered irrelevant by the telecommunications revolution, the marginal cost of transmitting knowledge, and especially tacit knowledge, rises with distance.

Von Hippel (1994) demonstrates that high context, uncertain knowledge (which he terms "sticky" knowledge) is best transmitted via face-to-face interaction and through frequent and repeated contact. Geographic proximity matters in transmitting knowledge because, as Kenneth Arrow (1962) pointed out four decades ago, such tacit knowledge is inherently nonrival in nature. Knowledge developed for any particular application can easily spill over and have economic value in very different applications. As Glaeser and colleagues (1992, p. 1126) have observed, "intellectual breakthroughs must cross hallways and streets more easily than oceans and continents."

The importance of local proximity for the transmission of knowledge spillovers has been observed in many different contexts. Recent scholarship has overcome the data constraints highlighted by Krugman (1991a) to provide precise estimates of the extent of knowledge spillovers and to link them to the geography of innovative activity. The empirical evidence consistently supports the notion that knowledge spills over from university research laboratories and from industry R&D laboratories as well. Location and proximity clearly matter in exploiting these knowledge spillovers. Jaffe, Trajtenberg, and Henderson (1993), for instance, found that patent citations tend to occur more frequently within the state in which patented inventions were made than outside of that state. Audretsch and Feldman (1996) found that the propensity of innovative activity to cluster geographically tends to be greater in industries where new economic knowledge plays a more important role. Prevezer (1997) and Zucker, Darby, and Armstrong (1998) show that in biotechnology, an industry based almost exclusively on new knowledge, firms tend to cluster together in just a handful of locations, a finding extended by Andrew Toole in this volume. Audretsch and Stephan (1996) demonstrate that an outside scientist is more likely to be located in the same region as the firm that he advises when the relationship involves the transfer of new economic knowledge. However, when a scientist is providing a service to a company that does not involve knowledge transfer, local proximity is much less important.

In addition, there is reason to believe that knowledge spillovers are not homogeneous across firms. In estimating the impact of knowledge spillovers on the innovative activity of large and small enterprises separately, Acs, Audretsch, and Feldman (1994) provide some insight into the puzzle posed by the recent wave of studies identifying vigorous innovative activity emanating from small firms in certain industries. How are these small, and frequently new, firms able to generate innovative output while undertaking negligible amounts of investment in knowledge-generating inputs, such as R&D? The answer appears to be that they exploit knowledge created by expenditures on research in universities and on R&D in large corporations, a finding affirmed by Nathan Rosenberg in his contribution to this volume. These findings suggest that the innovative output of all firms rises along with an increase in the amount of R&D inputs, both in private corporations as well as in university laboratories. However, R&D expenditures made by private companies play a particularly important role in providing knowledge inputs to the innovative activity of large firms, whereas expenditures on research made by universities serve as an especially key input for generating innovative activity in small enterprises. Apparently large firms are more adept at exploiting knowledge created in their own laboratories, while their smaller counterparts have a comparative advantage at exploiting spillovers from university laboratories.

THE ROLE OF ENTREPRENEURSHIP

That small entrepreneurial firms would emerge as more important in the knowledge economy seems to be contrary to many of the conventional theories of innovation. The starting point for most theories of innovation is the firm. In such theories the firms are exogenous and their performance in generating technological change is endogenous (Arrow 1962). For example, in the most prevalent model found in the literature of technological change, the model of the knowledge production function, formalized by Zvi Griliches (1979), firms exist exogenously and then engage in the pursuit of new economic knowledge as an input into the process of generating innovative activity. Knowledge as an input in a production function is inherently different from the more traditional inputs of labor, capital and land. Whereas the economic value of the traditional inputs is relatively certain, knowledge is intrinsically uncertain and its potential value is asymmetric across economic agents.[4] The most important source of new knowledge usually considered in this framework is R&D. Other sources of new economic knowledge include a high degree of human capital, in the form of a skilled labor force and a high presence of scientists and engineers.

There is considerable empirical evidence supporting the model of the knowledge production function. The empirical link between knowledge inputs and innovative output becomes stronger as the unit of observation gets larger. Among countries, for example, the relationship between R&D and patents is very strong. The most innovative countries, such as the United States, Japan, and Germany, also make large investments in R&D. By contrast, little patent activity is associated with developing countries, which have very low R&D expenditures. The link between R&D and innovative output is also very strong when the unit of observation is the industry. The most innovative industries, such as computers, scientific instruments, and pharmaceuticals also tend to be the most R&D-intensive. Audretsch (1995) finds a simple correlation coefficient of 0.74 between R&D inputs and innovative output at the level of four-digit standard industrial classification (SIC) industries.

---

[4] Arrow (1962) pointed out that this is one of the reasons for inherent market failure.

However, when the knowledge production function is tested at the firm level, the link between knowledge inputs and innovative output becomes tenuous and weakly positive in some studies and nonexistent or even negative in others. The model of the knowledge production function becomes particularly weak when small firms are included in the sample. This is not surprising, since formal R&D is concentrated among the largest corporations, whereas a series of studies (for example, Acs and Audretsch 1990) has clearly documented that small firms account for a disproportional share of new product innovations given their low R&D expenditures. The breakdown of the knowledge production function at the level of the firm raises the question, *Where do innovative firms with little or no R&D get the knowledge inputs?* This question becomes particularly relevant for small and new firms that undertake little R&D themselves, yet contribute considerable innovative activity in newly emerging industries such as biotechnology and computer software (Audretsch 1995). One answer that has recently emerged in the economics literature is that they draw on other firms and research institutions such as universities. Economic knowledge spills over to these firms from these outside organizations.

Why should knowledge spill over from the source of origin? At least two major channels or mechanisms for knowledge spillovers have been identified in the literature. Both of these spillover mechanisms revolve around the issue of appropriability of new knowledge. Cohen and Levinthal (1989) suggest that firms develop the capacity to adapt new technology and ideas developed in other firms and are therefore able to appropriate some of the returns accruing to investments in new knowledge made externally.

By contrast, Audretsch (1995) proposes shifting the unit of observation away from exogenously assumed firms to individuals, such as scientists, engineers, or other knowledge workers – agents with endowments of new economic knowledge. When the lens is shifted away from the firm to the individual as the relevant unit of observation, the appropriability issue remains, but the question becomes, *How can economic agents with a given endowment of new knowledge best appropriate the returns from that knowledge?* If the scientist or engineer can pursue the new idea within the organizational structure of the firm developing the knowledge and appropriate roughly the expected value of that knowledge, he has no reason to leave the firm. On the other hand, if he

places a greater value on his ideas than does the decision-making bureaucracy of the incumbent firm, he may choose to start a new firm to
appropriate the value of his knowledge. In the metaphor provided by
Albert O. Hirschman (1970), if voice proves to be ineffective within
incumbent organizations, and loyalty is sufficiently weak, a knowledge
worker may exit from the firm or university where the knowledge was
created. In this spillover channel the knowledge production function
is actually reversed. The knowledge is exogenous and embodied in
a worker. The firm is created endogenously in the worker's effort to
appropriate the value of his knowledge through innovative activity.

What emerges from this line of scholarship on entrepreneurship is
that markets are in motion, with a lot of firms entering and exiting
knowledge-intensive industries. But is this motion horizontal, so that
the bulk of firms exiting are firms that had entered relatively recently,
or vertical, such that a significant share of the exiting firms had been
established incumbents that were displaced by younger firms? In trying
to shed some light on this question, Audretsch (1995) proposes two
different models of the evolutionary process of industries over time.
Some industries can best be characterized by the model of the conical
revolving door, where new businesses are started, but there is also
a high propensity for them to subsequently exit the market. Other
industries may be better characterized by the metaphor of the forest,
where incumbent establishments are displaced by new entrants.

Which view is more applicable apparently depends on three major factors: underlying technological conditions, scale economies, and
demand. Where scale economies play an important role, the model of
the revolving door seems to be more applicable. Although start-up and
entry of new businesses are apparently not deterred by the presence
of high scale economies (in itself a rather startling result), a process of
firm selection analogous to a revolving door ensures that only those
establishments successful enough to grow will be able to survive beyond more than a few years. The bulk of new entrants that are not so
successful ultimately exit within a few years after entry.

When new entrepreneurial firms employ a strategy of innovation,
they typically start at a very small scale of output. They are motivated by
the desire to appropriate the expected value of new economic knowledge. But if scale economies in the industry are large, the firm may not
be able to remain viable indefinitely at its start-up size. In this case, the

new firm must grow to survive. The temporary survival of new firms is presumably supported by a strategy of compensating factor differentials that enables the firm to discover whether or not it has a viable product.

The empirical evidence has found that the postentry growth of firms that survive tends to be spurred by the extent to which there is a gap between the minimum efficient scale of output and the size of the firm. Innovation also figures in the selection process. New firms employing a strategy of innovation to attain competitiveness are apparently engaged in the selection process. Only those new firms offering a viable product that can be produced efficiently will grow and ultimately approach or attain the minimum efficient scale of output. The remainder will stagnate and exit the industry. Thus, in highly innovative industries, there is a continuing process of entry of new firms, but not necessarily the continuation of the same small firms over the long run. Although the skewed size distribution of firms persists with remarkable stability over long periods of time, a constant set of small entrepreneurial firms does not appear to be responsible. Rather, by serving as agents of change, small entrepreneurial firms provide an essential source of new ideas and experimentation that otherwise would remain untapped in the economy.

A series of studies have identified a positive link between entrepreneurial activity and growth for spatial units of observation[5] ranging from the city and region (Carree 2002; Fritsch 1997; National Commission on Entrepreneurship 2001b; Reynolds et al. 2000; Reynolds, Hay, Bygrave, Camp, and Autio 2000) to the country (Carree, van Stel, Thurik and Wennekers 2000; Carree and Thurik 1999). In particular, Fritsch (1997) and Reynolds (1999) provide compelling evidence that fast growing regions are experiencing higher levels of entrepreneurial activity, as measured by start-up rates and turbulence rates. Carree and Thurik (1999) provide empirical evidence from a 1984–1994 cross-sectional study of the twenty-three member countries of the Organization for Economic Co-operation and Development (OECD), which reveals that increased entrepreneurship, as measured by business ownership rates, is associated with higher rates of employment growth

---

[5] Spatial units of observation refer to a geographic dimension such as a city, county, region, or country.

at the country level. Similarly, the Global Entrepreneurship Monitor (GEM) Study (Reynolds, Hay, Bygrave, Camp, and Autio 2000) also establishes an empirical link between the degree of entrepreneurial activity and economic growth, as measured by employment, at the country level. Thus, there are not only theoretical arguments but also empirical evidence that suggest that the growth of places is positively associated with an entrepreneurial advantage. The strategic management of places emerged in order for places to capitalize on the growth associated with entrepreneurship. As a consequence, a new role for government emerged.

ENTREPRENEURSHIP POLICY

The link between entrepreneurial activity and growth for spatial units of observation, which has only systematically been established by scholars in recent years, captured the attention of policymakers much earlier. They witnessed the decline of large manufacturing corporations that had once been the mainstay of employment growth in industries such as steel, autos, and tires, in places like Pittsburgh, Detroit, and Akron. Their eyes told them that the regions enjoying the highest rates of growth and job creation also exhibited the highest rates of entrepreneurial activity. The emergence of knowledge as a source of competitiveness, combined with the propensity for knowledge to remain localized, resulted in a new policy opportunity for places – cities, regions, states, and countries. The policy goal of growth and employment creation could be attained, it was hoped, by strategically managing the climate of these places so as to generate entrepreneurial activities and thus economic growth.

The policy mandate for promoting entrepreneurship was based on the market failure associated with knowledge activities. Arrow (1962) recognized that knowledge was inherently a public good, so that its production generated externalities. As Audretsch and Feldman (1996) point out, however, local proximity is essential for accessing these knowledge spillovers. Thus, both knowledge-based firms and workers place a greater value on locations with clusters than those without clusters. Because of knowledge spillovers, the value of an entrepreneurial firm is greater in the (local) presence of other entrepreneurial firms (Audretsch and Stephan 1996). Yet individual firms and workers are reluctant to invest in the creation of such a cluster, which involves the creation of other entrepreneurial firms, because of their inability to appropriate the returns from such a cluster, due to the public nature of knowledge. Policymakers, whose interest lies in generating growth for a particular location, had to step in.

Market failure also stimulated policy through the positive economic value created in entrepreneurial firms that ultimately failed. The high failure rates of new firm start-ups has been widely documented (Bruderl et al. 1992; Carroll 1983; Hannan and Freeman 1989), and the failure rates in knowledge-based activities are especially great (Audretsch 1995). These rates are not surprising since knowledge activities are associated with a greater degree of uncertainty than traditional economic activities. The failure of a knowledge-based firm does not necessarily mean, however, that no value was created by that firm. Evidence suggests that ideas created by failed firms and projects often become integral parts of successful products and projects in successful firms (Holbrook 1995; Holbrook et al. 2000). For example, although Fairchild Semiconductor failed, the ideas generated by the firm were used by numerous other firms and helped to spawn Silicon Valley. The externalities associated with failed firms lead to market failure in the valuation of (potential) new enterprises between private investors and policymakers. The private investor can only appropriate her investment if the particular firm succeeds. If the firm fails but knowledge externalities contribute to the success of other firms, the private investor still does not appropriate anything from her investment. However, the public policy perspective is considerably different. From the public policy perspective it does not matter which firms succeed, as long as some do. Thus, policymakers should be willing to address the market failure associated with high rates of firm failure.

As comparative advantage has become increasingly based on new knowledge, public policy has responded in two fundamental ways. The first has been to shift the policy focus away from the traditional triad of instruments that constrained the freedom of firms to contract – regulation, antitrust, and public ownership of business. The policy approach of constraint was sensible as long as the major issue was how to restrain large corporations in possession of considerable market power. That this policy is less relevant in a global economy is reflected by the waves of deregulation and privatization throughout the OECD.

The new policy approach enables the creation and commercialization of knowledge through R&D, venture capital, and entrepreneurship.

Sternberg (1996) has shown that a number of government-sponsored technology programs have triggered entrepreneurial ventures, a finding further supported in the chapter by Auerswald and Branscomb in this volume. These programs aim to eliminate particular bottlenecks in the development and financing of new firms. Sternberg (1996) examines the impact that seventy innovation centers have had on the development of technology-based small firms. He notes that the majority of the entrepreneurs find advantages from locating at an innovation center.

The second fundamental change involves shifting the locus of such enabling policies to the state, regional, or even local level. The downsizing of national agencies charged with the regulation of business in many of the OECD countries has been interpreted by many scholars as the eclipse of government intervention. But to interpret deregulation, privatization, and the increased irrelevance of antitrust as the end of government intervention in business ignores an important shift in the locus and target of public policy. The last decade has seen the emergence of a broad spectrum of enabling policy initiatives that fall outside the jurisdiction of the traditional regulatory agencies. Sternberg (1996) shows that the success of several high-technology clusters spanning a number of developed countries is the direct result of enabling policies, such as the provision of venture capital or research support. For example, the Advanced Research Program in Texas has provided support for basic research and the strengthening of the infrastructure of the University of Texas, which has played a central role in developing a high-technology cluster around Austin (Feller 1997). The Thomas Edison Centers in Ohio, to cite another case, link leading universities and medical institutions, businesses, foundations, and civic and state organizations in Ohio in order to create new business opportunities (Carlsson and Braunerhjelm 1999).

The plethora of science, technology, and research parks provide further examples of entrepreneurship policy at work. Lugar and Goldstein (1991) conducted a review of research parks and concluded that such parks are created to promote the competitiveness of a particular region. Lugar (2001: 47) further noted that, "The most successful parks . . . have a profound impact on a region and its competitiveness."

A distinct exemplar of this effect is the Research Triangle Park in North Carolina. In the 1950s, the traditional industries of North Carolina, such as furniture, textiles, and tobacco, had lost international competitiveness, resulting in declines in employment and stagnation in real incomes. In 1952, only Arkansas and Mississippi had lower per capita income than North Carolina. A movement emerged in this period that advocated exploiting the rich knowledge base of the region, formed by the three major universities (Duke University, University of North Carolina-Chapel Hill, and North Carolina State University), for economic development (Link and Scott, 2003). This movement arose initially in the business community, but it eventually fell into the hands of the Governor's office, which carried it to fruition (Link 1995). Empirical evidence provides strong support that the initiative creating the Research Triangle Park has led to fundamental changes in the region. Link and Scott (2003) document the growth in the number of high-technology companies there from none in 1958 to fifty by the mid-1980s and over 100 by 1997. At the same time, employment in these companies increased from zero in the late 1950s to over forty thousand by 1997. Lugar (2001) credits the Research Triangle Park with directly and indirectly generating one-quarter of all jobs in the region between 1959 and 1990, and shifting the nature of those jobs toward high value-added knowledge-based activities.

One of the most interesting examples of entrepreneurship policy for the strategic management of places involves the establishment of five EXIST regions in Germany, where start-ups from universities and government research laboratories are encouraged (Bundesministerium fuer Bildung und Forschung 2000). The program has the explicit goals of (1) creating an entrepreneurial culture, (2) commercializing scientific knowledge, and (3) increasing the number of innovative start-ups and SMEs. Five regions were selected among many applicants for START funding: (1) Rhein-Ruhr region (bizeps program), (2) Dresden (Dresden exists), (3) Thueringen (GET UP), (4) Karlsruhe (KEIM), and (5) Stuttgart (PUSH!).

CONCLUSIONS

The role of entrepreneurship and small business policy has evolved considerably since World War II. What was once considered to be a necessary drain on Western economies has become a central strategic instrument for competitiveness in global markets. Globalization has shifted the comparative advantage in the OECD countries away from land, labor, and capital toward knowledge. This shift has triggered a divergence between the competitiveness of firms and the competitiveness of locations. As the strategic management of firms dictated a response to globalization of outward foreign direct investment combined with employment downsizing at high-cost locations, public policy has responded by developing the strategic management of places. Entrepreneurship policy plays a central role in the strategic management of places, because entrepreneurial activity is the conduit between investments in knowledge and economic growth at the particular location.

Just as it has been important to understand how to manage entrepreneurial firms, it has now become at least as important to understand how to achieve an entrepreneurial society. Although this emphasis on small entrepreneurial firms as engines of dynamic efficiency may seem startling after decades of looking to the corporate giants as engines of growth and development, it in fact may not be so new. That great observer of early American life, Alexis de Tocqueville, reported in 1835, "What astonishes me in the United States is not so much the marvellous grandeur of some undertakings as the innumerable multitude of small ones."

3

Entrepreneurship, Creativity, and Regional Economic Growth

Richard Florida

> If one wanted to select the best novelist, artist, entrepreneur, or even chief executive officer, one would most likely want someone who is creative.
>
> – Robert Sternberg, *Handbook of Creativity* (Sternberg 1999)

Entrepreneurship, both in the conventional wisdom and the academic view, has long been seen as the province of great individuals. Scores of books and articles have been written extolling the virtues of heroic entrepreneurs. This chapter starts from the assumption that this "great man" theory misses the fundamental mechanisms that spur entrepreneurship and economic growth. Indeed, entrepreneurship is more than an economic process and extends beyond the process of new business formation. At bottom, entrepreneurship is a social process that stems from a broad set of social and cultural conditions.

In the contemporary United States, the entrepreneurial impulse has become embedded in a social ethos. The forces that produced this ethos have been building at least since the 1960s, and perhaps longer, but the rise of the entrepreneurial society – or way of life – has become apparent just recently. Entrepreneurship is part of a broader social movement, a shift in what Americans want out of their lives. Consider the following facts.

- Some 60 percent of teenagers and young adults say they want to be entrepreneurs, according to a recent survey (Kourilsky and Walstad 2000).
- A survey of research on entrepreneurship by Patricia Thornton points out that 4 percent of Americans at any given time are involved in starting businesses (Thornton 1999).
- A 26-year-old woman I interviewed in the course of my research put it this way: "Me, I always felt like the weirdo. I can only imagine the number of times it was said, just do it that way because that's the way it's done. I always have felt a sense that to be or do anything outside of the realm of the norm was not different but wrong. I wish I had a dime for every time people said, get a real job. You see? You're seen as the weirdo if you take risks and build something different. I know I always wanted to create things for myself but I didn't know how to do it. I finally realized what it is. What I want to do to build things isn't weird; it's called entrepreneurship. I'm an entrepreneur" (interview by author 2000).

These facts hint at the broad shift occurring in American society, a shift that goes beyond the conventional notion that we now live in an "information" or "knowledge" economy. This economy is powered not by information or by knowledge, but by human creativity. Creativity – "the ability to create meaningful new forms," as *Webster's Dictionary* puts it – is now the decisive source of competitive advantage. As Paul Romer likes to say, the big advances in the standard of living – not to mention the big competitive advantages in the marketplace – come from "better recipes, not just more cooking" (Romer 1993).

Creativity is multifaceted and multidimensional. I identify three interrelated types of creativity: (1) *technological creativity* or innovation, (2) *economic creativity* or entrepreneurship, and (3) *artistic and cultural creativity*. I argue that these three types of creativity are mutually dependent. In order to generate entrepreneurship (evident in higher rates of new business formation), a region must create conditions that stimulate innovation, arts, and culture. The three types of creativity stimulate and reinforce one another.

Creativity requires diversity. As the great urbanist Jane Jacobs observed forty years ago, creativity thrives when the environment allows people of all lifestyles, cultures, and ethnicities to interact (Jacobs 1961). Regions that wish to encourage economic creativity must also encourage diversity. My focus groups and interviews with young, talented people indicated time and time again that one of the most important attributes they seek in looking for a place in which to live and work is diversity. In order to become an entrepreneurial center, a region must nurture a community that encourages all forms of creativity, which means supporting populations that are highly linked to creativity.

Entrepreneurship of the Schumpeterian sort – that is, the creation of technologically dynamic, high-value added, high-growth firms, with which this volume as a whole is mainly concerned – is intimately linked to creativity, defined in this broad fashion (Schumpeter 1947; Mokyr 1990). I have reached this conclusion after years of research on entrepreneurship, technological innovation, and economic growth at the regional level with a team of students and colleagues at Carnegie Mellon University. My qualitative research, drawing on interviews and focus groups, lays bare the changing attitudes and desires of creative people and ties these to key factors in the social environment. Our quantitative work substantiates these findings, using new measures that are more reliable and more focused on the dependent variable of interest – Schumpeterian entrepreneurship – than previous research in this vein (Florida 2002).

This chapter provides an empirical assessment of the relationship between entrepreneurship and other forms of creativity and diversity at the regional level. The next section reviews prior work and introduces some of the central precepts of my creativity-based perspective. The third section presents the basic designs, methods, and indicators used in our research. I then examine the relationship between entrepreneurship, technological and cultural creativity, and diversity. The last section discusses the implications of these trends and findings for the emerging field of entrepreneurship policy.

CREATIVITY, ENTREPRENEURSHIP, AND REGIONAL ECONOMIC GROWTH

Economists and geographers have always accepted that economic growth is regional, that it is driven by and spreads from specific regions, cities, or even neighborhoods. Robert Park, Jane Jacobs, and Wilbur Thompson, among others, long ago pointed to the role of places as incubators of creativity, innovation, and new firms and industries (Park et al. 1925; Jacobs 1969, 1984; Thompson 1965). The earliest explanation of this phenomenon was that places grow either because they are located on transportation routes or because they have endowments of natural resources that encourage firms to locate there. According to this conventional view, the economic importance of a place is tied to the efficiency with which one can make things and do business. Governments employ this theory when they use tax breaks and highway construction to attract business. But these cost-related factors are no longer key to success.

Another major theory of regional growth suggests that place remains important as a locus of economic activity because of the tendency of firms to cluster together. This view builds on the seminal insights of the economist Alfred Marshall. The contemporary variant of this view, advanced by Michael Porter, has many proponents in academia and in the practice of economic development (Porter 1998; 2000a; 2000b). It is clear that similar firms tend to cluster. Examples of this sort of agglomeration include not only Detroit and Silicon Valley, but the *maquiladora* electronics-and-auto-parts districts in Mexico, the clustering of makers of disk drives in Singapore and of flat-panel displays in Japan, and the garment district and Broadway theater district in New York City.

The question is not whether firms cluster but why. Several answers have been offered. Some experts believe, as Marshall did, that "agglomerations" of similar firms capture efficiencies generated from tight linkages between the firms. Others say it has to do with the positive benefits of co-location, which are sometimes referred to as "spillovers." Still others claim agglomeration occurs because certain kinds of activities require face-to-face contact (Feldman 2000). But these are only partial answers.

Over the past decade or so, a more powerful theory to explain city and regional growth has emerged. The basic idea behind this theory is that people are the motor for growth. Its proponents thus refer to it as the "human capital" theory of regional development. The proponents of the human capital theory argue that the key to regional growth lies not in reducing the costs of doing business or inducing the clustering of firms, but rather in enhancing regional endowments of highly educated and productive people.

The human capital theory owes a particular debt to the work of Jane Jacobs. Decades ago, Jacobs noted the ability of cities to attract creative people and thus spur economic growth (Jacobs 1984). For a long time academic economists ignored her ideas, but in the past decade or two, they have been taken up with gusto. The Nobel Prize-winning economist Robert Lucas, for instance, sees the productivity effect that comes from the clustering of human capital as the critical factor in regional economic growth, referring to it as a "Jane Jacobs externality." (In a widely circulated e-mail Lucas went so far as to suggest that Jacobs should be considered for a Nobel Prize in economics.) Building on Jacobs' seminal insight, Lucas contends that cities would be economically infeasible if not for the productivity effect associated with endowments of human capital:

If we postulate only the usual list of economic forces, cities should fly apart. The theory of production contains nothing to hold a city together. A city is simply a collection of factors of production – capital, people, and land – and land is always far cheaper outside cities than inside ... It seems to me that the 'force' we need to postulate to account for the central role of cities in economic life is of exactly the same character as the 'external human capital' ... What can people be paying Manhattan or downtown Chicago rents for, if not for being near other people? (Lucas 1988)

Studies of national growth find a clear connection between the economic success of nations and their human capital, as measured by the level of education. This connection has also been found in regional studies of the United States. In a series of studies, Edward Glaeser and his collaborators, for example, have found considerable empirical evidence that human capital is the central factor in regional growth (Glaeser 1998; Glaeser et al. 2001). According to Glaeser, such clustering of human capital is the ultimate source of regional agglomerations of firms. Firms concentrate to reap the advantages that stem from common labor pools and not to tap the advantages from linked networks of customers and suppliers, as Porter and others argue. Research by Spencer Glendon shows that a good deal of city growth over the twentieth century can be traced to cities' levels of human capital at the beginning of the century (Glendon 1998). Places with greater numbers of talented people grew faster and were better able to attract more talent. For our purposes, places with high concentrations of human capital both attract existing firms and provide the habitat required to create new entrepreneurial firms.

The human capital theory asserts that economic growth will occur in places that have highly educated people. It thus begs the question: Why do talented, creative, and entrepreneurial people cluster in certain places? My focus groups and interviews suggest three basic reasons.

- Thick labor markets: People don't just want a job, they want a lot of jobs. They know they're going to move around a lot, so they want a "thick labor market."
- Diversity: People in my interviews and focus groups look for visible signs of diversity, such as prevalence of various nationalities and ethnicities as well as a visible gay community. These are visual cues that a place is open to all and possesses "low entry barriers" to human capital.
- Quality of place: I define quality of place in terms of three attributes: what's there – the buildings, the neighborhoods, the physical design; who's there – the people, the diversity, the human energy; and what's going on – the bustling street life, sidewalk cafes, restaurants, music venues, and active outdoor recreation.

I argue, then, that regional economic growth is driven by creative people who prefer places that are diverse, tolerant, and open to new ideas. This "creative capital" theory thus differs from human capital theory in two respects. First, it identifies a type of human capital, creative people, that is the key to economic growth. Second, it identifies the underlying factors that shape the location decisions of these people, instead of merely saying that regions are blessed with certain endowments of them. Furthermore, it suggests that creativity is linked to diversity. Diversity increases the odds that a place will attract different types of creative people with different skill sets and ideas. Places with diverse mixes of creative people are more likely to generate new and novel combinations. Diversity and concentration work together to speed the flow of knowledge. Greater and more diverse concentrations of creative capital in turn lead to higher rates of innovation, high-technology business formation, job generation, and economic growth. This theory suggests that places that are open to creativity of all sorts (technological and cultural as well as economic) reflect an underlying environment or habitat that favors risk taking and thus will stimulate entrepreneurship.

In more pragmatic terms, my creativity-based theory of regional growth says that technological innovation, new firm formation, and regional growth are all related to what I call the "3 T's" of economic development: *technology, talent, and tolerance.* To spur innovation, economic growth, and other good things a region must have all three of them. The 3 T's explain why regions like Baltimore, St. Louis, and Pittsburgh fail to stimulate entrepreneurship and to grow despite their deep reservoirs of technology and world-class universities: They are unwilling to be sufficiently tolerant and open to attract and retain top creative talent and encourage risk-taking behavior. The interdependence of the 3 T's also explains why regions like Miami and New Orleans do not make the grade even though they are life-style meccas: They lack the required technology base. The most successful places – the San Francisco Bay Area, Boston, Washington, D.C., Austin, and Seattle – put all 3 T's together. They are truly creative places.

RESEARCH DESIGN AND METHODS

To test this theory, my team and I have developed a series of new and unique indicators of the social and economic factors that are associated with innovation, entrepreneurship, and regional economic growth. Conventional studies of regional entrepreneurship have been plagued by an absence of reliable and systematic measures of new firm formation. Researchers who have developed such measures typically fail to discriminate among types of businesses, which means that small service establishments swamp entrepreneurship of the Schumpeterian sort, which is of most interest in explaining regional economic growth.

High Technology Growth

In order to overcome this difficulty, I rely on an indicator of the regional concentration of high-tech firms developed by Ross De Vol and a team of researchers at the Milken Institute (DeVol 1999). I use the following indices:

High-Tech Entrepreneurship Index. Ranks a metropolitan area based on a combination of two factors: (1) its high-tech industrial output as a percentage of total U.S. high-tech industrial output; and (2) the percentage of the region's total economic output that comes from high-tech industries compared with the nationwide percentage. The first factor favors large metropolitan areas, whereas the second favors smaller regions with large technology sectors.

Diversity and Innovation

As Jacobs long professed, diversity of people is the catalyst for diversity of thought and innovation. To get at this phenomenon from a quantitative perspective, I use a variety of novel indicators to account for the social and economic factors that may condition or affect the process of high-tech entrepreneurship:

Innovation Index. This index is a measure of patents per capita, 1990–1999, based on data from the U.S. Patent and Trademark Office. Regions that have a high number of patents per capita are regions that my team and I consider highly innovative.

Gay Index. Drawing on research by Gary Gates and his collaborators (Black et al. 2000), this index is based on the decennial U.S. Census. The "gay index" is a location quotient ranking of gay households per capita, based on the percentage of all U.S. gays who live in the region divided by the percentage of the total U.S. population who live there. If the Gay Index is greater than 1.0, the region has a greater-than-average share of gays.

Bohemian Index. In the same way that the gay population represents a region's openness and tolerance, the Bohemian Index reveals a region's level of aesthetic creativity. The Bohemian Index is a measure of artistically creative people calculated in the same fashion as the Gay Index. The Bohemian Index includes authors, designers, musicians, composers, actors, directors, painters, sculptors, artist printmakers, photographers, dancers, artists, and performers. It is based on the 1990 U.S. Decennial Census Public Use Microdata Sample.

Talent Index. This index is a measure of human capital, based on a region's share of people holding a bachelor's degree and above. It is based on the 1990 U.S. Decennial Census Public Use Microdata Sample.

Melting Pot Index. This index measures the relative percentage of foreign-born people in a region, based on the 1990 U.S. Decennial Census Public Use Microdata Sample.

Composite Diversity Index (CDI). This index combines the Gay, Bohemian, and Melting Pot Indices. The CDI is a unique way to look at many different facets of creativity at the same time. Often, regions that are highly diverse in one element tend to be diverse in our other measurements, too.

The Importance of Being Creative

The rise of creativity as an economic force has registered itself in the rise of a new class. Some 38 million Americans, or about 30 percent of our work force, are members of the Creative Class, up from 15 percent in 1950 and less than 20 percent as recently as 1980. Their ranks will swell further as the "creative content" of many formerly rote jobs continues to increase. In order to gauge the level of creativity across the country, I created two new indices:

Creative Class. Creativity has become the most ubiquitous facet of many careers today. Scientists and engineers, artists and designers, as well as creative professionals, managers, and technicians in many fields who create marketable new forms or work primarily at creative problem-solving, are included in my definition of the Creative Class. This index draws on the Bureau of Labor Statistics OLS occupation categories for the year 1999 as percent of the work force (Florida 2002).

Creativity Index. To get at the full magnitude of creativity and its link to entrepreneurship, I combined a number of different indices that are representative of a region's openness, tolerance, and innovation. The Creative Index is a composite measure based on four indices for the most current year available: High-Tech Entrepreneurship Index (2000), Innovation Index (1999), Gay Index (2000), and the Creative Class (1999).

ENTREPRENEURSHIP, INNOVATION, AND THE CREATIVE CLASS

Using my measure of the Creative Class and the Talent Index, my research team examined these relationships for the forty-nine regions with more than one million people in the United States (see the appendix to this chapter for a full listing). The findings indicate that both innovation and the high-tech industry are strongly associated with the locations of the Creative Class and of talent in general. For example, four of the top five regions on the High-Tech Index also rank in the top five for the Creative Class, as do three of the top five Talent regions. The correlation between the Creative Class and the High-Tech Index (0.38) is positive and significant. (See Table 3.1.)

Economic and Cultural Creativity

I now turn to the less obvious relationship between economic and cultural creativity. In their studies of Chicago, Richard Lloyd and Terry Clark dubbed revitalizing urban areas "entertainment machines" (Lloyd and Clark 2001). Joel Kotkin found a similar shift to lifestyle amenities as the fuel for urban revitalization in the cities he examined (Kotkin 2000). In a detailed statistical study, Glaeser and his collaborators found considerable support for this view, which they referred to as a shift from the producer to the "consumer city" (Glaeser et al. 2001). Our Bohemian Index is an improvement over the measures used by these scholars because it directly counts the producers of cultural amenities using reliable Census data. (See Table 3.2.)

Table 3.1. *High-Tech Entrepreneurship and the Creative Class*

High-Tech Rank	Region	Creative Class		Talent	
		Share (percent)	Rank	Share (percent)	Rank
1	San Francisco	34.8	5	32.3	5
2	Boston	38.0	3	35.2	3
3	Seattle	32.7	9	26.4	12
4	Los Angeles	30.7	20	17.4	47
5	Washington, D.C.	38.4	1	35.3	2
6	Dallas	30.2	23	27.3	10
7	Atlanta	32.0	16	30.6	7
8	Phoenix	28.6	35	22.0	29
9	Chicago	32.2	14	25.1	15
10	Portland, OR	29.4	30	24.4	17
40	Buffalo	28.9	33	20.6	39
41	Oklahoma City	29.4	29	22.9	23
42	Las Vegas	18.5	49	13.9	49
43	Grand Rapids	24.3	48	20.1	42
44	Providence, RI	27.6	41	21.9	31
45	New Orleans	27.5	42	22.2	24
46	Louisville	26.5	46	19.3	44
47	Jacksonville	30.3	21	18.7	46
48	Memphis	24.8	47	23.1	22
49	Detroit	31.0	19	20.5	40

The Bohemian Index is strongly related to High-Tech Entrepreneurship. Five of the top ten and twelve of the top twenty Bohemian Index regions are among the nation's top twenty high-technology regions. Eleven of the top twenty Bohemian Index regions are among the top twenty most innovative regions. The Bohemian Index is also a strong predictor of both regional employment and population growth. A region's Bohemian Index in 1990 predicts both its high-tech industry concentration and its employment and population growth between 1990 and 2000. The Bohemian Index correlates with the High-Tech Index at 0.64 and with the Innovation Index at 0.60; both correlations are statistically significant. This evidence supports the view that places that provide a broad creative environment are the ones that also encourage entrepreneurship, and that entrepreneurship is one dimension of creativity, which is dependent on an environment that encourages other types of creativity.

Table 3.2. *High-Tech Entrepreneurship and
the Bohemian Index*

High-Tech Rank	Region	Bohemian Index
1	San Francisco	5
2	Boston	4
3	Seattle	7
4	Los Angeles	10
5	Washington, D.C.	13
6	Dallas	15
7	Atlanta	12
8	Phoenix	23
9	Chicago	26
10	Portland, OR	6
40	Buffalo	46
41	Oklahoma City	47
42	Las Vegas	9
43	Grand Rapids	31
44	Providence, RI	17
45	New Orleans	41
46	Louisville	33
47	Jacksonville	49
48	Memphis	40
49	Detroit	24

Creativity and Diversity

Economists have long argued that diversity is important to economic performance, but they have usually meant the diversity of firms or industries. The economist John Quigley, for instance, argues that regional economies benefit from the presence of a diverse set of firms and industries (Quigley 1998). Jane Jacobs was one of the few who understood diversity more broadly. As Jacobs saw it, great cities are places where people from virtually any background are welcome to turn their energy and ideas into innovations and wealth (Jacobs 1961).

Immigrants as a Source of Diversity

From Andrew Carnegie in steel to Andy Grove in semiconductors, immigrants have been a powerful source of innovation and entrepreneurship. People who choose to leave their countries of origin are predisposed to take risks and can be thought of as "innovative outsiders." It seems obvious too that people and groups facing obstacles in traditional organizations are more likely to start their own enterprises, and the facts bear this out. Roughly one-quarter of new Silicon Valley businesses established since 1980 were so started, according to Annalee Saxenian's study, a figure that increased to 30 percent after 1995 (Saxenian 1999). In *The Global Me*, G. Pascal Zachary contends that America's successful economic performance is directly linked to its openness to innovative and energetic people from around the world. Zachary attributes the decline of once-prosperous countries, such as Japan and Germany, to the homogeneity of their populations (Zachary 2000).

I explore this question with the Melting Pot Index (see Table 3.3). Four out of the top ten regions on the Melting Pot Index are also

Table 3.3. *High-Tech Entrepreneurship and Immigration*

High-Tech Rank	Region	Melting Pot Index
1	San Francisco	4
2	Boston	8
3	Seattle	16
4	Los Angeles	2
5	Washington, D.C.	14
6	Dallas	17
7	Atlanta	31
8	Phoenix	21
9	Chicago	7
10	Portland, OR	24
40	Buffalo	28
41	Oklahoma City	38
42	Las Vegas	13
43	Grand Rapids	36
44	Providence, RI	6
45	New Orleans	26
46	Louisville	49
47	Jacksonville	34
48	Memphis	46
49	Detroit	22

among the nation's top ten high-technology areas; and seven of the top ten are in the top twenty-five high-tech regions. The correlation between the Melting Pot Index and the High-Tech Index is 0.26 and significant.

The Gay Index and Regional Diversity

Immigrants are surely important to economic growth, but the gay population is an even stronger indicator of a region's openness, and in turn, its innovative and entrepreneurial activity. This relationship is primarily due to the fact that the gay population, historically, has been one of the groups most discriminated against. A region that is open to the gay population most likely will have low barriers to human capital for other populations as well. These low barriers to entry are critical for stimulating high-tech growth and innovation. Table 3.4 provides evidence for this claim.

Table 3.4. *High-Tech Entrepreneurship and the Gay Index*

High-Tech Rank	Region	Gay Index Rank (1990)	Gay Index Rank (2000)
1	San Francisco	1	1
2	Boston	18	22
3	Seattle	5	8
4	Los Angeles	3	4
5	Washington, D.C.	7	11 (tie)
6	Dallas	12	9
7	Atlanta	8	7
8	Phoenix	23	15
9	Chicago	17	24 (tie)
10	Portland, OR	22	20
40	Buffalo	49	49
41	Oklahoma City	40	40
42	Las Vegas	28	5
43	Grand Rapids	32	38
44	Providence, RI	31	32
45	New Orleans	25	11 (tie)
46	Louisville	47	36
47	Jacksonville	38	24 (tie)
48	Memphis	43	41
49	Detroit	42	45

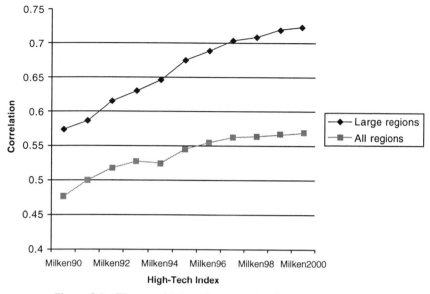

Figure 3.1. The gay–high-tech connection increases over time.

The Gay Index is a very strong predictor of a region's high-tech industry concentration. Six of the top ten 1990 and five of the top ten 2000 Gay Index regions also rank among the nation's top ten high-tech regions. The correlation between the 1990 Gay Index and the High-Tech Index is 0.57, and it is 0.48 using the 2000 Gay Index. Both are significant at the 0.001 level. Gays not only predict the concentration of high-tech industry, they also predict its growth. Four of the regions that rank in the top ten for high-technology growth from 1990 to 1998 also rank in the top ten on the Gay Index in both 1990 and 2000 (Growth Index). The correlation between the 1990 Gay Index and high-tech growth is 0.17, and it is 0.16 using the 2000 Gay Index. Again, both are significant at the 0.001 level. In addition, the correlation between the Gay Index (measured in 1990) and the High-Tech Index calculated for 1990–2000 increases over time (see Figure 3.1). The benefits of diversity may actually compound over the years.

The Gay Index also correlates highly with the Innovation Index; the correlation is 0.69. Again, this relationship supports my theory that places that are open to different backgrounds and cultures, especially the gay population, are places that have a strong creative, innovative, and entrepreneurial culture.

Table 3.5. *High-Tech and Diversity Go Together*

High-Tech Rank	Region	Composite Diversity Index
1	San Francisco	1
2	Boston	4
3	Seattle	8
4	Los Angeles	2
5	Washington, D.C.	7
6	Dallas	14
7	Atlanta	13
8	Phoenix	18
9	Chicago	15
10	Portland, OR	16
40	Buffalo	48
41	Oklahoma City	39
42	Las Vegas	26
43	Grand Rapids	36
44	Providence, RI	11
45	New Orleans	27
46	Louisville	49
47	Jacksonville	41
48	Memphis	44
49	Detroit	28

Diversity in the Broadest Sense

In order to fully measure a region's openness and tolerance for all walks of life, it is necessary to combine several different factors that capture the multiple meanings of diversity. The Composite Diversity Index (CDI) provides such a proxy. The CDI, which combines the Gay, Bohemian, and Melting Pot Indices, provides further support for the argument that openness and tolerance often beget innovation and entrepreneurial activity. (See Table 3.5.)

Five of the top ten regions on the CDI are also among the top ten high-tech regions: San Francisco, Boston, Seattle, Los Angeles, and Washington D.C. The statistical correlation between the High-Tech Index and the CDI rankings is also quite high. The correlation coefficient between CDI and High Tech is 0.475. The Spearman rank order correlation between the High-Tech Index and CDI is 0.63. Even more compelling, the CDI strongly predicts high-tech growth. When we estimate the effect of the CDI on high-tech growth from 1990 to 1998 and factor in the percentage of college graduates in the region, population, and measures of culture, recreation, and climate, the CDI continues to have a positive and significant effect. What this research tells us is that diversity may be the most crucial component for regions that hope to encourage entrepreneurship.

High-Tech Entrepreneurship and Overall Creativity

Finally, the Creativity Index provides a single baseline indicator of a region's overall standing in the creative economy, and it is also a strong indicator of its entrepreneurial capacity (see Table 3.6). Three of the

Table 3.6. *High-Tech Entrepreneurship and Overall Creativity*

High-Tech Rank	Region	Creativity Index Rank	Creativity Index Score
1	San Francisco	1	1057
2	Boston	3	1015
3	Seattle	5	1008
4	Los Angeles	12	942
5	Washington, D.C.	8	964
6	Dallas	11	960
7	Atlanta	14	940
8	Phoenix	19	909
9	Chicago	15	935
10	Portland, OR	16	929
40	Buffalo	46	609
41	Oklahoma City	42	668
42	Las Vegas	47	561
43	Grand Rapids	44	639
44	Providence, RI	40	698
45	New Orleans	43	668
46	Louisville	45	622
47	Jacksonville	37	715
48	Memphis	49	530
49	Detroit	39	708

top five regions and four of the top ten regions on the Creativity Index are also among the leaders on the High-Tech Index.

PUBLIC POLICY IMPLICATIONS

Entrepreneurship has become the driving force of wealth and growth across the country. As this chapter has shown, entrepreneurship requires a supportive social context that can stimulate and nurture creativity. Openness to people of all cultures and walks of life underlies entrepreneurship. In order to succeed as a region and promote innovation and entrepreneurship, a region must establish a multidimensional creative community.

Much of what government does to support economic growth right now is targeted at the wrong goals and is often counterproductive. The traditional formula for economic development revolves around the use of financial incentives to attract manufacturing facilities, branch plants, big-box retail outlets, and (in its more recent iterations) call centers. The other main prong of regional development strategy revolves around downtown revitalization through massive public subsidies for sports stadiums, convention centers, and retail malls of various sorts. The economists Andrew Zimbalist and Roger Noll, among others, have shown the limits of these strategies. Recent research actually finds that sports stadiums tend to reduce net local income, rather than adding to local economies (Zimbalist and Noll 1997).

My research indicates that such approaches have little if any effect on the location decisions of the talented and creative people who are the driving force behind regional development. Not once in my focus groups and interviews around the country did anyone mention sports stadiums or traditional economic development packages. These economic development strategies are those of the industrial age. New approaches are needed for regions to compete and prosper in the Creative Age.

State and local governments need to broaden their visions of entrepreneurship policy. Over the past two decades, interest in so-called "grow your own" strategies to support local entrepreneurship and the formation in particular of high-tech companies has proliferated, as described by Pages and his colleagues in this volume. The typical formula in this realm revolves around a combination of entrepreneurial assistance, high-tech incubation, technology transfer, and support for local venture capital funds. Josh Lerner and others have shown the limits of these direct entrepreneurial assistance strategies (Lerner 1999a). The gist of their critique is that such approaches are too narrow. Local support that is targeted for venture funds is a particularly problematic strategy.

The main task of regional development policy should be – and is – to set in place the broad environment or habitat that can attract people and in which creativity and entrepreneurship can flourish. That means investing in talent as well as technology and ensuring that regions are open and tolerant of diversity and risk taking. What it boils down to from my perspective is moving beyond the notion of a business climate and supplementing or replacing that concept with a "people climate." Cities and regions need to invest in creating the broad people climate that can attract creative and talented people of all sorts. And since people are different, a people climate must be broad enough to appeal to a wide range of them, regardless of age, gender, race, ethnicity, or marital status and sexual orientation.

Cities and regions alike must look beyond traditional methods of economic development and start encouraging a creative climate that allows people of all backgrounds to plug into their milieu. Only thus will a region become a truly creative and entrepreneurial center.

APPENDIX

Ranking Regions: The Creativity Index

Rank	Region	Creativity Index	Overall Rank	Creative Class	High-Tech	Innovation	Diversity
1	San Francisco	1057	1	12	1	5	1
2	Austin	1028	2	7	13	6	23
3	Boston	1015	3	6	2	12	41
3	San Diego	1015	3	30	14	13	4
5	Seattle	1008	5	20	3	34	11
6	Raleigh-Durham	996	6	5	16	8	52
7	Houston	980	7	22	19	39	16
8	Washington, D.C.	964	9	4	5	85	18
9	New York	962	10	25	15	54	20
10	Minneapolis	960	11	14	28	11	60
10	Dallas	960	11	55	6	40	15
12	Los Angeles	942	13	46	4	79	5
13	Atlanta	940	14	32	7	87	10
14	Denver	940	14	17	65	29	25
15	Chicago	935	16	29	10	56	46
16	Portland, OR	929	18	73	11	32	31
17	Philadelphia	927	19	27	17	36	70
18	Hartford, CT	922	21	16	41	35	61
19	Phoenix	909	22	92	8	46	21
20	Indianapolis	891	24	68	20	55	42
21	Rochester, NY	877	25	34	51	4	115
22	Sacramento	872	26	40	26	103	34
23	West Palm Beach	852	32	123	40	44	17
24	Columbus, OH	832	33	70	48	102	24
25	Kansas City	818	35	24	25	135	73
26	Tampa–St. Petersburg	804	38	76	42	128	26
27	Salt Lake City	798	41	139	35	45	59
28	Charlotte, NC	787	42	69	46	124	51
29	Miami	775	43	99	62	138	2
30	Cleveland	774	44	71	57	42	134
31	St. Louis	770	45	57	24	76	153
32	Orlando	752	49	108	43	164	9
33	Cincinnati	742	52	119	50	23	141
34	San Antonio	737	55	84	34	126	93
35	Milwaukee	736	56	111	61	38	128
36	Pittsburgh	734	57	53	31	50	210
37	Jacksonville, FL	715	64	50	95	168	47
38	Nashville	711	66	79	70	171	45
39	Detroit	708	68	42	147	27	150
40	Providence, RI	698	70	120	80	108	71
41	Greensboro, NC	697	71	128	53	119	78
42	Oklahoma City	668	83	72	72	150	113
42	New Orleans	668	83	122	87	180	19
44	Grand Rapids, MI	639	95	197	76	52	110
45	Louisville	622	100	150	91	131	83
46	Buffalo	609	105	83	71	73	240
47	Las Vegas	561	117	257	74	178	8
48	Norfolk–Virginia Beach, VA	555	120	97	60	200	162
49	Memphis	530	132	184	100	141	119

PART TWO

HIGH-TECH ENTREPRENEURSHIP

The University-Industry-Government Connection

4

Start-ups and Spin-offs

Collective Entrepreneurship Between Invention and Innovation

Philip E. Auerswald and Lewis M. Branscomb

The function of entrepreneurs is to reform or revolutionize the pattern of production by exploiting an invention, or more generally, an untried technological possibility for producing a new commodity or producing an old one in a new way, by opening up a new source of supply of materials or a new outlet for products, by reorganizing an industry, and so on.... To undertake such new things is difficult and constitutes a distinct economic function, first because they lie outside of the routine tasks which everybody understands and secondly, because the environment resists in many ways that vary, according to social conditions, from simple refusal either to finance or buy a new thing, to physical attack on the man who tries to produce it.

– Joseph A. Schumpeter (1942: 132)

We thank Richard Zeckhauser for his input into this chapter via numerous conversations, as well as for allowing us to incorporate into this chapter jointly authored material. David Hart provided editorial guidance and comments. We have benefited from ongoing conversations with David Audretsch, Maryann Feldman, Paul Reynolds, Hans Severiens, and Jeffrey Sohl. Brian Min contributed to analysis of data. Pat McLaughlin assisted with editing. We acknowledge research support from the Advanced Technology Program of the U.S. Department of Commerce. Many of the findings reported in this chapter draw on the insights of practitioners who participated in five workshops (three held in Cambridge, MA, and one each in Palo Alto, CA, and Washington, D.C.) and in a set of structured interviews undertaken under the direction of the authors by the management consulting firm of Booz, Allen and Hamilton. For further information see Branscomb and Auerswald(2002), or our website at <www.fundinggap.org>.

61

INTRODUCTION

The most successful new technology ventures generate tremendous returns for their investors (see Scherer and Harhoff 2000). Interest in capturing a share of such potentially large returns has stimulated rapid growth in recent years in both the number and diversity of institutions specialized in supporting the commercial development and marketing of new technologies. These include venture capital firms, corporate venture funds, incubators of various types, niche law firms, university and government offices of technology transfer, and networks of individual private equity, or "angel," investors.[1] The funds available for the support of technology entrepreneurship have grown accordingly. Indeed, at present, by some measures, the supply of such funds seems to exceed the demand.[2] Yet, even in such an environment, practitioners report that the process of translating a basic science "invention" into a commercially viable "innovation" is not only extremely difficult, but getting more so (see Branscomb and Auerswald 2001, 2002; Preston 1993, 1997; Hall 2002).[3] The economic and technological factors driving this trend are not new. Four years ago, then Undersecretary of Commerce Mary Good testified before the Senate Committee on Governmental Affairs: "As the competitive pressures of the global marketplace have forced American firms to shift more of their R&D

---

[1] The term "angel" investor comes from the theater, where wealthy individuals take very high risks in funding the production of Broadway shows. By analogy, angels in high-tech investing are traditionally individuals with a successful record of commercial innovation who use their wealth and experience to invest very early in new, high-tech businesses.

[2] As of February 2002, the magnitude of commitments from the limited partners (such as pension funds, banks, endowments, and wealthy individuals) that invest in venture capital funds exceeded industry-wide disbursements by a total of $75 billion, more than the cumulative total venture capital investments from 1990 to 1998 (data from Venture Economics/National Venture Capital Association).

[3] Entrepreneurs in many settings also report a particular difficulty in raising funds in the range of $200,000 to $2 million. The hypothesis of such a "capital gap" in seed stage funding for new ventures is discussed by Sohl (1999), and consistently supported by practitioners (see, for example, comments by participants at a Senate Small Business Committee Forum, <www.senate.gov/~sbc/hearings/internet.html>). The hypothesis is not restricted to the United States. In 1999 the U.K. Department of Trade and Industry published a report titled "Addressing the SME [small and medium enterprise] Equity Gap." At a recent National Science Foundation-sponsored conference, Jian Gao of Tsinghua University (Beijing, PRC) reported that an analogous "capital gap" phenomenon has been observed in China.

into shorter term product and process improvements, an 'innovation gap' has developed. . . . Sit down with a group of venture capitalists. The funding for higher risk ventures . . . is extraordinarily difficult to come by" (Gompers and Lerner 1999: 2).[4] Furthermore, markets, technologies, and their interrelation are becoming increasingly complex. As Martin Weitzman (1998: 333) has noted, "the ultimate limits to growth may lie not as much in our ability to generate new ideas, so much as in our ability to process an abundance of potentially new seed ideas into usable forms."

In this chapter we ask: Is there an "innovation gap" or "funding gap"? If so, how is it defined and manifested? In proposing answers to these questions, we argue that specific institutional and behavioral disjunctures in the process of technology development may systematically impede the flow of financial and other resources to even the most promising nascent technology ventures. Our particular focus is on the role of technology entrepreneurs in managing "early stage" technology development (ESTD) projects – the transition from invention to innovation. Thus we will contrast the personal qualities of entrepreneurship that are critical in radical, science-based innovations with the institutional context in which the entrepreneur is enmeshed. Our aims are (1) to characterize the sources and channels of ESTD finance, enhancing understanding of the processes that govern entrepreneurship during this high-risk transition, and (2) to inform public policies intended to encourage commercial innovations based on scientific and technological research.

The chapter begins by setting our problem in the larger context of recent scholarship on invention, innovation, and entrepreneurship. We then map the region of the technology development process that lies "between invention and innovation." Defining as our unit of analysis the technology project, backed by a champion, rather than the firm as

---

[4] Gompers and Lerner (1999) quite accurately point out an apparent contradiction in the quote from Dr. Good, which appears in its edited form to suggest that venture capitalists are reluctant to provide risk capital. Of course, this is not the case. As these authors describe, the venture capital mode of finance is precisely that which is specialized in providing finance in contexts where uncertainty is high and information asymmetries severe. At the same time, however, as Morgenthaler (2000) and other venture capitalists report, the risk/reward ratio for seed stage, technology-based ventures is not so attractive to venture capital firms as that for slightly later stage ventures. We develop this argument further below.

a whole, we characterize the institutional context for early stage technology development. Elaborating on Arrow (1962) and Zeckhauser (1996), we observe that the particular uncertainties and risks inherent in technology entrepreneurship, and the challenge of integrating technical and market knowledge, significantly complicate the process of writing contracts for technical information. At the same time, a complex mix of motivations and skills is required to bring a technology project to fruition. We introduce the term "collective entrepreneurship" to describe the trust- and reputation-based process by which these linked challenges are overcome. We then examine in some detail two paradigmatic contexts in which collective entrepreneurship occurs: university-based "start-ups" and corporate "spin-offs." In each of these contexts, the technology development process is shepherded by an ESTD "angel" – a term we employ in reference not only to private equity investors, but also to the small subset of corporate technology managers and Federal program officers who act as the *external* champions of high-risk, nascent technology ventures. We conclude by elaborating on the implications of the work for public policy.

EARLY STAGE TECHNOLOGY DEVELOPMENT IN CONTEXT

Forty years after Nelson (1959) and Arrow (1962), the scientific and technological enterprise of the United States – sources of funding, characteristics of performing institutions, and motivations of researchers – is reasonably well understood by academics and policymakers alike (Stephan 1996). Similarly, corporate motivations, governance, finance, strategy, and competitive advantage have been much studied and are relatively well understood. But the process by which a technical idea of possible commercial value is converted into one or more commercially successful products – the transition from invention to innovation – is highly complex, poorly documented, and little studied. Most of the relevant data are either private or not tabulated to begin with. Yet technological innovation is critical to long-term economic growth, and the core driver of technological innovation is, in turn, the capacity to turn inventions into innovations. Understanding this transition is critical to the formulation both of public policies and private business strategies designed to make the conversion of the nation's research assets into economic assets more effective.

Institutions that fund basic research and those that fund new ventures tend to hew to dissimilar investment policies. Most government agencies that fund R&D in the universities use peer review to select the projects; this process gives priority to research leading to new insights into the natural world, to the disadvantage of those motivated by the promise of commercial applications. On the other hand, venture capital firms and banks are reluctant to invest or lend if the technical content of a business proposal is not sufficiently well established to provide reliable estimates of product cost, performance, and reliability in the context of an identified market that can be developed in a reasonable length of time. For many high technology innovations the research required to bring a technical concept to the point of supporting such a business case is expensive and time consuming. It is the funding of this technical bridge – from invention to innovation – that is the focus of this chapter and the basis for the notion of an "innovation gap" or "funding gap."[5]

Data analysis of funding for ESTD projects, reported in Branscomb and Auerswald (2002), provides a further motivation for our argument here. In that parallel work, we demonstrate that support for start-ups and spin-offs comes predominantly from three relatively (that is, as compared with venture capital) unheralded sources: angel investors, corporations, and the Federal government. Entrepreneurs who are advancing ESTD projects reside in a wide variety of institutional settings, and receive funding and mentoring from an equally wide variety of sources. Throughout this chapter we employ the terms "start-ups" and "spin-offs" in particular ways to distinguish two categories of ESTD projects. A "start-up" in our usage is a technology firm whose genesis lies outside of the commercial world in a university or other academic setting. In a start-up, the transition of a technology from invention to innovation is accompanied by the migration of its inventors from academia to a new business. In

---

[5] The existence of an "innovation gap" or "funding gap" in the textbook economics sense of a shortfall from a social optimum would be extremely difficult to establish empirically. Doing so would require not only reliable data on both the demand for and supply of early stage technology funding, but also computation of the marginal social benefits of such funding. Such a project would be an interesting and valuable one, and it has been rigorously pursued by Griliches (1992) and Jones and Williams (1998), among others. It is not our objective here, however, to offer conclusive results regarding the *appropriate* distribution of inputs into ESTD projects.

contrast, a "spin-off" is an ESTD project initiated in a large corporation but advanced toward the market in an entrepreneurial venture. These definitions allow us to distinguish the motivations and challenges involved in these two important contexts.

Start-ups based on university-licensed intellectual property and new technology firms backed by venture capital – two particular types of ESTD ventures about which data are readily available, and which thus have been studied intensively – represent only a small portion of all ESTD activity. The bulk of ESTD activity occurs in the relative obscurity (from the standpoint of data availability) of university-originated start-up firms *not* based on the licensing of university-held intellectual property; corporate research projects undertaken outside of business divisions; spin-offs from corporations; and other undertakings by technology entrepreneurs backed by a mix of angel investment, Federal grants and procurement, direct corporate funding, and partnerships.

Yet, regardless of whether the new venture is a start-up or a spin-off and no matter what its source of funding, the collectivity that is engaging in technology entrepreneurship must include individuals with the skills to assess simultaneously both technologies and markets. Mentoring is as important as funding for entrepreneurs embarked on the invention to innovation transition. The most effective angel investors are unique in that they possess both experience and financial resources to assist technology entrepreneurs. Having "been there and done that," they are better suited to the mentoring of the inexperienced entrepreneur than more institutionally grounded investors. The need for mentoring poses a challenge for Federal programs such as the government-wide Small Business Innovation Research program (SBIR) and the Commerce Department's Advanced Technology Program (ATP). It is unclear the extent to which such programs can (or should) engage technology entrepreneurs in partnerships that are as rich in mentoring as those created by angels.

The geographical dimension of entrepreneurship is explored by several other contributors to this volume (including David Audretsch, Richard Florida, Maryann Feldman, and Andrew Toole); we have relatively little to say here on that subject. We note, however, that our analysis leads us to policy recommendations distinct from, but complementary to, those that flow from the economic "cluster" approach developed in Porter (1990) and subsequent work. Historical evidence amply supports the presence of significant geographically localized knowledge spillovers, within given industries (see, for example, Jaffe, Trajtenberg, and Henderson 1993; Feldman 1994b). Persuasive theoretical arguments, and some empirical evidence, however, support the parallel claim that sustained regional growth also requires a degree of economic diversity (see, for example, Glaeser et al. 1992; Feldman and Audretsch 1999). In an era in which technologies, products, and services are increasingly developed on shared platforms, with networks of research centers, suppliers, and customers linked in complex ways across industry boundaries, the identification of key economic clusters presents policymakers with a severe practical challenge. Even when clusters can be identified, the question remains: what are the critical points of leverage, if any, for public policy?

Our analysis suggests that regions seeking to build a capacity for technology-based innovation should complement programs emphasizing the targeted development of clusters with generic policies supporting collective entrepreneurship. Barriers to entry in the field of any complementary capability will hurt entrepreneurial activity in general.[6]

With this context in mind, we turn to a more rigorous definition of ESTD.

THE DISJUNCTURE BETWEEN INVENTION AND INNOVATION

The Unit of Analysis

Entrepreneurship is a broad category of economic activity. By one operational definition, it encompasses "any attempt at new business or new venture creation, such as self-employment, a new business organization, or the expansion of an existing business, by an individual, a team of individuals, or an established business" (Reynolds, Hay, and Camp 1999: 3). According to survey work by Paul Reynolds and colleagues, there are in the United States at present about 15 million entrepreneurs actively engaged in launching new ventures as varied as catering services, consulting firms, educational software companies,

---

[6] This line of argument echoes some of the themes in the chapter by Pages, Freedman, and Von Bargen in this volume.

and biotechnology start-ups. Most of these entrepreneurs create or manage firms to deliver an existing, well-defined product or service at a small scale to a new or growing market. A few are engaged in bringing to market products or services that are new (the sort of activity emphasized by Schumpeter) and based on fundamental advances in technology and science. These "technology entrepreneurs" represent, according to the same survey results, no fewer than 3 to 4 percent of all entrepreneurs – about a half million individuals, involved in roughly 200,000 nascent science- and technology-based ventures (Reynolds 2000). Our unit of analysis in the study of technology-based innovation is a member of this group – not a firm, but rather the champion of a technology project.[7]

The Interval Between Invention and Innovation

A diagram of the innovation process that allows us to define the "invention to innovation" transition is presented in Figure 4.1.[8] The arrows across the top of, and in between, the five stages of technology development and funding are intended to suggest the many complex ways in which the stages interrelate. The first two stages lie within the world of research and development, beginning with the research base on which innovative ideas rest, followed by the demonstration (proof of principle or concept) of a technical device or process speculated to have unique commercial value. The end of stage 2 is the point for which we are using the shorthand label "invention." The device or process invented is not always – perhaps not often – patent protected, but it does represent a technical achievement whose value can be protected in some manner.

The third stage, the link between invention and innovation, begins when a new product and market are identified. In this stage, product

---

[7] Low and MacMillan (1988) and Audretsch (1995) take a similar approach. In cases of innovations created within established firms, an innovative project is generally small relative to the firm. In other important cases, however, the project/team is the link that binds a set of firms sequentially created out of a single core idea. An example is the so-called Shockley Eight, eight engineers, including Gordon Moore, who left Shockley Semiconductor and founded first Fairchild Semiconductor, then Intel and numerous other path-breaking Silicon Valley firms.

[8] The literature on technology management contains innumerable variants on this diagram. A good example is that developed in Lane (1999). Formal models involving staged technology development include Aghion et al. (2002) and Judd et al. (2002).

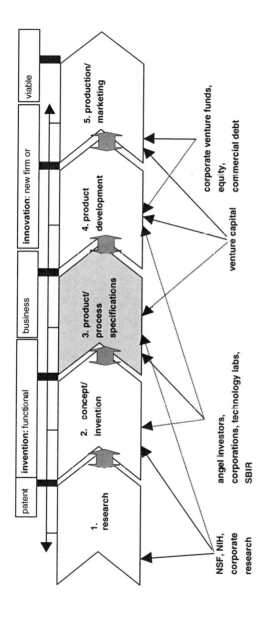
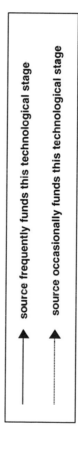

Figure 4.1. Sequential model of development and funding. The region corresponding to the hypothesized "invention to innovation" transition is shaded in gray. The boxes at top indicate milestones in the development of a science-based innovation. The arrows across the top of, and in between, the five stages represented in this sequential model are intended to suggest the many complex ways in which the stages interrelate. Multiple exit options are available to technology entrepreneurs at different stages in this branching sequence of events.

specifications appropriate to the identified market are demonstrated. Production processes begin to be developed, allowing estimates of product cost. At the end of stage 3 the entrepreneurial team has articulated a business case. The entrepreneurial venture can now hope to attract levels of capital sufficient to permit initial production and marketing, moving the project into stage 4. At the end of stage 4, the product has been introduced to the market. An "innovation" in the Schumpeterian sense has occurred. If the innovation is commercially successful, investors can expect to see early returns on their investment in stage 5.

Our focus, then, is stage 3 of this model. We use the phrase "early stage technology development" (ESTD) to describe this region of technology development space.[9] *It is this stage that we propose corresponds with the "innovation gap" identified by practitioners.* Initially a scientist or technologist demonstrates *to his or her own satisfaction* that a given breakthrough could form the basis for a commercial product (proof of principle). A substantial amount of difficult and potentially costly research (sometimes many years' worth) will be needed, however, before the envisioned product is transformed into a commercial reality with sufficient functionality, low enough cost, high enough quality, and a big enough potential market to survive economic competition. Few scientists engaged in academic research (or the agencies funding their work) possess the full set of skills and access to the resources to undertake ESTD. As we will discuss in detail below, a collective effort is required.

Before moving forward, we note that our usage of the terms "start-up" and "spin-off" is more narrow than the usage in common parlance. Specifically, in reference to Figure 4.1, a "start-up" here refers to an ESTD project where stages 1 and 2 (invention) occur in

---

[9] With a slight abuse of language, we employ the phrase "invention to innovation transition" interchangeably with "early stage technology development." Since an innovation is defined as successful entry to market, these phrases should embrace, strictly speaking, stages 3 and 4 as they appear in Figure 4.1. But our concept of the critical "gap" between the established institutions of R&D and those of business and finance really concerns only stage 3. There is no generally agreed term for the point between stages 3 and 4 except "reduction to practice," which refers only to the technical activities in stage 3, and "seed and startup finance," concepts specific to venture capital, which is only one of the potential sources of funding for traversing stage 3. In our analysis of capital flows, we attempt to focus on only phase 3, the gap between invention and a validated business case.

association with a university, whereas 4 and 5 (innovation and commercial development) take place in a new firm.[10] In contrast, a "spin-off" refers to an ESTD project initiated (stages 1 and 2) in a corporation, and continued (stages 4 and 5) in a new technology venture.

Who Funds Early Stage Technology Development?

Technology entrepreneurs make use of a wide variety of funding options to keep their projects alive. These include not only successive rounds of sales of their firm's equity to investors willing to bear substantial risks, but also contract work, and income from such sources as the licensing of intellectual property and the sale of spin-off firms. Complementing all these approaches is old-fashioned cost cutting. Each funding source is associated with its unique costs and benefits. As much as possible, entrepreneurs try to preserve both financial and managerial control over their projects. Most also recognize, however, that they need to gain access not only to funding, but also (as or more important) to relationship networks and mentoring. In practice, as opposed to theory, decisions regarding funding sources (like other complex matching processes) depend heavily on timing and past events. Rather than optimizing over all possible future pathways of financing, most entrepreneurs simply take the best deal they can get, when they can get it.

In contrast with the relatively well understood institutional sources of equity and debt capital for advancing existing businesses incrementally, the transition from invention to innovation is financed by a great variety of mechanisms. These parallel, but are distinct from, the wide variety of funding *strategies* employed by technology entrepreneurs. Institutional "species" comprising the ESTD ecosystem include not only well recognized entities such as venture capital firms, large corporations, and universities, but also new forms such as angel networks, angel funds, university and corporate venture capital funds and incubators, experimental R&D programs supported by Federal and state government, fast track regulatory clearance services by state

---

[10] Commercially promising research ideas are pursued not only by faculty and students in university departments and centers proper, but by graduate students and others who choose to pursue commercial ventures outside the formal embrace of the university but who still draw sustenance from many links in the extended university community.

and local governments, and specialized services firms (for example, in law, real estate, or accounting).

The institution most closely identified with support for technology entrepreneurs is the venture capital firm. Gompers and Lerner (1999) point out that the venture capital form of funding is particularly appropriate to situations in which there is a high degree of information asymmetry: Venture capitalists must overcome "tremendous incentive and informational problems. Venture capitalists typically concentrate in industries with a great deal of uncertainty, where information gaps among entrepreneurs and investors are commonplace. These firms typically have substantial intangible assets which are difficult to value and may be impossible to resell if the firm fails. Similarly, market conditions in many of these industries are highly variable." The magnitude of venture capital disbursements in 2001 was an imposing $37 billion, down from about $100 billion at the peak of the dot-com boom, but substantially larger than previous cyclical low points (Gompers and Lerner 2002).

Does venture capital dominate support for ESTD projects? Our analysis suggests not. As noted above, the best available data imply that there are roughly 200,000 technology ventures in the United States, many involving just one or two self-employed entrepreneurs. Surveys of angel networks conducted by a team at the University of New Hampshire's Whittemore School of Business and Economics suggest that perhaps 10 percent of these ventures per year, or about 20,000 new firms, receive funding from angel investors in amounts typically ranging from $100,000 to $1 million per deal.[11] In contrast, fewer than 500 companies a year receive venture capital "seed stage" funding. The total number of firms that ultimately succeeded in raising money from public markets through initial public offerings (IPOs) in 2001 was 91; in 1999, there were 537 (Hale and Dorr LLP 2001).

As a rule, venture capital firms specialize in acquiring promising technology firms, not in building such firms from scratch. Venture capital firms support nascent ventures through mechanisms other than investments categorized as "seed stage" (such as bridge loans),[12]

---

[11] Estimates based on preliminary survey results presented by Jeff Sohl at the "Between Invention and Innovation" workshop, January 25, 2001, summarized in Branscomb and Auerswald (2002). See also Sohl (1999).

[12] Bridge loans represent a particularly important source. These (usually small) loans are provided to early stage ventures prior to an initial round of funding. If a funding round

but only a fraction of venture capital funding at all stages of company advancement directly supports the development of new technology (as opposed to other activities of new firms such as management, production, and marketing). Furthermore, anecdotal evidence backed by data on disbursement trends suggests that the risk/reward ratio is most favorable from the standpoint of venture capital in the first and second round of financing. Seed stage investments require a great deal of attention, and involve high risk.[13] Later, third and fourth round, investments offer inadequate returns. As a consequence, the distribution of venture capital deals has trended away from early stage investments, and toward first and second round investments.[14]

In Branscomb and Auerswald (2002) we sought to identify the portion of reported R&D investments and expenditures that are directed to early stage technology development. Doing so is a challenging task. Existing data[15] are not gathered in a way that allows direct comparison of flows of funding from different public and private institutional sources in support of ESTD projects. Blurred distinctions between the traditional categories of basic research, applied research, and development further complicate analysis of existing data.[16] Such distinctions are often based more on the motivations of the investigator than those of the investor, and as such are of little use in our effort to track funding supporting early stage commercialization efforts. There is no straightforward way to use government R&D data to identify

takes place, the loans are converted to equity. We thank Josh Lerner for emphasizing this point.

[13] As Hans Severiens (founder of Silicon Valley's first angel network, the Band of Angels) points out: "Early stage investment is a tough area. A lot of work has to be done. I think that is one of the reasons VCs do tend to shy away from it." For the same number of hours mentoring a seed stage venture as opposed to a company ready for its first or second round funding, "why not invest $10 million rather than $1 million?"

[14] Data from NVCA/Venture Economics. We thank Michael Horvath (Tuck School of Business, Dartmouth) for bringing these trends to our attention.

[15] Important sources are the NSF surveys on research and development funding and expenditures, data on the venture capital industry from Venture Economics, and the limited data on angel investing reported by Sohl (1999) and van Osnabrugge and Robinson (2000).

[16] See, for example, Council on Competitiveness (1996): "The old distinctions between basic and applied research has proven politically unproductive and no longer reflects the realities of the innovation process."

the portion of aggregated funding that is directed at ESTD activities. Attempts at a "top down" interpretation of existing data require the subtraction from a large, aggregate number (such as total industry R&D) of a speculative estimate of the portion *not* directed toward ESTD, leaving a small and uncertain residual. Attempts at a "bottom up" approach involve either dramatic extrapolation from anecdotal testimony or the sort of large-scale data gathering effort that has not been done and is outside the scope of the current project. (See Figure 4.2.)

The methodology in Branscomb and Auerswald (2002) does not overcome these fundamental constraints. Rather, it represents an attempt at benchmarking the existing data in a manner that takes the limitations of the data as given. Because of these challenges, we present two models that we believe represent underestimates and overestimates of ESTD funding from its main sources. We have not attempted a "best-informed estimate" lying between these two limiting cases for each funding source. Instead, we have focused on estimating the fraction of ESTD funding flowing through each of the channels discussed, since this fraction seems relatively invariant to the model selected and is the figure most relevant for informing public policy.

We wish to determine what fraction of U.S. national R&D expenditures, or of the investments involved in creating the half million new firms founded in the United States each year, is directed at ESTD. Since the unique feature of the transition from invention to innovation is the intimate interdependence of technical research and market sensitivity to product specifications, we suggest that the intent of the investor to develop a *new* high-tech product or service should be the central criterion used to identify ESTD investments. Such a definition suggests, for example, that the Federal SBIR and ATP programs, which expressly have this intent, are clear examples of Federal programs on which our attention should focus and represent a lower bound to the ESTD estimate for Federal contributions. Similarly, angel investments and some venture capital funds that focus on the seed and early stages of a technology-based business enterprise can be assumed to share such an intent. So too do efforts by companies and universities to spin out new ventures based on inventions made by their employees in areas outside their core businesses.

Lower ESTD Estimate: $5.4 Billion

Upper ESTD Estimate: $35.6 Billion

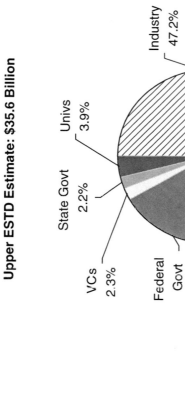

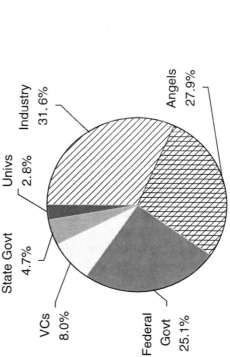

Figure 4.2. Estimated distribution of ESTD funding, based on narrow (lower estimate) and broader (upper estimate) definitional criteria.

We estimate that, of the $266 billion spent in 1998 on national R&D and invested by angels and venture capitalists in the United States, investments and expenditures flowing into ESTD activities made up roughly 2 to 14 percent, or $5 to $36 billion. We preserve this broad range to remind the reader that these estimates are primarily meant to provide policymakers with information on the relative importance of different sources of ESTD funding – in particular, the magnitude of Federal investment relative to that from corporations, venture capitalists, angel investors, states, and universities. We find that expenditures on ESTD by angel investors, corporate "out of the core business" seed investments, and Federal agency programs are roughly comparable to one another in magnitude (see Figure 4.2). The importance of each of these three funding sources greatly exceeds state programs, university expenditures, and the small part of venture capital investment that goes to support early stage technology projects. Notably – even excluding as we do the impact of government procurement – the Federal role in this process is substantial. In our estimates roughly 20 to 25 percent of the total ESTD comes from Federal sources. Although small in absolute terms when compared to total industrial R&D, ESTD investment significantly impacts long-term economic growth by converting the nation's portfolio of science and engineering research into innovations generating new paths for industrial growth.

An "Innovation Gap"?

The notion of an "innovation gap" or "funding gap" is controversial. Yet, from the standpoint of theoretical fundamentals as set forth in Arrow (1962), the existence of a "market failure" in the funding of ESTD projects should come as no surprise. Generically, perfect competition may fail to achieve optimal resource allocation whenever products are indivisible (marginal cost pricing rules apply imperfectly), economic actors are unable to appropriate the full returns from their activities (social and private benefits diverge), and/or outcomes are uncertain (future states of nature are unknown). Clearly, all three of these attributes characterize ESTD projects. Of the three, it is instructive to note that the discussion in Arrow (1962) begins not with inadequate incentives to innovate due to imperfect appropriability, but rather with contracting problems due to uncertainty. In particular, Arrow points out that the activity of "invention" has particular characteristics that complicate the ability of economic actors to relieve themselves of risks due to uncertainty. Arrow notes that success in highly risky business activities, including "invention" depends on

an inextricable tangle of objective uncertainties and decisions of the entrepreneurs and is certainly uninsurable. On the other hand, such activities should be undertaken if the expected return exceeds the market rate of return, no matter what the variance is. The existence of common stocks would seem to solve the allocation problem . . . But then again the actual managers no longer receive the full reward of their decisions; the shifting of risks is again accompanied by a weakening of incentives to efficiency.[17]

Elaborating on Arrow (1962) and Zeckhauser (1996), we argue that the most critical fixed factor in the support of technology entrepreneurs is not financial capital per se, but human capital and time, in particular, the time of those few individuals with the skills to assess both technological possibilities and market opportunities. Every high-technology innovation, by its nature, calls for specialized technical knowledge. And every radical innovation that is supposed to create a market that does not yet exist can only be evaluated by someone with experience in new market creation in that segment of the business world. Talent at this level to assess both technologies and markets is scarce. Furthermore, the value of a technical idea close to commercial application depreciates rapidly. Consequently, as Zeckhauser (1996) argues, technological information (TI) is not, as is widely assumed in the economics literature, a public good. Indeed, "excessive focus" on the public good character of technological information has led economists "to slight the major class of market failures associated with TI that stems from its amorphous quality."[18] Zeckhauser

---

[17] Hellman (1998) describes the manner in which control rights in venture capital contracts mitigate the sorts of risks described by Arrow (1962).

[18] To emphasize this point, Zeckhauser (1996: 12746) offers the following illustration: "A thought experiment might ask what would happen if information remained a public good, but were susceptible to contract. Fortunately, there are public goods that offer relatively easy contracting, such as songs or novels, which offer an interesting contrast with information. Such goods appear to be well-supplied to the market, with easy entry by skilled low-cost songwriters and novelists."

identifies five distinguishing characteristics of technical information that complicate contracting:

- Technical information is difficult to count and value.
- To value technical information, it may be necessary to "give away the secret."
- To prove its value, technical information is often bundled into complete products (for example, a computer chip or pharmaceutical product).
- Sellers' superior knowledge about technical information makes buyers wary of overpaying.
- Inefficient contracts are often designed to secure rents from technical information.

Congressman Vern Ehlers, among others, uses the term "Valley of Death" to dramatize the particular challenges facing entrepreneurs engaged in the transition from invention to innovation.[19] The imagery of the Valley of Death suggests a barren territory. In reality, however, between the stable shores of the S&T enterprise and the business and finance enterprise is a sea of life and death of business and technical ideas, of "big fish" and "little fish" contending – with survival going to the creative, agile, and persistent. Thus instead of "Valley of Death" we suggest that the appropriate image is that of the "Darwinian Sea."

Despite the large amounts of capital looking for lucrative private equity investments, the ability to place the money is limited by the ability to match the needs of technical entrepreneur and business investor. Research funds are available (typically from corporate research arms, government agencies, or, more rarely, personal assets) to support the creation of the idea and the initial demonstration that it works. Investment funds can be found for a market-ready prototype, with validated specifications and processes, supported by a validated business case. In

---

[19] A seasoned consultant on corporate strategy related to technology elaborates (Branscomb and Auerswald 2002): "I would define [the] Valley of Death [as occurring] when the amount of money you're starting to ask for – the bill – starts to add up to the point where management says, 'What are you guys up to, what are you doing, and what am I going to get out of it?' But yet it is sufficiently early in the process that you don't feel you can answer that question. If you are fortunate enough that the questions come when you have an answer, you, in fact, have scooted over the Valley. If not, you are squarely in that Valley."

between, however, there are typically few sources of funding available to aspiring innovators seeking to bridge this "disjuncture" in funding sources. From the perspective of the technology entrepreneur, this situation will look like an "innovation gap."

TECHNOLOGISTS AND EXECUTIVES: DIVERGENT SKILLS, SHARED MOTIVATIONS

On opposite sides of the "Darwinian Sea" stand apparently very different groups of people. Scientists and technologists populate the invention shore; managers and investors reside on the innovation side. Each of these groups has different training, expectations, information sources, and modes of expression. The scientists and technologists know what is technologically interesting, what may be technically feasible, and what is fundamentally novel. In the event of failure, these experts risk a loss of reputation, as well as forgone pecuniary returns. They are personally dedicated to realizing a vision of what could be.

Managers and investors know about the process of bringing new products to market, but may have to trust their expert counterparts when it comes to the technical particulars of projects. Investors are generally putting at risk other people's money. The investor is committed to producing a profitable return on his investments, regardless of the technology or market through which that return is realized. To the extent that scientists and technologists on the one hand and investors and managers on the other do not fully trust one another or cannot communicate effectively, the disjunctures between invention and innovation become even more severe.

These groups also assess opportunities differently. The decisions of inventors to pursue given lines of inquiry are driven by complex sets of criteria varying substantially from individual to individual. Yet among the defining characteristics of academic inquiry in particular is the freedom to pursue research motivated solely by the researcher's *interest* in the question posed. Inventors in corporate settings have less freedom, but often share the intrinsic motivations of academic scientists. Although the criterion of "interestingness" does not directly correlate with the stage of the research in the context of the model above – applying as well to research classified as "basic" as it does to that classified as "applied" – it does contrast sharply with a decision rule based on commercial potential. A fundamental challenge involved in taking a project from invention to innovation is accomplishing the shift from decisions based on the criterion of "interestingness" to one based on the criterion of commercial value.

Thus, the role of entrepreneurship in creating successful innovations is likely to embrace not one entrepreneur but several – the inventor with her dream of a new way to serve human needs, the business visionary willing to embrace the inventor's dream, and the financier willing to take unusual risks in the quest for an extraordinary return. This concept of "collective entrepreneurship" not only emphasizes the difficulty of assembling this set of talents into one project but also the importance of the networks of relationships that bring them together. It also makes one appreciate all the more how unusual it is when one individual actually embraces all these talents and single-handedly, so to speak, traverses the Darwinian Sea successfully. The names of such individuals are as well known as they are rare: among them, Edwin Land, founder of Polaroid; Bill Gates, founder of Microsoft; and David Packard and William Hewlett, founders of HP.

By "collective entrepreneurship" we do not mean a committee, but rather the complicated process through which inventors engage with managers and together mobilize early-stage funding from investors. The inventor might mature into the business leader, the CEO of the enterprise. Or the investor may insist on replacing the initiating CEO with another more experienced in management. If there is sufficient trust and common interest and if egos do not get too much in the way this process can be successful and ultimately the emergent leader may have acquired the basic skills in all three areas – technology, management, and finance. She or he is then prepared, perhaps, for a second venture with a much higher likelihood of success.

The likelihood of success is then quite dependent on the context in which the founders find themselves, and this context will also influence the patterns of finance most likely to be available for the venture. The technical entrepreneur is the initiator of the innovation. Where are such people found? Let us now consider two situations: start-ups from academic settings and spin-offs from existing business enterprises. This discussion will bring us back to the modes of finance and to the increasingly important role of angel investors.

Start-ups: The Similar Motivations but Different Skills of Academic Scientists and CEOs

Just as most business entrepreneurs focus on building small-scale ventures that offer at most small, incremental improvements on existing goods or services, most academics build stable careers out of small, incremental contributions in increasingly narrowly defined disciplines. Indeed, as knowledge advances and markets become increasingly complex, pressures grow on both entrepreneurs and academics alike to "define your niche" and subsequently "stick to your knitting." Regardless of whether one emphasizes vision, culture, calculation, or adaptation as the decisive factors in the "entrepreneurial event," the question remains: Why work on a hard problem for uncertain reward rather than work on an easier problem for more predictable returns? The motivation to take those risks and reach for the level of self-fulfillment and recognition that drives entrepreneurs is surprisingly similar in both academic and business entrepreneurs.

Consider first those university professors who take an entrepreneurial approach to their professional lives. For these academics, what is at stake in the decision to leave the (presumed) security of an academic department for the uncertainty of a new firm? The following excerpt from an interview with deCODE Genetics founder Kari Stefansson provides the beginnings of an answer:

Interviewer: What has it been like for you to be a CEO instead of an academic scientist?
Stefansson: The difference between the two is vastly overrated. What mostly drives you is the desire to win, to perform, to control your own fate, whether you do it through money, or the admiration of people who follow your work, or whatever. It's a larger scale: I was running a lab of 10 or 15 people; I'm now running a company of about 450 people. But it's basically the same thing. You put together certain ideas, you gather the people who can execute them. The fact that you can create value out of the results of your research doesn't alter in any way the weight or the importance of the fundamental questions you are asking.[20]

According to this account, which is supported by sociological studies (see, for example, Etzkowitz 1989), technology entrepreneurs who

---

[20] *Technology Review,* April 2001, p. 52.

start new firms previously were usually technology entrepreneurs who worked in academic research laboratories. The roles are fundamentally linked by "the desire to win, to perform, to control your own fate, whether you do it through money, or the admiration of people who follow your work." In each setting, the academic researcher or CEO "put together certain ideas" and gathered "the people who can execute them." Both, as Etzkowitz (1989) points out, must be entrepreneurs, but of different types. Wealth, Nobel Prizes, high rankings in citations indices, and photos on the cover of *Fortune* magazine all constitute high returns to a risky venture in terms of the underlying currency of recognition: "recognition" as an authority, "recognition" by awards and/or high salary; and in the more primitive sense of the word, "recognition" by name or by face. Junior academics who have not yet earned tenure and young business entrepreneurs both face the related challenges of developing a distinctive vision, contending with culture, and engaging in complex risk/return calculations in the face of substantial uncertainty. The academic who pushes toward the frontier of knowledge and takes daring intellectual positions may be a future candidate for prizes and other forms of peer approbation. If the positions taken are too speculative or prove unfounded, however, the junior academic's career may be jeopardized. Many commercial entrepreneurs from academia are students or fellows who find the risk/return profile of a business career more favorable than that of an academic one.

To say that the decision problems facing academic scientists and those of technology CEOs are isomorphic is not, however, to say that the skills required for success in each setting are the same. Quite to the contrary, as emphasized above, the apparently distinct roles of professor and CEO are actually rooted in the radically different skill set required of each – technical for the former, financial/managerial for the latter.

This similarity of entrepreneurial motivations and dissimilarity of skills required from technical and business entrepreneurs is dramatically illustrated by the fate of many founding CEOs of newly formed high-tech ventures. Venture capitalists on the boards of such firms often find it necessary to ask the founding CEO to step aside or assume the more limited role of Chief Technical Officer to make room for a proven manager. As the experienced venture capitalist David Morgenthaler said, "I can remember no case where we intervened to replace a CEO too soon" (Branscomb and Auerswald 2001: 101). Only rarely will a single individual possess, or acquire with sufficient speed, all the skills needed to make a successful transition from scientific visionary to CEO. The disjuncture in the skills required for success as an academic scientist and those required to lead a technology-based start-up is a critical component of the challenge facing the transition from a science-based "invention" to a commercial "innovation" ready for market.

Spin-offs: The Fruit of Frustration

For technology entrepreneurs within corporations seeking to advance "radical" technologies not directly tied to the core business, frustration is common. Pressures to achieve steady revenue growth drive corporations to pursue mostly incremental technological opportunities that leverage their existing value chain (Christensen 1997) and lend themselves to known business models (Chesbrough and Rosenbloom 2001). As Bruce Giffing of General Electric's corporate research center notes:

What we do is develop great evolutionary products that don't have a lot of technical risk. Most of the development that goes on in [a large corporation] is of that character. Revolutionary products require taking substantial technical risks, and that's basically the job of a lot of the people we have at the R&D center – to pursue those things that are difficult, frankly, to do in the environment that we're in. . . . Even in big companies that have a lot of resources, there is this valley [of death] that you talk about. And it's not always easy to overcome, and there are a lot of projects where this doesn't happen.[21]

Within nearly all large, technology-based corporations, formal processes exist for assessing the commercial prospects of early stage technology projects (Branscomb and Auerswald 2001). Such processes are effective in boosting near-term profitability based largely on continual evolutionary improvements to core products (Christensen 1997). When tied closely to near-term profitability, such processes may tend to suppress projects involving high magnitudes of technical risks and departures from the core business. In other cases such processes are

---

[21] Observation offered at "Between Invention and Innovation" workshop, Washington, DC, January 25, 2001.

constructed to ensure that the corporation maintains a fair share (often in the range of 10 to 15 percent) of its R&D outside of core business activities, in early stage projects directed toward returns in the longer term.

Often only two options exist for out-of-core innovations: give up or spin-off. Intel founder Gordon Moore remarks:

> In a pattern that clearly carries over to other technological ventures, we found at Fairchild that any company active on the forefront of semiconductor technology uncovers far more opportunities than it is in a position to pursue. And when people are enthusiastic about a particular opportunity but are not allowed to pursue it, they become potential entrepreneurs. As we have seen over the past few years, when these potential entrepreneurs are backed by a plentiful source of venture capital there is a burst of new enterprise. (Moore and Davis 2000: 11)[22]

Reviewing the literature on spin-offs, Klepper and Sleeper (2000: 4) note that "spinoffs occur when employees are frustrated with their employer. The frustration is often related to innovation. Sometimes employees want to pursue innovative ideas their employers are not willing to undertake. Relatedly, sometimes employees feel they have better insights than their employer about how to capitalize on an innovation developed by their employer or elsewhere." Some firms may cooperate with an inventor in the firm who desires to leave and start his or her own business. In other cases firms undertake to do this with corporate funds, perhaps engaging a venture capital firm like Ampersand in Boston that specializes in creating spin-off businesses from large firms. The more aggressive large corporations have established venture capital funds[23] to develop products or processes for internal use or sale by the firm; to capture returns from in-house inventions and boost retention of top research talent by displaying a willingness to support the development of innovations outside of the core business; and to develop markets for core products.

Larger, established, high-tech firms often encourage entrepreneurship. These firms try to create a larger scope for invention by their

---

[22] The early history of the semiconductor industry is described by Braun and Macdonald (1978).

[23] Impressively, corporate venture capital funds accounted for one-third of all venture capital disbursements in the peak year 2000.

top technologists by being prepared to "excubate" such ideas for development outside the firm.[24]

Overcoming Barriers to Innovation: Angels Are Everywhere

Start-ups and spin-offs both require champions who are pursuing visions for which there is no ready source of management and financial support.[25] In the case of start-ups, especially those from universities, the vision and commitment of the technical entrepreneur is rarely matched by the business experience and access to capital required to build a viable business. In the spin-off, the originating firm's pockets may be deep but they are not readily accessible to inventors whose projects diverge from the firm's core competencies. Furthermore, few technical entrepreneurs spinning new ventures out of a large firm have the right kind of business experience; they are not necessarily even so well-prepared as the academic entrepreneur. In these situations, the initial finance is most likely to come from a source prepared to mentor these technical visionaries through the acquisition of the networks of relationships required to overcome their limitations – a source that has "been there and done that." Increasingly, this source is the angel investor and mentor.

A critical element in the success of an angel investor, as in that of a venture capital firm, is the ability to gain and maintain good knowledge of the abilities of a large group of potential participants in early stage ventures, particularly those individuals with high levels of technological ability. As Leonard and Swap (2000) emphasize, the process of building a network of contacts is one that involves strategy and concerted effort. Private equity investors employ their networks not only in evaluating potential deals but also, and importantly, in building companies in which they have invested. Such mentors contribute to building companies by directly helping them develop business plans, products, and

---

[24] "Excubating" is a term employed by McGroddy (2001). It refers to looking outside the firm for partners to commercialize an innovation. This is an increasingly common way of compensating for the limitations of technical scope in the firm and reducing the institutional constraints on creating new, out-of-core products. Buyer-supplier co-development and the formation of research joint ventures similarly allow corporations to distribute risks and to benefit from increasing returns to scale and scope in research.

[25] The final two subsections of the chapter draw upon material jointly authored with Richard Zeckhauser.

marketing strategies, and (extensively) by providing them with access to networks of contacts – making introductions and attesting to quality. The success of the best venture capital firms (those that capture a disproportionate share of the returns in the industry) depends far less on their ability to *pick* winners than on their ability to *build* winners out of the companies that they support. This capability both adds value to the firms they fund and enables them to attract the most promising business propositions. Barriers to entry will be high, so individuals and firms that successfully manage such contracting should reap high rewards – a theoretical prediction readily supported by data.

The best of the angels are so-called cashed out entrepreneurs – entrepreneurs who have been through the collective entrepreneurship experience one or more times. They have learned the vital importance of trust and competence in all the skills required for success. They have built the networks of relationships, with other investors, with banks, lawyers, government regulators, and with all the other actors who can facilitate or impede the creation of a successful venture. They are a reservoir of "virtual entrepreneurs" who did acquire in their own entrepreneurial experience the range of skills that a Bill Gates or Edwin Land were somehow able to acquire as undergraduates, to successfully lead in each of the skills required for success.

Like their storybook counterparts, ESTD angels seek regular and direct engagement with the subjects of their beneficence. However, this category of angels, unlike the other, does not like to fly: More than 50 percent reportedly limit the geographical range of their investments to fifty miles from home (Sohl 1999; Wong 2002). Among the most robust findings of research concerning individual private equity investment is that it is a highly localized phenomenon. In the following section we close the chapter with a discussion of the regional dimension of the "innovation gap."

Putting Innovation in Its Place: Collective Entrepreneurship and Regional Economic Development

To the extent that financial resources are mobile and technical information is a public good that can be copied and transmitted at low cost, one would expect the invention-to-innovation transition to occur with comparable intensity wherever technical and business talent are located. However, a number of regions that lead in inventive activity (for example, as measured by per capita patenting) are relative laggards in terms of innovation.[26] Noting such "variation among advanced economies in their ability to innovate at the global frontier," Stern, Porter, and Furman (2000: 1) ask: "If inventors can draw on technological and scientific insights from throughout the world, why does R&D productivity depend on location?" The dominant theories offering answers to this question take a very aggregated perspective. Stern, Porter, and Furman highlight three: ideas-driven endogenous growth theory (Romer 1990),[27] the cluster-based theory of national industrial competitive advantage (Porter 1990), and the literature on national innovation systems (Nelson 1993). An aim of this volume, the present chapter included, is to complement these dominant analyses by reiterating the role of entrepreneurs, not only in economic development in general (ground ably covered by Schumpeter nearly a century ago), but particularly in *regional* economic development.

The cluster-based approach of Porter (1990) merits particular attention in this context. This approach emphasizes the importance for regional competitiveness of networks of functionally defined institutions supporting either the creation of final products (for example, wine-making in Napa Valley) or the development of a technology area (for example, biotechnology in the greater Boston area). As noted above, there is strong evidence that knowledge spillovers within given industries are geographically localized. Yet sustained regional growth also requires a degree of economic diversity. The advent of emerging fields such as bioinformatics and agricultural biotechnology signals an increasing integration between technology and industry areas, further complicating policymakers' attempts to define clusters. What is more, on both a theoretical and an empirical level, the identification of clusters is problematic for regions at both ends of the development spectrum: undeveloped regions where no identifiable collection of activities constitutes a viable economic cluster, and highly developed

---

[26] Documented examples include Cleveland, Ohio, and Stockholm, Sweden.

[27] The antecedent for Romer (1990) is found in Shell (1966; 1967). On national innovation systems, see Nelson (1993) and Branscomb and Keller (1998).

regions where the clusters are so densely interlinked that separating
them is a somewhat artificial undertaking.[28]

Our analysis suggests that regions seeking to build capacity for
technology-based innovation should complement programs emphasizing the targeted development of clusters with generic policies supporting collective entrepreneurship, bridging the invention to innovation
transition. Not surprisingly, the most innovative regions of the country
have seen rapid growth of critical institutional infrastructure, such as
venture capital or technology-oriented law firms. Policies may be de-
vised to overcome deficiencies in any complementary capability that
fails to support entrepreneurial activity in general. Competition favors
regions that have strong industry clusters yet whose economies are
not excessively specialized, and regions without rigid regulatory structures for investment and other barriers to activities that complement
knowledge creation and entrepreneurship.

An approach emphasizing the creation of generic infrastructure
to support collective entrepreneurship has relevance across the entire spectrum of the development process. A central characteristic
of much-publicized microlending initiatives in developing countries,
modeled after the Grameen Bank in Bangladesh, is the creation of entrepreneurial support and mentoring networks. In the United States, a
growing number of universities and regions have launched programs
targeted solely on building relationships and trust among participants
in ESTD activities.[29] Such programs do not focus on specific industry
clusters, nor do they seek to attract new firms to the region or build
human capital. They are, instead, investments to build the region's
"social capital" and shared infrastructure that support entrepreneurs
in making the transition from idea to business, invention to innovation,
or both.

---

[28] A 1992 study of the greater Boston area identified the four leading clusters as: information technology, health care, knowledge creation, and financial services. Over
the past decade, the increased integration of these four areas has been dramatic. For
further discussion of long-term trends in technological convergence at a national and
global scale, see Ernst and Young (2000) and National Research Council (2002).

[29] Notable examples include Ben Franklin Technology Partnerships in Southeastern
Pennsylvania (Philadelphia, PA), the IC2 Institute (Austin, TX), MIT Enterprise
Forum (Cambridge, MA), and USCDConnect (San Diego, CA). See National Commission on Entrepreneurship (2001) for a discussion of strategies employed by regions
toward building entrepreneurial networks.

CONCLUSION: PUBLIC POLICY IN SUPPORT OF COLLECTIVE ENTREPRENEURSHIP

Beginning with Nelson (1959), public policy studies relating to research and development investment have tended to emphasize the hypothesis of systematic underinvestment due to imperfect appropriability of returns. Recent analyses by Zeckhauser (1996) and others (see Hall 2002) have shifted the focus of attention in this area from the appropriability problem to that of asymmetric information and resultant "challenges in contracting for technical information." Increasingly, research and policy alike have focused on strategies to mediate the complex relationships between technology entrepreneurs, business managers, and financial backers. In this chapter we have sought to advance this line of work by exploring the hypothesis of an "innovation gap" or "funding gap" in the process of early stage technology development (ESTD) – the stage after a basic science breakthrough ("invention") and prior to the development of a potentially viable product or process linked to a specific target market ("innovation") (see, for example, Jaffe, Trajtenberg, and Henderson 1993; Feldman 1994a).

The growing complexity of both technologies and markets also suggests that the effort to value technological information – assessing the market possibilities of new, perhaps recombined, technologies – is severely constrained, and may become more so in the coming decades. Few skilled individuals are available to evaluate new combinations. There will always be many more potential new combinations of technologies – imaginable, but not tried – than there are companies and their financial supporters to try them out. The gap between potential breakthrough ideas and the number that receive a fair trial may grow in the future, as the execution of new technological combinations increasingly requires the collaboration of different actors with specialized skills. As Romer (2000) and Good (2001) have emphasized, the future vitality of the U.S. innovation system may be severely constrained over coming decades by a shortage of trained scientists and engineers. If this is the case, the shortage of individuals with *both* technical and market training is likely to be even more severe.

In this invention to innovation transition, mentoring is as important as funding. The most effective mentors supporting early stage technology development projects possess both the direct experience and access to financial resources and networks of personal contacts to assist technology entrepreneurs. Having "been there and done that," they are better suited to the mentoring of the relatively inexperienced entrepreneur than a more institutionally grounded, financially oriented venture capital firm.

The proliferation of new institutional types involved in the process of early stage technology development has been of a magnitude sufficient to prompt the National Commission on Entrepreneurship (Zacharakis et al. 1999: 33) to note that "the substantial amount of funding provided through informal channels, orders of magnitude greater than provided by formal venture capital investments and heretofore unknown and unappreciated, suggests some mechanisms for filling the gap may have developed without recognition." Yet the proliferation of institutional types is as much an indication of the particular informational challenges and structural disjunctures that define the "innovation gap" as it is one of a resolution to the challenge.

Some government agencies such as the National Institute of Standards and Technology (NIST) – the home of the Advanced Technology Program (ATP) – have a century of experience assessing a broad array of highly sophisticated technologies. There is no doubt about their ability to undertake such assessments. Yet these institutions cannot, and do not, pretend to be able to offer mentoring to a fledgling start-up or spin-off in a manner similar to that of an experienced angel investor who lives in the same community as the entrepreneur. In this sense, we know of no government program (including ATP) for which the designation "public venture capital" is, strictly speaking, appropriate. The managers of government programs like SBIR and ATP can, of course, consult the experienced angels and seed venture capital investors for strategic advice about promising areas of new industrial growth. But the role of Federal technology programs such as ATP should not be to bridge the Darwinian Sea – acting as commercialization programs – but rather to assist technology entrepreneurs in lowering the technical risks associated with reducing a new technical idea to practice – acting as technology development programs. When projects are rigorously selected for support and this technology development function is performed effectively, the validation provided to ESTD projects can be as valuable to a nascent venture as the funding. In this manner, even at a modest scale of activity, such programs have the potential to reduce the magnitude of the "innovation gap" significantly for supported firms.

Knowledge creation and entrepreneurship are increasingly dominant components of regional and national strategies for economic development across the globe. As other authors in this volume emphasize, political leaders and economic planners from Bangalore to Boston recognize that their future economic well-being depends on the innovative capacity of the people and institutions they attract and retain, not only to grow and expand their technology sectors, but all industries. This critical capacity to innovate depends on more than inventive capacity and physical infrastructure. Technology entrepreneurs and supporting institutions must be linked to one another by trust, incentives, and shared objectives. Innovation in all contexts requires a capacity for collective entrepreneurship.

5

Entrepreneurship and American Research Universities

Evolution in Technology Transfer

Maryann P. Feldman

American research universities have long served as a source of invention and technological expertise for industry (Rosenberg and Nelson 1994). This relationship, traditionally at arm's length, has entered a new era marked by closer interaction as universities actively manage their intellectual property in a process known as technology transfer. Moving beyond publication and teaching, the traditional modes of disseminating academic inventions, many universities now have technology transfer offices dedicated to securing invention disclosures from campus research and establishing intellectual property rights over them. These offices work to license to firms the rights to use the intellectual property, sometimes encouraging the formation of new firms for this purpose.

This chapter employs the term "entrepreneurship" in two distinct senses. The first, drawing on Clark (1998), who coined the phrase "entrepreneurial universities," conveys the broader and more active role that American research universities now play in facilitating technology diffusion and promoting economic growth within the national system of innovation. The second meaning of the term coincides with

Earlier versions of this chapter were presented at the conference *Entrepreneurship and Public Policy*, Harvard University, April 10, 2001 and National Academy of Sciences' conference *Academic Intellectual Property: Effects of University Patenting and Licensing in Commercialization and Research*, April 17, 2001. The chapter has benefited from discussions with Janet Bercovitz, Richard Burton, Irwin Feller, and Pierre Desrochers as co-authors on other papers. The research is supported by a grant from the Andrew W. Mellon Foundation.

Hart's definition in the introductory chapter to this volume, referring to the formation of firms based on university research.

Entrepreneurship in this second, narrower sense has become a favored mechanism by which universities transfer technology to the commercial realm. Based in part on the examples of the Massachusetts Institute of Technology (MIT) and Stanford University, which played active roles in the genesis of industrial clusters along Route 128 and in Silicon Valley respectively, university spin-off firms are seen as a means to transform local economies and a mechanism that provides a way for these economies to capture the benefits of proximity to research universities. Although university licenses have no locational constraints in principle, entrepreneurship is a decidedly local phenomenon in practice. As universities have been leveraged by policymakers to serve as engines of local economic development over the past twenty years, the rate of start-up formation has become an increasingly important indicator that they are succeeding in producing benefits (Feller 1990a). Miner et al. (2001) find that the idea of universities acting as "magic beanstalks" for economic development resonates with university administrators and economic development officials and has found broad acceptance. We may question the desirability of university-based entrepreneurship (Nelson 2001), but a wide variety of resources are devoted to it.

This chapter begins by examining the establishment by universities of dedicated technology transfer offices (TTOs) that serve as a focal point for universities' interaction with commercial interests. Three central mechanisms that universities may use in technology transfer, sponsored research, licensing, and the formation of entrepreneurial ventures, are explored in the next section. The chapter then considers the empirical literature that demonstrates that universities are important to local innovative activity. I conclude with an assessment of the place of research universities and university entrepreneurship in state economic development strategies.

UNIVERSITY TECHNOLOGY TRANSFER OFFICES: TIMING, STRUCTURE, AND MOTIVES

University technology transfer efforts have intensified over the past thirty years due to four interrelated and reinforcing factors

(Geuna 1999). One factor is the economic importance of new, high-opportunity technologies arising out of such disciplines as computer science, molecular biology, and materials science. Basic scientific research in these fields is conducted primarily at universities. The new generic technologies have widespread commercial applications and are associated with the emergence of new firms and the creation of new industries. Second, many industrial products outside the high-technology areas have become increasingly science-based and technology-intensive, creating an even broader array of potential users of university research. Together these two factors create a demand for technology transfer. On the supply side, universities faced a need, beginning in the 1970s, to find new sources of funding due to budgetary stringency and fiscal uncertainty on the part of federal and state governments, traditionally the largest sources of university funding. As a result, universities turned to industry for financial support. The fourth and final factor was a series of government policies aimed at raising the economic returns of publicly funded research by stimulating university technology transfer. The Bayh-Dole Act of 1980, which established a uniform policy that gives universities ownership of intellectual property developed from federally funded research, is a landmark in the history of university entrepreneurship.[1]

In response to these four factors, universities have organized formal technology transfer operations to manage their intellectual property. Many of these operations are housed in new administrative units within universities. However, several state universities are restricted by statute from engaging directly in any commercial activity, such as receiving fees, royalties, or stock in a company in exchange for the use of university-held patents. Consequently, these universities have established independent technology transfer organizations to engage in such transactions. Whatever the organizational form, TTOs have responsibility for keeping track of inventions made by university-employed

---

[1] The Bayh-Dole Act (Public Law 96-517, since amended to PL 98-620) established a uniform federal patent policy that allowed universities, and other nonprofit organizations, to retain title to their inventions developed using federal funds. Prior to the Bayh-Dole Act federally sponsored inventions could only be licensed from the government and then only on a nonexclusive basis. The Bayh-Dole Act enabled universities to directly control and benefit from inventions made by their faculty. The ownership rights of universities were further expanded under Public Law 98-620 in 1984.

researchers, preparing patent applications, and negotiating licensing agreements with firms for the use of university-owned intellectual property.

Although all universities gained greater intellectual property rights under the Bayh-Dole Act, there is diversity in the timing of the establishment of dedicated TTOs. At the time that Bayh-Dole was enacted, twenty universities already had such offices. The oldest of these is the Wisconsin Alumni Research Foundation (WARF), which was founded in 1925 to hold Professor Harry Steenbock's Vitamin D patents (Apple 1989). WARF's principal objectives were to seek patents to protect inventions made by university scientists and to promote the public benefit of these inventions through licensing agreements with companies. WARF was so successful in achieving public dissemination and returning substantial revenues to the university that it became the de facto model for other universities. The University of Iowa is credited with establishing a TTO in 1935, with MIT (1940), the Kansas State University Research Foundation (1942), and the University of California system (1950) not far behind. The pace of TTO founding accelerated after 1980. In 1999, the latest year for which data are available, three universities established TTOs: West Virginia University, the University of New Orleans, and California State Polytechnic University.

Figure 5.1 presents the type of classic S-shaped diffusion curve that economists use to describe a process for which the rate of adoption first increases rapidly and then gradually slows down as the process approaches saturation. In general, two factors are associated with early institutionalization of technology transfer: the presence of a medical school and the status of the university as a land grant institution. It is no accident that the presence of a medical school would hasten the establishment of a TTO; most commercially valuable university intellectual property arises from biomedical research (Mowery et al. 1999, Feller et al. 2002). The link to land grant institutions is a little less obvious. The Morrill Act of 1862 established at least one land grant college in the agricultural and mechanical sciences in each state, and these colleges became integral to the agricultural and industrial extension programs that aided local economies. The extension philosophy and mission proved easy to adapt to active technology transfer.

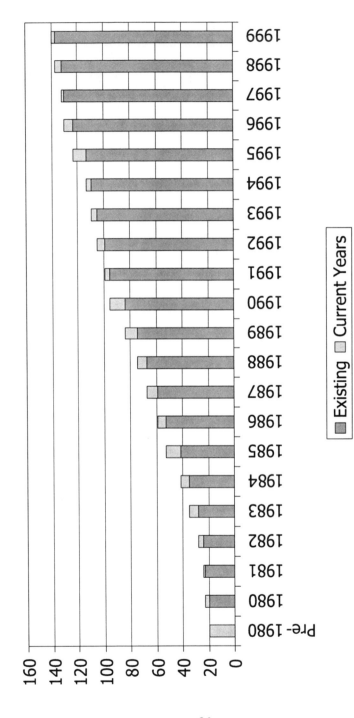

Figure 5.1. Diversity in entry in technology transfer: year of establishment of office. *Source:* AUTM Licensing Annual Surveys. *N* = 139 Universities.

Universities are engaged in an ongoing search for the best way to organize technology transfer operations (Feller et al. 2002). Bercovitz et al. (2001) identify three structural features associated with effectiveness in performing the technology transfer function. One such feature is the TTO's ability to coordinate its activities with those of several other administrative units, such as sponsored research, corporate giving, and industrial liaison. Another is its ability to receive, interpret, synthesize, and disseminate information both within and outside the university. The final key feature is an effective alignment of incentives between and among the TTO, faculty, and other administrative units. In sum, the performance of the TTO can only be assessed within its broader organizational setting within the university.

TTOs vary significantly in the ways in which they define their missions. Feldman and colleagues (2002) surveyed technology transfer managers in order to rank the importance of five distinct but related motives in technology transfer. Knowledge dissemination is the most traditional objective for universities, and it would be natural for TTOs to adopt it as a mission. Service to industry, a specific objective for land grant institutions, reflects the type of more intense interaction with industry that was promoted by the Bayh-Dole Act and other legislation in the 1980s. The objective of fostering local economic growth also reflects this emphasis, but with a local focus. Revenue generation may be another motivation for TTOs; exploitation of intellectual property may augment university budgets in the face of fiscal austerity. Finally, service to the faculty reflects an orientation by TTOs to serve an internal constituency as a part of the university.

Table 5.1 presents our findings. Service to the faculty was named the most important objective by a plurality of TTOs, followed closely by the traditional university motive of dissemination of knowledge. Revenue generation ranked third, despite the fact that many TTOs have yet to break even. Service to industry and the generation of local economic growth tied for last place. If one adds the scores for these two closely related motives together, however, the combined total would equal that for revenue generation. Overall, these results are not surprising and compactly say that TTOs tend to rank traditional goals of the university highest. Newer objectives such as generating revenue and having an economic impact rank lower.

Table 5.1. *Technology Transfer Motivations, by Type of University*
(percent)

Criteria Ranked as Most Important	All Respondents	Land Grant Universities	Private Universities	With Medical Schools
Service to the Faculty	36	16	63	38
Knowledge Dissemination	35	44	21	32
Revenue Generation	18	20	16	22
Service to Industry	9	16	–	5
Promoting Local Economic Growth	9	4	–	3

Note: $n = 67$ responses, or 58% of the 124 Carnegie I and II research universities that have active technology transfer operations (see Feldman et al. 2002).
Source: Feldman et al. 2002.

Different types of universities rank these motivations differently. For example, as shown in Table 5.1, land grant institutions rated knowledge dissemination higher and service to the faculty relatively lower. Sixty-three percent of private universities ranked service to the faculty as the most important goal, whereas universities with medical schools gave more weight to revenue generation. These categories are not mutually exclusive, since universities with medical schools may be land grant or private institutions. The results do highlight the diversity in the objectives of universities in carrying out technology transfer.

THE MECHANISMS OF UNIVERSITY TECHNOLOGY TRANSFER

Universities use a variety of mechanisms to transfer technology to industry. Each mechanism offers trade-offs in terms of achieving the TTO's objectives. Because technology transfer is a relatively new activity for universities, there has been experimentation in the use of these mechanisms and the terms of the agreements made with industry (Feller et al. 2002). Formal mechanisms include sponsored research agreements with industry, licensing of university intellectual property to firms, and the formation of spin-off companies. Informal mechanisms, such as industry hiring of students, faculty consulting, and knowledge trading among friendship networks also contribute to technology transfer, but do not fall under the auspices of the TTO. (Informal mechanisms of technology transfer are the focus of Nathan Rosenberg's chapter in this volume.)

Technology transfer depends on technology creation, the "Eureka!" moment of a university employee that results in a discovery that may have commercial value. Such a discovery is the basis of university intellectual property. When the discoverer files an invention disclosure with the TTO, a claim is made that begins the formal technology transfer process. The TTO legally establishes the university's intellectual property rights in the form of patents, copyrights, or trademarks. Only a small subset of invention disclosures generates any intellectual property, much less licensing interest; of those that do, very few generate sizeable net returns. The rule of thumb in university technology transfer is that for every one hundred invention disclosures, ten patents and one commercially successful product result (Blake 1993).

The technology transfer process is fraught with peril. The knowledge being transferred is by its nature difficult to value and to appropriate (Zeckhauser 1996). Indeed, uncertainty about the value of knowledge is highest for the most upstream, basic research activities conducted at universities. Technology transfer agreements must be negotiated in the shadow of this uncertainty. The parties to these negotiations base their positions on subjective estimates of that portion of the value flowing from the knowledge that the firm will be able to appropriate. These imperfect estimates of the value of the knowledge acquired by the contracting firm may lead to a market failure: the contractual price may be different from the social value of the knowledge involved in the transaction. The spillovers may be positive if the contractual price paid by the firm is below the social value or negative if the resulting private value is less than the contractual price. Negotiation under high uncertainty is characteristic of most formal technology transfer processes, such as sponsored research or licensing agreements.

There are two other general factors that shape the technology transfer process in addition to the attributes of the knowledge that is transferred. First, firm strategy and characteristics affect the choice of mechanisms for technology transfer. Large firms, for example, are more likely to sponsor research. If the research proves fruitful, the company may be able to devote substantial resources of its own to moving it forward without necessarily negotiating a license from the university. Second, commercializing a university technology typically involves multiple, complementary transactions. The use of one mechanism does not exclude the use of others. The three mechanisms explored below, sponsored research, licenses, and spin-off firms, should be viewed as potentially complementary elements in the larger technology transfer process, along with the informal mechanisms described by Rosenberg.

Sponsored Research

Research is the process that creates knowledge and ideas that form the basis for university intellectual property. In 2000, an estimated $30 billion was spent on sponsored research and development (R&D) projects at U.S. academic institutions. Through the National Science Foundation (NSF) and mission agencies, such as the National Institutes of Health (NIH), the federal government is the largest source of funding (58 percent) for university-based research (National Science Board 2002). Federal funds usually support basic research, which is conducted without concern for practical use but is instead oriented to fundamental understanding and discovery. The Bayh-Dole Act gave universities ownership of any intellectual property resulting from federally funded projects.

Companies and other industrial organizations also sponsor university research projects. Industry support of academic research has grown from less than $264 million in 1980 to $2 billion in 2000. There is great diversity among universities in the receipt of industrial research funding. Those schools most favored by these sponsors, such as Georgia Institute of Technology and Duke University, receive 20 percent of their total R&D funding from industry. The average for all universities is about 7 percent (National Science Board 2002).

Sponsored research is a mechanism for transferring technology involving a quid pro quo. The university gains financial resources, while the contracting firm gains research results and access to university scientists. Industry-sponsored research is typically more applied in nature than federally funded research and, thus, closer to practical application and realization of commercial potential. A research agreement between a university and industrial sponsors will specify the distribution of any intellectual property that results from the project. In addition, the agreement will differentiate between the background knowledge created within the university (and which may derive from a variety of different funding sources) and the foreground knowledge created by the new project. The industrial sponsor will typically retain ownership of intellectual property resulting from the sponsored research or will have the right to review such property with the first option to license. Again, firm strategy and market characteristics shape such agreements. If the technology is broad-based and involves network externalities, the sponsor may choose to let the university retain ownership and license the technology on a nonexclusive basis to other companies.

Licenses

Licenses are contractual agreements that provide firms with rights to use intellectual property. The number of licenses executed by TTOs has grown rapidly from a mere handful in 1970 to 936 in 1991 to 3,295 in 1999. In return for the use of university intellectual property, the licensee will typically provide an up-front payment at the time of signing the agreement and make periodic payments at certain milestones, such as when regulatory or technical hurdles are cleared. In addition, licensing agreements typically include provisions for royalty payments, calculated as a percentage of product sales, which become a steady revenue stream when the product reaches the commercial market. TTOs typically have great latitude and flexibility in negotiating these agreements (Mowery et al. 1999). For example, in licensing the Cohen-Boyer patents on recombinant DNA technology, Stanford University asked for a one-time licensing fee of $10,000 and royalty rates ranging from 0.5 percent on sales of end products such as insulin to 10 percent on sales of research vectors and enzymes (Scherer 1999: 55). This approach facilitated licensing, so that at the time the patents expired in 1997, their university owners had over 400 licensees.

The typical licensing agreement has changed significantly over time. Initially, most university licenses were granted on an exclusive basis to one company. This approach limited the potential number of transactions and the amount of potential revenue. Universities are now more likely to negotiate licenses that are calibrated to certain applications or specific geographic markets. There is also significant variation in licensing agreements with respect to royalty rates, duration, and future option rights (for example, Raider 1998; Barnes, Mowery, and Ziedonis 1997). More research is warranted to understand how these contracts are negotiated and which partner, the university or the corporation, exerts the greatest bargaining power and under what circumstances.

The distribution of licensing revenues is highly skewed, with a few big commercial successes generating large returns for a small number of universities. For example, the cancer-fighting drug Taxol, which is based on intellectual property owned by Florida State University, has worldwide annual sales worth $1.2 billion and yielded some $60 million in licensing revenue in 2000 (Zacks 2000). Successes like Cohen-Boyer, Taxol, Gatorade (University of Florida), cisplatin and carboplatin (Michigan State), and fax technology (Iowa State) are well known, but they are exceptional. Most university technology transfer operations do not break even. Their licensing revenues are not sufficient to cover administrative costs and the costs of filing and maintaining patents.

American universities continue to experiment with the licensing process. One example of such experimentation is the practice of taking an equity interest in the licensing company in lieu of traditional licensing fees (Feldman et al. 2002). This practice originated with cash-starved start-up firms that had little other than an ownership stake to offer, but it is now used in a variety of situations to streamline the negotiation process and align the interests of the university and the industrial partner. If the company succeeds, the university stands to make a larger financial gain than might be expected from a traditional agreement. Another experiment involves the monetization of licensing royalties. In Yale University's agreement with Royalty Pharma (Blumenstyk 2001), for instance, the university sells the stream of future royalties from its intellectual property in exchange for a lump-sum, up-front payment. These experiments aim to improve the financial rewards from technology transfer and illustrate a commitment to learning on the part of TTOs.

There is some evidence, however, that licensing has not been an entirely satisfactory mechanism from industry's perspective. In a survey of industry licensing executives, Thursby and Thursby (2000a) found that 66 percent (199 business units out of a total of 300) had not licensed intellectual property from universities. The reasons given included the feeling that university research is generally at too early a stage of development (49 percent); that universities rarely engage in research in a related line of business (37.4 percent); that universities refuse to transfer ownership to a company (31 percent); that universities have policies regarding delay of publication that are too strict (20 percent); and that faculty cooperation for further development of the technology would be too difficult to obtain (16 percent).[2] Others have found that universities may place too high a value on their technologies, move too slowly in negotiating licenses, or simply not be receptive enough to a firm's circumstances. These results suggest that there may be some additional evolution in licensing agreements or in the organization of technology transfer operations.

UNIVERSITY-BASED SPIN-OFFS

Spin-offs are an increasingly important means of commercializing university research. Given the difficulty of evaluating the economic potential of university intellectual property, the researchers who made the relevant discovery may be in the best position to carry the work forward toward commercialization. (This process is analyzed in more detail in the chapter in this volume by Philip Auerswald and Lewis Branscomb.) Life-cycle models suggest that scientists invest heavily in human capital early in their careers to build reputations and establish positions of primacy in their fields of expertise (Levin and Stephan 1991). In the later stages of their careers, they are more likely to seek an economic return on this investment. Starting a company may serve the purpose of realizing that return. It also allows the founders to appropriate the value of the intellectual property they created while

---

[2] Twenty-eight percent of the respondents indicated some other difficulty such as "general attitude is poor," "complexity of deal and . . . weird expectations," "too cumbersome," and "high licensing fees" (Thursby and Thursby 2000a).

at the university and to accelerate progress on their research agenda by providing access to additional funding. The potential financial rewards of starting a company coupled with tightening university budgets and competition for the relatively fixed pool of public funding create incentives for scientists to engage in entrepreneurial activity (Powell and Owen-Smith 1998).

The Association of University Technology Managers (AUTM) is the main source of data on university-based spin-off companies. AUTM defines a university spin-off as a firm formed around a university license of intellectual property. This definition is not the only one that may be employed. Two caveats are worth mentioning in this context. First, many more spin-offs are likely to be formed by individuals with some association with the university other than the licensing of intellectual property. Thus, the AUTM numbers may understate the impact of universities on entrepreneurship. There is a countervailing influence, however. Discussions with university technology transfer officials reveal that they are under pressure to report as many spin-offs as they can in order to compare well with other universities in the AUTM reports and other benchmarking activities. These anecdotes suggest that universities may not strictly adhere to the AUTM definition in their reporting.

The reader should bear these caveats in mind, when interpreting Figure 5.2, which reports figures on university-based spin-off firms from AUTM's surveys. In 1999, there were 275 firms of this type, an average of about two companies per university. This average is somewhat deceptive. The distribution of spin-offs among universities is highly skewed. The majority of universities report no spin-offs. At the high end of the range is a university that produced nineteen companies in 1999. In addition, it should be noted that the total number of spin-off companies reported has increased simply because the number of universities actively involved in technology transfer has increased.

Figure 5.3 provides spin-off data for a constant set of universities that have consistently reported to AUTM since 1993. These universities were asked to report on the number of start-ups prior to that date as well. Using data on TTO founding dates, I have calculated that the average annual total for these universities prior to 1993 was about 80 start-ups. The 1999 AUTM survey reported a total of 179 start-ups for this group.

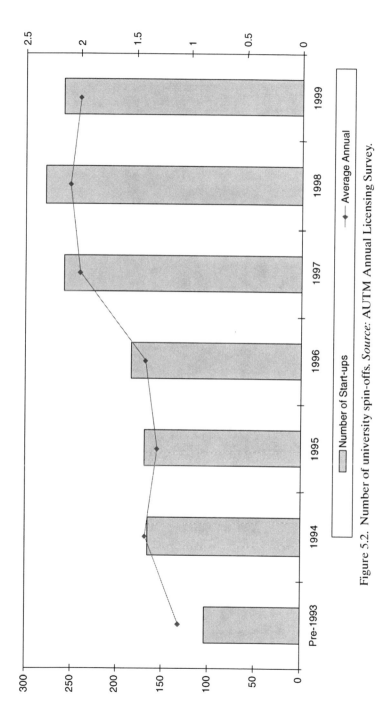

Figure 5.2. Number of university spin-offs. *Source:* AUTM Annual Licensing Survey.

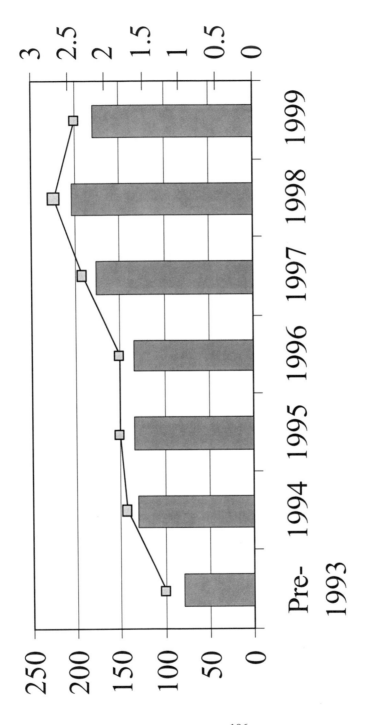

Pre-
1993   1994 1995 1996 1997 1998 1999

■ Number of Start-ups ─■─ Average

Figure 5.3. Number of university spin-offs: constant set of AUTM respondents (*N* = 76). *Source:* AUTM Annual Licensing Survey.

THE LOCAL EFFECTS OF ACADEMIC RESEARCH

Spin-off firms are local phenomena. In general, entrepreneurs who start companies do not relocate but stay close to the source of their perceived competitive advantage, which is typically the referent organization where the founders were previously employed (Feldman and Francis 2002). For university-based spin-offs the university serves as the source of advantage, providing skilled labor, specialized facilities, and expertise. In addition, university personnel who start companies often split their time between the university and the firm, making close location advantageous. As universities and state governments have provided incentives for faculty to start companies or engage in joint research projects with companies, the attraction of proximity to universities has grown. In 1999, AUTM reported that 82 percent of firms formed around university licenses operated in the same state as the university that provided the license.

This pattern in university-based entrepreneurship fits what we know about entrepreneurship in the larger knowledge economy. In a pioneering study, Jaffe (1989) found that university-based research had significant local spillovers. Patents are granted to inventors in the same states in which public and private knowledge-generating inputs (such as academic and industrial research) are the largest. These results held up even after controlling for industrial R&D, indicating the localized value of university research. In addition, Jaffe found an important indirect or induced effect in which university research increases industry R&D, which in turn increases patents. This effect is quantitatively larger than the direct effect of university research spending. Feldman (1994) corroborates and extends these findings, using market introduction in place of patents as an indicator of innovation. She also demonstrates that the presence of related industries and business services contributes to the geographical clustering of innovative activities in the neighborhoods of universities.

As one might expect, the knowledge spillovers from universities are most important in knowledge-intensive industries. Audretsch and Feldman (1996) follow Krugman's (1991a) example and calculate Gini coefficients for the geographic concentration of activity to demonstrate this relationship.[3] We also add skilled labor as a mechanism by which knowledge spillovers occur; workers move between jobs in an industry, taking their accumulated skills and know-how with them. The results suggest a greater propensity for innovative activity to cluster spatially in industries in which industry R&D, university research, and skilled labor are important inputs, even after taking into account the geographic concentration of production.

"Star scientists" are a particularly important form of skilled labor, better termed "intellectual capital," which transforms scientific knowledge into commercial applications. Star scientists embody knowledge of break-through techniques that are initially available only at their lab benches, making it costly for others to obtain or use. Zucker and Darby (1996) show that such intellectual capital is key in the development of the biotechnology industry and that its economic effects tend to be geographically bounded within the regions where star scientists reside. The entrepreneurial venture is one important pathway through which this intellectual capital yields returns. Zucker, Darby, and Brewer (1998) document linkages between star scientists and biotechnology start-ups near their home universities. Firms with access to leading-edge scientists perform better than enterprises lacking such access in terms of products in development, products on the market, and employment growth in the firm.[4] (See Andrew Toole's chapter in this volume for a critique and revision of the work by Zucker, Darby, and their colleagues.) Almeida and Kogut (1997) extend this approach to consider the interfirm mobility of star patent holders. Their results suggest that even the transfer of ideas between firms tends to be geographically confined.

---

[3] The Gini coefficients are weighted by the relative share of economic activity located in each state. Computation of weighted Gini coefficients enables us to control for size differences across states. The Gini coefficients are based on the share of activity in a state and industry relative to the state share of the national activity. The locational Gini coefficients for production are based on industry value-added and are calculated as the amount of value-added in an industry and a state, divided by state share of national value-added for the industry. This ratio is normalized by the state share of total manufacturing value-added to account for the overall distribution of manufacturing activity. An industry that is not geographically concentrated more than is reflected by the overall distribution of manufacturing value-added would have a coefficient of 0. The closer the industry coefficient is to 1, the more geographically concentrated the industry.

[4] Zucker, Darby, and Brewer (1998) also find that firm scientists had a higher total number of citations than scientists in universities or in research institutes and hospitals.

The economic benefits of knowledge spillovers from universities are significant. Beeson and Montgomery (1992) examine the relationship between universities and labor-market conditions. They find that universities raise the average skill level of the surrounding area and positively affect wage and employment rates. The study focuses on employment growth rates for the time periods 1975 to 1980 and 1980 to 1989 and finds that employment growth is related to increases in university R&D funding as well as to the number of nationally rated science and engineering programs at local universities. These results are consistent over the two time periods.[5]

Taken together, the results reviewed in this section indicate that universities can play a significant role in economic development. Of course, not all universities and all geographical regions benefit equally. Many factors affect the transmission of knowledge spillovers.[6] Most important, a university's founding mission, institutional context, and prior experiences with commercial activity influence its interaction with industry and ultimately affect the ability of the university to impact its local economic and innovation environment (Feldman and Desrochers forthcoming).

STATE ECONOMIC DEVELOPMENT INITIATIVES AND UNIVERSITIES

State policymakers in the United States are increasingly keen to leverage the presence of universities for economic development. In 1997, the fifty state governments spent over $400 million on programs to encourage technology-based economic development (State Science and Technology Institute 1998). Local universities figure prominently in these initiatives. Although university research may provide ideas for

---

[5] The results regarding income, employment rate, and net migration are somewhat mixed. Choice of time period does not include the turnaround prompted by innovation in the computer industry known as the Massachusetts miracle, nor does it capture the computer revolution, which certainly are two incidents of high innovative activity that anecdotally are associated with increased local earnings, higher employment rates, and net in-migration.

[6] Other factors may inhibit the absorption of university spillovers such as attributes of the region and its industrial composition, characteristics of the labor force, and social capital variables. In addition, the historical relationship of local industry with the institution may be instructive. These are not considered in this chapter.

existing firms, entrepreneurial ventures occupy a unique position in the minds of state economic development officials. As Pages, Freedman, and Von Bargen describe in their contribution to this volume, states first became active in providing business assistance programs during the economic depression in the 1930s. The focus of state interest changed over time from stabilizing local economies to attracting relocating firms and branch plants. The 1980s heralded a new era in state economic development that complements the adoption of formal technology transfer practices in universities with attempts to promote new firm formation.

Universities are attractive for economic development purposes for several reasons. First, universities are perhaps less mobile than any other institution. Although it is common for universities to establish programs in new locations, they are relatively fixed in place due to historical accident. Firms change headquarters locations; universities do not. Second, state governments provide funding for both public and private universities. States provide an average of 8 percent of university R&D expenditures (National Science Board 2002), but this commonly cited figure understates their contribution. States fund capital improvements in university laboratories and research facilities, contribute to the operating costs of universities, and earmark special programs, contributions that are not included in the R&D figures.

States have instituted a diverse array of programs that aim to enhance knowledge spillovers to small, technology-intensive firms (Schachtel and Feldman 2000). State programs provide grants to encourage cooperative research projects between companies and university faculty, subsidize space in incubator facilities, and provide assistance in new venture formation and business planning (Feldman and Kelley 2002). Perhaps the greatest need in new firm formation is for financing, and states have been active in this domain as well. Traditional venture capital investors are typically interested in companies that are three to five years old and have a clearly defined product concept. In contrast, university entrepreneurs form companies around embryonic ideas that require patient seed funding (see Auerswald and Branscomb, this volume). State-funded venture capital programs help to meet this need and typically give preferential treatment to start-ups located in their jurisdictions. For example, the state of Maryland has a family of three investment vehicles that attempt to address the continuum of needs of technology-based start-ups. At this point, we have only limited understanding of how state technology programs contribute to firm growth and regional vitality.

Universities are now investing their own funds in start-up companies as well. For example, Vanderbilt University established a $10 million Chancellor Fund to invest in university spin-offs. There are concerns about the feasibility of these investments, as witnessed by Boston University's financing of its start-up firm, Seragen, which absorbed $120 million of BU's money between 1987 and 1997. The company was not successful. The failure is not a surprise; only about 5 percent of venture-capital-backed firms are very successful, and another 30 percent are moderately successful (Micklethwait 1997). In this case, the university only recovered a fraction of its investment, raising concerns about its fiduciary responsibility and objectivity. There is great potential in these relationships for conflict of interest and the threat of a fundamental re-ordering of university priorities.

REFLECTIVE CONCLUSIONS

The United States has entered a new era in technology transfer and in the process has become a model that the rest of the world is trying to emulate. Nelson (2001) worries that the new system of technology transfer will interfere with the norms of open science and adversely affect the role of universities in the national system of innovation. These are important questions to ask in light of the aggressive moves that this chapter has described. The process may be viewed as a natural experiment. Scholars are only beginning to understand the impact of this experiment on the broader national system of innovation (*Journal of Technology Transfer* 2001). The numbers are only part of the story and mask great diversity in the organizational motives, strategies, and incentives at the various institutions.

The same questions are also worth thinking about at the regional level as universities are asked to become engines of local economic development. Universities have demonstrated great adaptability in fulfilling their commitment to active technology transfer. Their attempts to spin off new companies satisfy an increased expectation that they be engaged in local economic development and demonstrate their relevance. Yet, universities add more to their local economies than the metrics of technology transfer capture, and there are certainly many different models for assessing how universities interact with and enrich their local economies. Thus, we may question whether university programs intended to encourage entrepreneurship and local economic growth make the best use of state and university resources. The examples provided by WARF, Stanford, and MIT may have established an unrealistic standard against which American research universities are currently being judged.

As this chapter has demonstrated, virtually all American research universities actively participate in technology transfer and have accepted the new mantle of promoting local economic development, specifically through the promotion of entrepreneurial start-up firms. In addition, a variety of new mechanisms to put licenses into circulation are being used, and used more creatively. Certainly, only time and additional research will reveal the long-term effects of these changes on the American system of innovation.

6

America's Entrepreneurial Universities

Nathan Rosenberg

It is difficult to discuss American universities in the specific context of entrepreneurship without falling into a celebrationist (but not, one hopes, a complacent) mode. I say this because, from an international comparative perspective, one can hardly reject the conclusion that American universities have been uniquely successful in the scope and intensity of their contributions to entrepreneurship. This success stems largely from their own capacity for novelty and dynamism, which deserves the adjective "entrepreneurial" as well. The entrepreneurial perspective is only one of many possible perspectives from which one might examine the operation of American universities, and not necessarily the most important one. The European continent is endowed with numerous universities of great intellectual distinction, many of which have faculties who would look with deep disdain, if not total disbelief, at the idea that centers of learning should ever be judged by such a philistine standard. I have more than a little sympathy with that point of view. But in a world in which economic activity is becoming, indeed already has become, highly knowledge-intensive, it would be unrealistic, and perhaps even impolitic, to expect universities to remain withdrawn from the changing needs of their economic environments. The high degree of responsiveness to these changing needs has long been the most distinctive feature of American universities, at least as far back as the passage of the Morrill Act of 1862, which established the land grant college system.

The historical background fact, then, is that the transition to greater economic relevance has been easier to achieve in the United States than elsewhere because American institutions of higher education have always had to be sensitive and responsive to the changing requirements of industry, agriculture, and business. If we compare American universities with those of continental Europe, a conspicuous feature is that American universities are decentralized and highly autonomous. There has never been a federal Ministry of Education in the United States that bears responsibility for determining the size of university budgets, how the budgets ought to be allocated, or the intellectual priorities they ought to observe. The fact that Washington, D.C., with its extraordinary archival and library resources, has never become home to a leading research university, in spite of numerous proposals to make it so over the past two centuries, going all the way back to Alexander Hamilton, is evidence, if further evidence is needed, of a long-standing political aversion to centralizing tendencies in the academic sphere. Even the Morrill Act, whose enabling legislation provided each state with federally owned lands as the financial basis for the operation of state universities, also provided that the subsequent governance of these universities, as well as their financing, would reside in each separate state.

In the American context, then, the university president has always had to have a sort of talent in common with entrepreneurs in business: skills that led to success in fund-raising. It might be thought that state universities would be exempt from the need for such entrepreneurship, but this has not been the case. Since there are many state universities, it has been incumbent on each of these public institutions to demonstrate to the legislature of its home state that it is uniquely fulfilling the needs of the state's economy. Such demonstration has been a political precondition for imposing the necessary taxes on citizens to support their state university. Furthermore, state legislatures usually provided only modest financial support to their universities (financial support heavily concentrated on the cost of teaching). State universities were therefore under considerable pressure to seek further financial support from nongovernment sources, especially to finance their research activities. For example, MIT's aggressive (and successful) search for industry sponsorship early in the twentieth century was largely triggered by reductions in funding by the state of Massachusetts.

A second distinctive feature is that the United States has always had a large private university sector. Until after the Second World War the most prestigious universities were, overwhelmingly, private. These universities, in spite of their endowments, have almost always had to charge substantial tuition fees, since their ambitions always exceeded their grasps as defined by their current sources of income. Stanford, for example, charged no tuition when it first opened its doors in 1891, but found that such fees were an unavoidable necessity after the First World War. (An important part of the problem in Stanford's case derived from the fact that Leland Stanford had provided an endowment that was excessively encumbered with railroad bonds!)

The important point for present purposes is that the mere existence of a large private university sector has created an important reality for state universities. In order to have a distinguished faculty (as well as better students), they have had to compete for professorial talent in a labor market in which private universities had more flexibility with respect to salaries as well as more financial resources for other purposes. These circumstances have been important in preventing state universities from falling into a continental European civil service mode. State university competition in faculty hiring has led them to be more competitive in the search for funds to support faculty research as well. In the pre-World War II world, private industry and philanthropic institutions, such as the Rockefeller and Carnegie foundations, were the main objects of these efforts. This situation changed drastically after the war, when the federal government became, for the first time, the predominant patron of university research (see Mowery and Rosenberg 1998; Shils 1997).

A critical consequence of the need for financial support and other distinctive features of the American system is that both public and private universities were very quick to introduce new course material that was relevant to the needs of newly emerging industries, wherever that new material may have originated. This facility was not confined to the curriculum; in the course of the twentieth century American academics also played increasingly prominent roles in the development of new technologies and new disciplines that were relevant to the economy, especially in engineering, computer science, and applied sciences (Nelson and Rosenberg 1993). In part, this adaptability has to be understood as a way of competing for higher tuition fees by offering an education that would command a greater value in the labor market for college graduates. In this sense, America's decentralized higher education system can be fairly described as "market-driven," rather than locked into a centralized system in which the reallocation of budgets and personnel is severely restricted by political and bureaucratic considerations – as well as by the constraints of past history.

Central to the argument of this chapter, then, is that American commercial success in high-technology sectors of the economy – semiconductors and microelectronics generally, computer hardware and software, the Internet and World Wide Web, and medically related technologies, including medical devices and biotechnology – owes an enormous debt to the entrepreneurial activities of American universities. The nature of that debt, however, varies considerably from one sector of the economy to another.

In the past couple of decades, an important extension of this traditional behavior has emerged that fits even within the narrow definition of entrepreneurship employed in most of this volume. There has been a rise in the willingness (often eagerness) of university faculty to depart from their traditional teaching and research responsibilities and move into the commercial arena wearing the hat of the business decisionmaker. The scale of such activities has recently become so large that the success of research universities is now often measured by the number of start-up firms to which they have given birth.

Defining academic entrepreneurship solely in terms of start-up firms is far too restrictive to capture the full scope of the interaction between research universities and high-technology entrepreneurs. But even if one sticks with the narrow definition, one must be careful to include not only successful start-up firms but also those that never get very far off the ground (and perhaps some that never get going at all). The first substantial attempts at commercial introduction of technological innovations usually fail, as even Karl Marx acknowledged well over a hundred years ago, when he called attention to "the far greater cost of operating an establishment based on a new invention as compared to later establishments arising *ex suis ossibus*. This is so very true that the trail-blazers generally go bankrupt, and only those who later buy the buildings, machinery, etc., at a cheaper price make money out of it" (Marx 1959). Marx clearly understood the limitations of so-called first mover advantages.

ACADEMIC ENTREPRENEURSHIP, CURRICULAR INNOVATION, AND HIGH-TECHNOLOGY INDUSTRY

There is widespread agreement that no single location in the United States provides more evidence of academic entrepreneurship, especially in the past thirty years or so, than Silicon Valley. Boston's Route 128 area was the hub of industrial development in electronics in the early post-World War II period, building on the preeminent role of MIT in those years, but the rise to prominence of Silicon Valley beginning in the 1960s is simply the most dramatic demonstration of academic entrepreneurship (see Saxenian 1994). Indeed, to the extent that one can identify a single academic entrepreneur of truly protean dimensions, it would be difficult to find one who could share Fred Terman's accomplishments. Terman, dean of engineering at Stanford and later its provost, spent the war years at Harvard, but came back to Stanford proclaiming that he was patterning his plans after "the MIT model."[1]

Consider the integrated circuit (IC), which became available in 1961. Very shortly thereafter, Stanford University's Department of Electrical Engineering introduced a course in the design and fabrication of ICs. Each subsequent improvement in ICs was followed, within just a couple of years, by a new course in the teaching curriculum that prepared future electrical engineers for working with the newly available technology (Harayama 1998).[2] Integrated circuits have been of far greater commercial importance than the original transistors. After they were introduced in the 1960s, ICs were critical to the transformation of the computer into a widely used technology. By the beginning of the 1970s, the IC had evolved into the microprocessor, which became the platform for the personal computer and much else. Stanford's commitment to the improvement of integrated circuitry led eventually to the university's establishment of its own Center for Integrated Systems.[3]

Stanford became highly competitive in the new field of integrated circuitry partly through a most unorthodox hiring technique.

---

[1] Terman's entrepreneurial activities were not universally admired. For critical appraisals, see Leslie 1993 and Lowen 1997. For Terman's views as spokesman for an exportable "Silicon Valley Model," see Leslie and Kargon 1996.

[2] I am grateful to Ms. Harayama for permission to quote from this manuscript.

[3] This center, which receives financial support from government and industry, conducts research on microelectronic materials, devices, and systems.

Terman sought out the most knowledgeable and talented electrical engineers in Silicon Valley. He "anointed" them as adjunct professors at Stanford, because Stanford faculty were not yet sufficiently conversant with the new technology to be able to teach it. In effect, Terman said to these leading industrial engineers: "Come in on Tuesday and Thursday afternoons and teach us – faculty as well as students – about integrated circuitry." Note that in this formulation I am suggesting that the IC originated in industry, not in the university (see Moore 1996). This judgment has been confirmed by the recent award of a Nobel Prize in Physics to John Kilby for work carried out at Texas Instruments in inventing the IC. Had Robert Noyce of Intel (previously at Fairchild) not died prematurely, he would almost certainly have shared the prize with Kilby. The first patent for the integrated circuit was awarded to Noyce in April, 1961, but after litigation it was agreed that this was a case of independent simultaneous inventive activity. According to Richard Langlois and Edward Steinmueller:

In 1958 and 1959, two Americans, Jack Kilby of Texas Instruments and Robert Noyce of Fairchild, were the first to devise practical monolithic circuits. Noyce's approach, based on the planar process that had revolutionized transistor production, was the more immediately practical. After struggling over patent claims, the two companies forged a cross-licensing agreement in 1966 that effectively gave them joint claim on the invention. Each company granted licenses to all comers in the range of 2 to 4 percent of IC profits. (Langlois and Steinmueller 1999: 31–32)

Stanford's responsiveness in the case of the IC lay in the speed with which it diffused the knowledge of an invention that had already been developed in industry and not in the academic world, a speed that was of great competitive significance for both Stanford and Silicon Valley.

The role of U.S. universities in the emergence of new technology has been even more significant in the computer industry than in semiconductors. This statement applies to both computer hardware and software, although the roles were vastly different in each of these two spheres.

American universities played a leading role in the early history of computer hardware, a role heavily financed by the federal government. Academic personnel at the Moore School of Electrical Engineering at the University of Pennsylvania conceptualized, designed, and eventually constructed the first prototype of an electronic digital computer, the ENIAC (Electronic Numerical Integrator and Computer), over the period 1943–1946. The ENIAC was financed by a contract with the Army Ordnance Department, which was concerned to improve the accuracy of its ballistic tables. As with many innovations of major significance, there were several claims for priority (see Stern 1981). The design of the ENIAC was heavily indebted to a differential analyzer that had been developed in the early 1930s by MIT's Vannevar Bush in order to solve differential equations. A crucial difference, however, is that the Bush machine was analog, whereas the ENIAC was digital.

Professors J. Presper Eckert and John W. Mauchly, who led the ENIAC effort at Penn, undertook to form their own company, the Eckert-Mauchly Corporation, to commercialize the first electronic digital computer, the UNIVAC, in 1946. As Marx might have predicted, these two academic entrepreneurs encountered serious financial difficulties in developing a general purpose commercial computer, and their firm went bankrupt in 1950. The corporation was sold to Remington Rand which, in turn, merged with the Sperry Gyroscope Company to form Sperry Rand (Stern 1981: 1–2). A number of other universities, most notably MIT, participated in important projects during the 1950s involving the application of computers, especially SAGE and Whirlwind, the two key projects behind the development of a strategic air system (Flamm 1988: 53–58; Wildes and Lindgren 1985; Langlois and Mowery 1996).

Although the role of universities in computer hardware declined later in the 1950s as private firms, particularly IBM, expanded their presence in the industry, academia remained critical to the later expansion of software which, in effect, built on the new discipline of computer science (Flamm 1988; Mowery 1996). In the realm of software, the role of American universities was massive.

It is important to remember that the original ENIAC was "hardwired" to solve a particular set of problems. Even after von Neumann's conceptual breakthroughs made stored-program computers possible in the 1950s, software remained closely bound to hardware; the organization that designed the hardware generally designed the software as well. The software industry was effectively born in 1969, when IBM, confronted with the prospect of an antitrust suit, agreed to unbundle its software from its hardware. The industry then experienced what was certainly one of the most rapid growth rates of new, high-tech, start-up firms in American history.[4]

In terms of commercial success, American dominance of the computer software industry was overwhelmingly due to the remarkable speed with which its university faculties were able to develop and introduce an entirely new academic curriculum in computer science after the launching of the Soviet *Sputnik* in 1957. As late as 1959 there were no formal programs in computer science at American universities. The majority of skilled personnel in the industry had been trained in other fields, primarily mathematics and various fields of engineering. By 1965, however, it was possible to speak of computer science as a "distinct academic discipline," with doctorates and bachelor's degrees in the subject available in at least fifteen universities, and master's degrees at more than thirty (Norberg and O'Neill 1996). By the early 1980s, computer science had become an extremely popular subject at American universities, an achievement that was not even remotely approached in Europe. By 1983, American universities were awarding far more bachelor's degrees in computer science than in any other field of science or engineering (Computer Science and Telecommunications Board 1999).[5]

---

[4] It should also be remembered, however, that a particular hardware innovation, the microprocessor, set the stage for the explosive growth of software firms after 1980. As Mowery has observed: "The epochal innovation for the U.S. computer software industry, of course, was the microprocessor, which was subsequently incorporated into the microcomputer. The rapid adoption of the microcomputer within the United States after 1980 created opportunities for entry by independent software vendors. But these entry prospects were made still more attractive by the rapid emergence of 'dominant designs' within the U.S. microcomputer market, the IBM PC and the Apple Macintosh architectures" (Mowery 1996: 144).

[5] An important contribution of private industry to the rapid emergence of the discipline of computer science in American universities was the willingness of computer firms to make their computers available at heavily discounted prices as well as to provide complementary inputs that were necessary in the academic world. "For example, in addition to offering price discounts on its machines, Control Data Corporation (CDC) offered research grants, free computer time, and cash contributions to U.S. universities ... In addition to donating computer time to establish regional computing centers at MIT and UCLA in the mid-1950s, IBM rented some fifty of its model 650 computers to universities at reduced rates ... For example, the IBM 650 at the Carnegie Institute of Technology's new Graduate School of Industrial Administration, which was used by Herbert Simon, Allen Newell, and Alan Perlis in their early work on artificial intelligence, was acquired with funds from private foundations, although Simon and others also received support as consultants to the Rand Corporation" (Langlois and Mowery 1996: 58).

The contributions of American universities in generating powerful new computer-based technologies led directly to the creation of today's Internet. The history of the Internet is a story of university-based research, supported with extensive federal funding (primarily from the Department of Defense's Advanced Research Projects Agency [ARPA]). These efforts produced a series of innovations in software, computer architecture, and computer networking that led from the ARPANET to the NSFNET, which, in turn, came to underpin national and international electronic mail. Spin-off firms from academic research, such as Bolt, Beranek and Newman, which originated at MIT, were contracted to provide specific technical components, in this case the first packet switch.

The research management structure at ARPA was heavily dominated by academics on leave from their universities.[6] The present day global communications network, involving Internet and the World Wide Web, traces its origins directly back to ARPA's effort to link more closely together the research activities of four universities (Carnegie-Mellon, MIT, Stanford, and the University of California at Berkeley). Each of these universities was, at the time, performing research for the Department of Defense. The remarkable degree of openness and accessibility that characterizes today's Internet and World Wide Web must surely owe a great deal to the fact that they were developed primarily in a university context. It is most unlikely that this technology would have developed in the directions that it has, and as quickly as it has, if it had originated in a commercial environment in which proprietary considerations loomed large.

ACADEMIC MEDICAL CENTERS AND THE NEW WAVE OF ACADEMIC ENTREPRENEURS

In addition to information technology, American universities have played a decisive role in biotechnology, which (as Andrew Toole's chapter describes) has evolved at an extremely rapid pace, especially

---

[6] For a valuable recent discussion, see Mowery and Simcoe 2001. As they point out: "Though it was not the first Internet browser, the program that launched the World Wide Web was a free browser named Mosaic, written by Marc Andreesen, a graduate student working at the University of Illinois' National Center for Supercomputing Applications" (p. 16).

in response to the revolutionary scientific breakthroughs in molecular biology. The industry within which these technological breakthroughs have become embedded is, even now, barely a quarter of a century old. Although it is not yet widely appreciated, American universities have already completed a dramatic transition to the world of industrial biotechnology. By the late 1980s a far higher percentage of university research resources were already committed to the life sciences in the United States than in any other OECD country (Irvine et al. 1990).

The extent to which American universities have been responsive to the expanded commercial opportunities created by molecular biology may be readily seen by considering the data for U.S. university R&D expenditures. These figures are startling to anyone who still considers physics and chemistry to be the central "core" of university science. In 2000, total academic R&D spending in the United States was $30.2 billion. The physical sciences (physics, chemistry, astronomy) received less than 10 percent of the total. The share of the engineering disciplines (including computer science) was less than 20 percent; the life sciences (biology, medicine, agriculture) totally dominated the picture, with well over half of the total. Moreover, biomedical research was substantially more than half of total life sciences expenditures. Thus, biomedical research alone is now more than three times the size of all the physical sciences (National Science Board 2002: A5–15). This is compelling evidence of the American university's responsiveness to the growth in demand for such research, partly due to the aging of the American population, partly also to the higher priority that the increasingly affluent American population and its congressional representatives have come to attach to improvements in the delivery of medical care, and partly to a growing consensus that great steps forward in medical technology lie just around the corner.

The role of the American university in the biotechnology revolution differs from the earlier roles played by universities in one very fundamental respect: The biotechnology industry has been, from its inception in the second half of the 1970s, and remains today, intimately tied to academic scientists, not only in their traditional capacity as researchers, but also as entrepreneurs. Many university scientists have been directly involved in starting up new firms and have served as business decision makers and strategists (see Kenney 1986). All the earliest start-ups in this new industry extensively involved university faculty, and many academics remain heavily involved in biotechnology enterprises while retaining their active academic appointments. (More detail on the evolution of biotechnology entrepreneurship can be found in Andrew Toole's chapter in this volume.) This situation is a reflection of the fact that the new process technology of recombinant DNA represented, simultaneously, a fundamental advance in science and an invention of great potential utilitarian and commercial value.

America's current commercial leadership in biotechnology can hardly be attributed to overwhelming U.S. leadership in the underlying science of molecular biology. European science as a whole has been competitive, and the scientific community in Cambridge, England, has played a towering role (see Judson 1979; Morange 1998). Rather, U.S. universities have responded, far more quickly than universities in other OECD countries, to the commercial opportunities held out by these discoveries as well as to the scientific opportunities.

The contributions of university research in the life sciences are only a portion of those made by American universities, and their academic medical centers, to the country's innovative capability in biomedical technology. If one consults the data for corporate patenting by the United States, Japan, and Germany, it is apparent that the largest U.S. patent classes are precisely in categories where academic medical centers play a predominant role. As Table 6.1 shows, in striking contrast to corporate patenting by Japan and Germany, the top five patent classes for American corporations in 1997 were all medical; three of the top five were either surgical instruments or closely connected to surgical procedures. Moreover, when one includes U.S. patent class 11 (molecular biology and microbiology) and patent class 15 (analytical and immunological testing), fully seven of the top fifteen U.S. corporate patenting categories were closely tied to medicine. Although past experience suggests caution in regarding health care sectors as relatively "immune" to cyclical phenomena, it is worth observing that, whereas health care companies accounted for only about 5 percent of all IPOs in 1998 and 1999, this figure has risen to around 20 percent since early 2000, when the dot-coms went into their recent precipitous decline.[7] Clearly America's international commercial successes in medically related

---

[7] These figures were compiled by Thomson Financial as reported in the *New York Times*, November 11, 2001.

Table 6.1. *Top Fifteen Most Emphasized U.S. Patent Classes for Corporations from the United States, Japan, and Germany, 1997*

	United States	Japan	Germany
1.	Surgical instruments	Photography	Printing
2.	Biology of multicellular organisms	Information storage and retrieval	Plant protecting and regulating compositions
3.	Surgery: light, thermal, and electrical applications	Electrophotography	Clutches and power-stop control
4.	Surgery: application, storage, and collection	Liquid crystal cells	X-ray or gamma ray devices
5.	Prosthesis	Facsimile	Organic compounds (includes classes 532–570)
6.	Computers and digital processing	Typewriting machines	Fabrication of plastics and earthenware
7.	Data processing	Television signal processing	Machine element or mechanism
8.	Special receptacle or package	Printing of symbolic information	Winding, tensioning, or guiding devices
9.	Telephone communications	Optics: systems and elements	Metal deforming
10.	Communications: directive radio wave systems	Active solid-state devices	Internal combustion engines
11.	Chemistry: molecular biology and microbiology	Radiation imagery chemistry	Coating or plastic fabrication
12.	Chemistry: natural resins or derivatives	Storage or retrieval of magnetic information	Paper making
13.	Information processing system organization	Internal-combustion engines	Power-driven conveyors
14.	Cryptography	Television	Sheet feeding or delivering
15.	Chemistry: analytical and immunological testing	Electrical generator or motor	Synthetic resins or natural rubbers

Note: Ranking is based on patenting activity of nongovernment U.S. or foreign organizations, which are predominantly corporations. Patenting by individuals and governments is excluded.

Source: U.S. Patent and Trademark Office, Office of Information Systems, TAF Program. Reprinted in *Science and Engineering Indicators, 2000*, 7–23.

technologies are deeply rooted in the research contributions of the faculties of the country's academic medical centers.

SPILLOVERS AND SPIN-OFFS: UNIVERSITY RESEARCH AS THE KNOWLEDGE BASE FOR ENTREPRENEURSHIP

There has been a specific organizational feature of American academic entrepreneurship since the end of the Second World War – a feature also of great potential significance for the future – to which I now turn. Recent research has shown that the "spillovers" from American university research have played a more important role in generating innovative activity in small firms than in large ones (Acs, Audretsch, and Feldman 1994; see also Acs and Audretsch (eds.) 1990a; Stephan 1996). In certain high-technology sectors small firms have proven to be extremely skillful in exploiting the research findings of the university world. Indeed, these skills may be interpreted as a way of compensating for the obvious fact that small firms, and especially small start-up firms, can have only a very modest capability for making investments in their own R&D. Clearly, the institutional and policy situations in the United States have created a far more congenial environment than in other OECD countries for newly established firms to play a prominent role in the commercialization of sophisticated new technologies – at least in certain specific sectors of the economy. The stark contrast, in this respect, between the American experience and that of the Europeans has been sharply delineated by patenting activity in the European Patent Office for the specific case of the biotechnology sector. According to a recent study based on EPO data, newly founded U.S. firms totally dominated patenting activity in this sector between 1978 and 1993 (Henderson et al. 1999).[8] (See Table 6.2.)

The study examined patent ownership for nine countries (United States, Japan, Germany, United Kingdom, France, Switzerland, Netherlands, Denmark, and Italy) according to the types of institutions owning the patents in each country: (1) new biotechnology firms, (2) established corporations, and (3) universities and other research

---

[8] I do not mean to suggest that the biotechnology industry is representative of other high-tech U.S. industrial sectors; it is, however, a sector currently on a sharply rising trajectory of economic importance.

Table 6.2. *Activity in Genetic Engineering by Type of Institution*

	NBFs	Established corporations	Universities & other research institutions
% Patents by Institution, European Patent Office Data 1978–1986			
USA	43.2	34.5	22.3
Japan	0.0	87.7	12.3
Germany	0.0	81.8	17.7
UK	27.3	49.1	23.6
France	18.7	21.5	59.8
Switzerland	0.0	92.9	7.1
Netherlands	12.7	56.4	30.9
Denmark	0.0	93.5	6.5
Italy	0.0	95.7	4.3
% Patents by Institution, European Patent Office Data 1987–1993			
USA	40.4	38.1	20.7
Japan	3.1	86.9	10.0
Germany	3.0	80.0	17.0
UK	23.7	44.7	31.6
France	16.7	35.0	48.3
Switzerland	4.7	89.0	6.3
Netherlands	20.0	62.5	17.5
Denmark	5.7	92.5	1.9

Source: Henderson et al. 1999: 291.

institutions. The fifteen-year period of the study was divided roughly in half. The contrasting roles of new start-up firms are very striking. Of American patents granted between 1978 and 1986, 43.2 percent were owned by new biotechnology firms. In the United Kingdom the share held by these kinds of firms was 27.3 percent; in all the other countries, new biotechnology firms accounted for less than 20 percent. In five of the nine countries new biotechnology firms accounted for none of the country's patents. Between 1987 and 1993, new biotechnology firms still accounted for more than 40 percent of all U.S. biotechnology patents in the EPO. Comparable studies are not available for other sectors, but no other country has shown anything like the massive increase in new business formations across a range of high-tech sectors (see Table 6.3 below for U.S. data).

How are we to account for the much greater prominence of small firms, especially new start-up firms, as prime agents in the commercialization of new technologies? Such small firm participation has been a distinguishing feature of U.S. high-technology sectors, by comparison with the United States in the years before World War II, and with the situation in other OECD countries over the past fifty years. In most of postwar Western Europe and Japan, the commercialization of innovations in electronics and pharmaceuticals was dominated by large, well-established firms, often supported as "national champions." In the United States, start-ups have been very prominent. In Silicon Valley, the epicenter of the U.S. electronics industry, there were once estimated to be nearly three thousand electronics firms (Saxenian 1994), the vast majority of which were very small and, it is important to note, highly specialized. One estimate of several years ago is that 70 percent of these firms had fewer than ten employees, and 80 percent had fewer than one hundred. To be sure, large firms continue to maintain a critical presence in U.S. high technology. AT&T remains a considerable presence in the world of microelectronics, for instance (although shorn of its former superb research capability), as does IBM in computers and Merck in pharmaceuticals. Nevertheless, the role of start-ups in the commercialization of new technologies has been far more prominent in the United States than in other industrial countries.

To a considerable extent, the prominence of small firms in the commercialization of new technologies has been an outcome of government policies. A key goal of these policies has long been to guarantee that large firms do not exclude potential new entrants into their industry. Government antitrust policy has compelled very large firms such as AT&T and IBM to pursue liberal licensing policies that have made their new technologies, including the transistor itself, more readily available to new entrants. AT&T suffered divestiture in 1984, an event that opened up the huge telecommunications market to new, far smaller entrants such as MCI and Sprint (as discussed by Eli Noam in his chapter in this volume). The possibility of an antitrust suit against IBM led that firm, in 1969, to "unbundle" its software from its hardware, thus creating the modern independent software industry (Mowery 1996). Furthermore, the Department of Defense (DoD) during the Cold War years maintained a policy of awarding contracts to small firms with little or no previous "track record," a policy that opened the door to newcomers such as Texas Instruments (which produced the first commercially successful transistor), Motorola, Fairchild, and Intel. DoD also maintained a so-called second sourcing policy that required its large contractors to share their technology with another firm, a policy that speeded up the diffusion of sophisticated technological capabilities. Nothing comparable to this occurred in military procurement in Western Europe (Mowery 1996).

A main observation, then, has been that start-up firms, a primary source of entrepreneurial talent, have come to assume a far more prominent role in high-technology sectors than ever before. Since, almost by definition, start-up firms do not have the financial resources to support the large-scale budgets usually required to be competitive in these sectors, a key question is: How do they do it? And what are the future prospects for the role of new start-up firms?

There is at least a partial historical explanation for the much greater prominence of start-up firms in the exploitation of university-based research in the second half of the twentieth century. The various virtues of small firms in the commercialization of new technologies (their ability to remain tightly focused, their more effective information exchange arrangements, their ability to change strategy rapidly) could not be tested in the pre-war period because start-up firms, almost by definition, possessed very limited financial resources for performing research of any kind. Moreover, university research resources in the pre-war years were minuscule by comparison with the postwar years when the federal government became an extremely generous patron of university research. There was virtually no federal support for basic research in the pre-war years; a sizeable phalanx of congressmen argued that using federal monies for such purposes was unconstitutional.

Thus, in the postwar years numerous new opportunities were opened up by the expansion of federal funding in support of research and a very large fraction of federal research funds went to universities. In effect, many financially strapped small firms could now exploit a major source of research activity that had no counterpart in pre-World War II years.[9]

---

[9] Start-up firms also figured prominently in the commercialization of research findings of large firms that failed to exploit the products of their own inventive efforts, but the subject is outside the boundaries of this chapter. Xerox's failure to harness the creativity of their Xerox PARC facility is the most notorious example, but there are many others.

The late Edwin Mansfield was a pioneer in establishing that innovations based on academic research are more likely to be made by small firms (Mansfield 1991). Mansfield's work addressed the further issue of the length of the time lags between investment in recent academic research projects and the industrial application of those findings. An especially interesting finding of Mansfield is that, in the seven manufacturing industries he examined (information processing, electrical equipment, chemicals, instruments, drugs, metals, and oil), the time lags were greater for large firms than for small ones. It would appear that small firms have a comparative advantage over large ones in the speedy commercial exploitation of university research findings.

This advantage contributes to an unusual structural characteristic of American high-technology industries, the coexistence of large numbers of small firms with a few very large ones. Whereas computer hardware was once dominated by a few large firms, including one super-large firm, this industry now contains hundreds of specialized component suppliers. Although, as noted earlier, the role of universities in innovation with respect to hardware declined considerably in the course of the 1950s, universities did play a significant later role in the minicomputer and microcomputer product lines, a role that involved the provision both of entrepreneurship and of valuable scientific knowledge. The Digital Equipment Corporation (DEC), which played a key entrepreneurial role in minicomputers, accounting for about one-third of sales in that segment for many years, had its origins in MIT's Lincoln Laboratory. Stanford and the University of Texas played key roles in microcomputers and work-stations as well. It would be difficult to find universities in Europe playing anything like a comparable role. As Bresnahan and Malerba have observed, "Only Cambridge in the United Kingdom has played a similar (albeit more reduced) role in Europe" (1999: 127–128).

Although Microsoft is currently a giant in the software industry, there are now literally thousands of small firms in that industry. More generally, as Gavin Wright has succinctly expressed it, commenting on the American chemical industry, "The coexistence and complementarity of large and small technology-based firms has been a persistent feature of the United States in major twentieth-century industries" (1999: 317; see also Arora and Gambardella 1998).

Table 6.3. *United States High-Tech Business Formations, by Technology Area*

Period formed	All high-tech fields	Automation	Biotechnology	Computer hardware	Advanced materials	Photonics & optics	Software	Electronic components	Telecom-munications	Other fields*
Total since 1960	31,819	2,155	812	3,003	1,155	944	8,020	3,292	2,240	10,198
1980–94	18,529	1,041	610	2,090	527	507	5,506	1,524	1,375	5,349
1980–84	7,478	487	195	804	213	201	2,274	669	416	2,219
1985–89	6,978	383	236	812	211	187	2,014	577	483	2,075
1990–94	4,073	171	179	474	103	119	1,218	278	478	1,055
1995–June'97	912	27	11	89	24	11	300	46	217	187

* Other fields are chemicals, defense-related, energy, environmental, manufacturing equipment, medical, pharmaceuticals, test and measurement, and transportation.

Data reflect the number of companies formed since 1960 that were still in business as of June 1997. Company mergers and acquisitions will tend to understate the data shown in this table.

Source: Corp Tech database Rev. 12.3 (Woburn, MA: Corporate Technology Information Services, Inc.). Special tabulations, July 1997. Reprinted in NSF, "Will Small Business Become the Nation's Leading Employer of Graduates with Bachelors Degrees in Science and Engineering?" January 1999.

Table 6.3, although its classificatory arrangements are not ideal, sheds considerable light on the profusion of start-up firms over a period of almost forty years. Note, first of all, that well over half of all high-technology start-ups in this database, which includes only firms that were still operating in 1997, were formed after 1979. The computer sector (hardware and software) accounted for about 40 percent of all new high-technology businesses formed after 1979, but the software numbers far exceeded those for hardware, as would be expected from my earlier discussion. In the case of biotechnology, a sector whose underlying technology began to be transformed in the 1970s, the figure was more than 75 percent. The relative growth rate for new telecommunications firms sharply accelerated in the 1995–1997 period.

TWO EXEMPLARY CASES: CT AND MRI

Some important insights into the complexities of academic entrepreneurship emerge from a brief consideration of the two most important medical diagnostic technologies of the post-World War II period: computed tomography (CT) scanners and magnetic resonance imaging (MRI) machines.[10] These machines are extremely expensive, involving an initial outlay of perhaps two million dollars and an annual operating cost of a million dollars or so. (In the case of the MRI machine there is usually a high cost involved in "insulating" the surrounding hospital area from the powerful magnets that are central to the operation of the machine.)

Like many other recent developments in medical technologies, CT scanners and MRI machines depend heavily on computers. Computers are essential for three-dimensional image reconstruction as well as extremely fast scanning time in both technologies. In both cases the development process, after the introduction of the first working prototype, has involved the reduction of scanning time. In the case of the CT scanner this has meant a reduction from around five minutes to as little as five seconds. Competitive survival for both diagnostic technologies has depended on the availability of plentiful financial support as a precondition for meeting the very high costs of this development process (see Gelijns and Rosenberg 1999).

---

[10] The following discussion of the CT scanner and MRI draws freely on Gelijns and Rosenberg 1999.

Several features of the history of these imaging technologies deserve emphasis. The first is that clinicians in American and British academic medical centers played a dominant early role, not only in conceptualizing the new technology, but in developing it all the way to a prototype stage. Second, these clinicians commonly sought out the technical expertise of electronic engineers or applied physicists within their own university for assistance in their R&D. Additionally, the clinicians themselves frequently played an entrepreneurial role, at which they hardly ever succeeded.

The CT scanner joined X-ray technology to the remarkable computational capabilities of the digital computer. CT scanning relies on X-rays but uses mathematical techniques and computer technology to produce images from which one can derive three-dimensional information. European radiologists first developed the concept and techniques of tomography, and clinicians at UCLA, Georgetown, and Columbia-Presbyterian Medical Center (along with Bell Labs) made substantial contributions, especially with respect to reducing image construction time. The first firm to bring the CT scanner to market in 1973 was the British firm, Electrical and Musical Industries Ltd. (EMI). Leadership in the development of the technology was supplied by Godfrey Hounsfield, an engineer who worked at the central research laboratory of EMI on pattern recognition and computer storage techniques.[11]

By mid-1975, EMI had installed over 120 CT scanners. It had orders for 416 more by the end of that year, and it held about 40 percent of the U.S. market. EMI encountered competition from a variety of sources, however, and by the end of the 1970s the firm had left the industry. After the shakeout, the American and European firms that came to dominate the market were overwhelmingly firms that had also played prominent roles in the market for conventional X-ray machines. Especially prominent were such huge multinational firms as GE, Siemens, and Toshiba. In 1981 GE held 60 percent of the American market.

The history of the MRI machine has much in common with that of the CT scanner. The role of university research, in both the United

---

[11] EMI's earlier core business had been in recording, broadcasting, and home entertainment equipment (including television). The firm had a considerable reputation for the high quality of its research in both basic and applied fields. After the Second World War it decided to diversify into civilian and defense-related electronics.

States and the United Kingdom, remained central throughout the early stages in the development of this new technology. I. I. Rabi of Columbia University confirmed the existence of the phenomenon of nuclear magnetic resonance in 1938, and in 1946 E. M. Purcell of Harvard and Felix Bloch of Stanford demonstrated the existence of NMR in solids and liquids, respectively. All three scientists subsequently received Nobel Prizes for their research. Prominent later participants in both the United States and United Kingdom came from the academic medical centers and physics departments of the universities of Aberdeen and Nottingham in the United Kingdom and the State University of New York at Stony Brook and the University of California at San Francisco in the United States. Raymond Damadian, a medical doctor who was also an assistant professor of biophysics at Downstate Medical Center of New York, was especially important in the commercialization process.

In the late 1970s and 1980s, after the basic technology had been proven, extensive further research was taken up by private industry in both the United States and Europe, including EMI in 1976, with financial support from the U.S. Department of Health and Human Services. The first American company, Fonar, was a single-product start-up firm that drew heavily on Damadian's work. Fonar was responsible in 1980 for the first commercial placement of an MRI machine. Yet neither Fonar nor any of the other start-ups survived the competition, especially after GE's relatively late entry into the market. Damadian, who had received a patent in February 1974, but whose firm was driven out of the market, sued GE. In the summer of 1997, the courts supported Damadian's patent suit and ordered GE to pay Fonar $128.7 million. Fonar had also sued Hitachi, Johnson and Johnson, Philips, and Siemens for patent infringement, and each of these firms agreed to settle out of court for undisclosed sums of money.

CT and MRI share several features that help to account for the failure of academic entrepreneurs to establish and maintain a competitive position in the high-technology medical diagnostics market. Both technologies passed through an intensely competitive phase after the first prototypes had been developed, a phase of rapid performance improvement during which the "table stakes" for maintaining competition were very high in terms of the required levels of R&D spending. Academic medical centers continued to play a major role in expanding the range of uses of the new technology, and in testing for safety and efficacy in clinical trials, functions essential to the many upgrades thrown up by the rapid rate of technological change. As a consequence, first-mover advantages do not seem to have been of decisive significance in either market, and first-movers failed to sustain themselves through the eventual shakeout period. Smaller firms that appeared to be promising in the early stages could not sustain the very high cost of the later product improvement process. Moreover, marketing these complex new diagnostic technologies required a great deal of professional sophistication not possessed by the start-ups (or by EMI), nor did they possess the reputation for reliability that is a major consideration in the markets for medical products. At the end of the day, after the shakeout, the American and European markets were dominated by a small number of large, well-known multinational firms already dominant in other imaging markets. Broadly speaking, the firms that came to dominate the MRI market were the same as those that dominated the CT scanner market.

THE ROLE OF VENTURE CAPITAL

I turn finally to a recent institutional innovation, the venture capital firm. The ability of start-ups to enter high-technology, high-risk sectors has been powerfully strengthened by this financial innovation, which now plays a crucial role in the exercise of entrepreneurship (see Gompers and Lerner 1999). The venture capital firm has been a key reason for American success in high-tech industries in the past quarter century, and for the prominence of small, start-up firms in those successes. As the National Science Board's biennial *Science and Engineering Indicators* puts it: "It appears that venture capital firms tend to cluster around locales considered to be 'hotbeds' of technological activity, as well as in states where large amounts of R&D are performed" (National Science Board 2000: 7–24).

It is estimated that almost two-thirds of venture capital resources are concentrated in three states: California, New York, and Massachusetts. The venture capital industry has vastly increased the supply of capital becoming available to high-risk sectors of the economy from such sources as pension funds (public and private), insurance companies, and university endowments. The amount of venture capital under management in the United States rose from around $4 billion in 1980 to $34 billion in 1990, declined slightly in the early 1990s, but then rose more than sixfold, from $35 billion to $234 billion, between 1994 and 2000 (National Science Board, 2002: 6–35).[12] As Table 6.4 shows, venture capital investments have been heavily concentrated in computer hardware and software, medical and biotechnology sectors, communications, and semiconductors. And, most recently, the spectacular growth of the Internet (which was followed by an almost equally spectacular fall) depended heavily on venture capital financing.

American venture capital firms, it should be emphasized in the present context, do a great deal more than merely supply capital to high-risk, high-tech enterprises. They have reshaped the nature of entrepreneurship by providing various kinds of sophisticated expertise that serve as powerful, professional filters in allocating risk capital as well as highly trained human capital. In a variety of ways they shape the start-up firm's decision-making process and prepare the firm for the marketplace. In a very serious sense, venture capital firms have been serving as suppliers of entrepreneurial talent.

A CLOSING CONJECTURE

With respect to the role of start-up firms, I would like to close with the conjecture that such firms may constitute a socially efficient vehicle for exploring new commercial opportunities in technologically dynamic economies. In the face of the high uncertainties attached to the innovation process in the realms of science and technology, it may make a great deal of sense to encourage exploration by small firms along a wide variety of alternative paths – along with high rewards to those risk-takers who succeed (see Nelson 1990; Rowen 2000; Rosenberg 1994).

Looking backward, what seems to have evolved in the United States in the past half century is a new set of networks and institutional modifications that compensate for some of the more obvious limitations to the research capabilities of small, start-up firms. In particular, the

---

[12] There has been a substantial decline in inflows in the past two years, 2001–2002. Comparable figures are not yet available.

Table 6.4. *U.S. Venture Capital Disbursements, by Industry Category: 1980–2000*

Priority country	1980	1982	1984	1986	1988	1990	1992	1994	1996	1998	2000
	Millions of U.S. Dollars Disbursed										
All industries	703.3	1,901.9	5,292.8	4,685.7	5,602.9	3,868.9	5,229.4	5,187.8	9,897.4	16,777.6	90,551.1
Biotechnology	50.0	87.0	124.1	328.3	395.5	309.6	586.4	515.8	675.6	1,031.8	2,458.6
Communications	74.8	231.4	497.8	620.7	914.5	472.8	1,169.2	922.7	1,531.8	2,870.6	14,807.7
Computer hardware	155.1	652.9	1,057.9	838.1	586.4	335.3	279.4	259.7	393.9	553.8	2,091.3
Consumer related	50.0	104.7	1,757.5	521.9	815.1	443.3	378.9	790.9	1,123.2	1,194.3	1,944.7
Industrial and energy	148.6	248.1	328.3	325.1	362.0	243.9	182.0	216.3	389.6	395.9	821.9
Medical and health	49.0	118.1	332.4	395.6	613.6	597.1	879.8	921.1	1,277.2	2,287.9	3,327.2
Semiconductors and other electronics	85.0	221.9	471.4	510.6	453.8	297.6	243.2	265.8	532.1	871.1	5,661.1
Software and services	19.3	154.0	492.2	499.1	469.4	673.9	685.2	851.3	2,560.4	5,750.8	13,010.1
Other products and services	71.4	83.8	231.1	646.4	992.6	495.4	825.3	444.1	1,413.5	1,821.4	5,535.0
Internet specific	NA	NA	NA	NA	NA	NA	NA	NA	NA	NA	40,893.6
	Percentage of Total Venture Capital Disbursements										
All industries	100.0	100.0	100.0	100.0	100.0	100.0	100.0	100.0	100.0	100.0	100.0
Biotechnology	7.1	4.6	2.3	7.0	7.1	8.0	11.2	9.9	6.8	6.1	2.7
Communications	10.6	12.2	9.4	13.2	16.3	12.2	22.4	17.8	15.5	17.1	16.6
Computer hardware	22.1	34.3	20.0	17.9	10.5	8.7	5.3	5.0	4.0	3.3	2.4
Consumer related	7.1	5.5	33.2	11.1	14.5	11.5	7.2	15.2	11.3	7.1	2.1
Industrial and energy	21.1	13.0	6.2	6.9	6.5	6.3	3.5	4.2	3.9	2.4	0.9
Medical and health	7.0	6.2	6.3	8.4	11.0	15.4	16.8	17.8	12.9	13.6	3.7
Semiconductors and other electronics	12.1	11.7	8.9	10.9	8.1	7.7	4.7	5.1	5.4	5.2	6.2
Software and services	2.7	8.1	9.3	10.7	8.4	17.4	13.1	16.4	25.9	34.3	14.3
Other products and services	10.2	4.4	4.4	13.8	17.7	12.8	15.8	8.6	14.3	10.9	6.0
Internet specific	NA	NA	NA	NA	NA	NA	NA	NA	NA	NA	45.2

Note: NA = not available.

Source: Special tabulations provided by Venture Economics (Newark, NJ, March 2001). Reprinted in *Science & Engineering Indicators – 2002*, appendix table 6–19, p. A6–64.

symbiotic relationship that now exists between university research and the world of industrial innovation is a powerful determinant of improved performance in the American economy. Much additional research is necessary to probe more deeply into the exact nature, and the extent, of interdependence of the various components of these networks, and how they might be modified in ways that will further strengthen the contributions of academic entrepreneurship.

PART THREE

EQUITY ISSUES IN ENTREPRENEURSHIP POLICY

7

Venture Capital Access

Is Gender an Issue?

Candida G. Brush, Nancy M. Carter, Elizabeth Gatewood,
Patricia G. Greene, and Myra M. Hart

Diana was a heroic woman, a huntress. Women seeking capital are
hunters rather than gatherers. They are hunting for capital in a traditionally male dominated arena.

Women's participation in entrepreneurship is vital to the growth of the
U.S. economy. It is not surprising, then, that breaking down gender barriers and facilitating the start-up and development of women-owned
businesses has been at the forefront of public policy for several decades.
Legislative changes such as the Civil Rights Act of 1964, the Equal
Credit Opportunity Act of 1975, and the Affirmative Action Act of
1978 were pioneering efforts to address some of the challenges that
women faced in starting and growing their own businesses. Baseline
data on women's participation as business owners in the wake of
these efforts were first made available in *The Bottom Line* (President's
Interagency Task Force 1979). Ten years later passage of the Women's
Business Ownership Act provided set-asides for women business
owners, created the National Women's Business Council, called for
additional data collection, and established new federal capacities to
guarantee loans to women-owned businesses.

More recently, women's entrepreneurship policy has been manifested in a wide range of federal, state, and local programs. Relevant

The authors are indebted to James Post, Alicia Robb, and Elaine Romanelli for their
thoughtful suggestions and ideas.

federal initiatives include the Small Business Administration (SBA)'s preferential procurement program (known as section 8(a)), which provides government contracts and other assistance to small businesses owned by socially and economically disadvantaged persons; the Women-owned Business Procurement Program, which teaches women how to market to the federal government; the Women's Demonstration Program, which provides women with long-term training and counseling for all aspects of owning and managing a business; and the Women's Network for Entrepreneurial Training, which arranges for experienced women owners to serve as mentors to others. Government-subsidized financing has been made available through the SBA's micro-loan program (the "7 (M)" program), which provides funds to nonprofit intermediaries that then make small loans to qualified women entrepreneurs; and through the SBA's loan guarantee programs, which increase incentives to financiers to lend to riskier businesses, including some that have no credit track record. Debt financing opportunities are further expanded by government initiatives (like the Women's Pre-qualification Loan Program), private banking programs (such as the Wells Fargo Bank and BankBoston programs for women business owners), and women's business organizations (like Women Inc.). In addition, the Small Business Investment Company (SBIC) program and its minority counterpart (MESBIC) attempt to foster investment in early stage businesses, including those owned by women.

POLICY IMPACT AND DEBT FINANCING

The success of these programs can be measured in part by the explosive growth of women's entrepreneurship in recent years. In 1990, women owned 32 percent of all nonfarm sole proprietorships (5,348,000), a number that had grown to 37 percent (6,833,000) by 1998 (*Women in Business* 2001). Other indicators of women's entrepreneurship have followed suit. A recent report by the Center for Women's Business Research estimates that between 1997 and 2002 sales made by women-owned firms grew by 40 percent and their employment increased by 30 percent, rates greater than those of their male-owned counterparts. Based on a Dun and Bradstreet sample of over 9 million firms, this research group estimated that 24.6 percent of the 1.4 million women-owned businesses had revenues greater than $1 million in 1997, and the proportion had increased to 25.5 percent of 1.5 million by 2000 (Center for Women's Business Research 2001). Although debates about the exact numbers continue,[1] it is indisputable that women's entrepreneurship has grown and has made a substantial contribution to the U.S. economy in the past decade.

This remarkable growth was financed almost entirely by debt. Considering that public policy programs targeting women entrepreneurs emphasized this form of finance, this is not surprising. The Survey of Small Business Finances indicates that 92 percent of women-owned firms used at least one form of financial services. Women business owners were less likely to use commercial banks as sources of credit than their male counterparts, but were more likely to use thrift institutions or credit unions. Women were also more likely to use credit cards than men to finance their businesses, presumably paying higher interest rates as a result. Women-owned businesses' share of SBA loans has fluctuated from 12.4 percent in 1991 to 24.3 percent in 1998 (*Women in Business* 2001).

Yet there is some question as to whether these programs have fully alleviated the barriers to credit encountered by women entrepreneurs. Some studies show that women have less access to initial financial resources than men, that their access to private banking sources is reduced as a result, and that bankers often perceive men to be higher on characteristics associated with successful entrepreneurship than women (Carter, Williams, and Reynolds 1997; Carter and Allen 1997; Buttner and Rosen 1998). In contrast, however, a study of access to bank financing in Canada showed few differences once firm age, size, and growth rate were controlled (Riding and Swift 1990; Fabowale, Orser, and Riding 1995). Research using bank data shows women-owned businesses are smaller and newer than men-owned businesses, and are less likely to use external financing, leading to the conclusion that there is no discrimination in lending based on gender

---

[1] Figures recently released by the U.S. Census report lower numbers for 1997 that reflect the adoption of new qualifying criteria. To be considered "women-owned" under the new definition requires 51 percent ownership, $1,000 minimum annual revenues (up from the previous criterion of $500), and that the business be privately held. The new criteria exclude many high growth ventures that are publicly held and at the upper end of the revenue continuum. The change in definition has depressed the reported contribution of women-owned businesses.

(Coleman 2000). Nonetheless, women often paid higher interest rates and met stricter collateral requirements than men (Coleman 2000; Fabowale et al. 1995).

EQUITY CAPITAL INVESTMENT

Although their access to debt financing has improved, women entrepreneurs' access to equity markets remains limited. A study of the venture capital industry conducted by Stout (1997) found that of the 1,200 companies that received venture funding in 1996, only 30 were women-led. Only 2 percent of the $33 billion invested by venture capitalists between 1991 and 1996 went to female-led firms. More recently, our "Diana Project"[2] utilized data from the National Venture Capital Association to deduce patterns of disparity between financing of women-led and men-led ventures. The NVCA data were originally collected by Venture Economics and contain information on companies funded by venture capital since 1957. The data set includes information on 20,000 portfolio companies, 34,000 executives, and 120,000 company investments and is provided by 4,500 private equity firms investing a total of 7,000 separate funds. The data are updated on a quarterly basis. Since only businesses receiving funding are included, comparisons to businesses not receiving funding are not possible with this data set.

Of the 8,311 venture-capital-financed businesses[3] for which the leader's gender could be identified, 395 (2.4 percent) were led by women. Between 1957 and 1980, there was no year in which more than three identifiable women-led ventures received venture capital. After 1980, the number of such investments grew. By 1987, 33 women-led ventures, representing 4.1 percent of all investments, were given the

[2] The "Diana Project" (for which the five authors of this chapter are principal investigators) was formed to investigate the apparent disconnect between opportunities and resources in equity funding for high-growth women-owned businesses. It is funded by the Kauffman Center for Entrepreneurial Leadership, the U.S. Small Business Administration, and the National Women's Business Council.

[3] Of the 16,135 investments in ventures between 1957 and 1998, we were able to identify the gender of the founder in 8,311 cases. For many cases, the name of the management contact for the business receiving the investment was only listed by last name or initial. In other instances, we could not assume that the first name was male or female. For all cases in which there was any question, the businesses were counted as "unidentifiable" by leader's name.

green light. The percentage receded, however, after hitting that peak. From 1988 to 1998, the average was only 3.5 percent, although by the end of this period, the figure again hit the 4.1 percent level. Still, allowing for measurement error, the best one can say is that women entrepreneurs receive no more than 5 percent of all invested venture capital, a disproportionately low share.

These findings are all the more remarkable when one considers the unprecedented growth rate of the venture capital industry. For decades venture capital played a quiet yet crucial role in the development and expansion of new ventures. Changes to the Employment Retirement Income Security Act (ERISA) in 1979, which permitted pension funds to make venture investments for the first time, marked a turning point. This revision resulted in a significant flow of pension assets into venture capital companies during the 1980s. In the early 1990s, this "ratchet-like growth" accelerated to explosive growth, and the industry became global and highly competitive (Timmons and Bygrave 1997). For the first time, commitments by limited partners exceeded $4 billion, and returns moved upwards of 20 percent per annum. During the late 1990s, venture capital investment skyrocketed to new highs every year. In 2000 alone $103 billion was invested, reflecting a 75 percent increase over 1999. Not only did the absolute amount of investment reach new highs, but also the number of companies receiving venture capital funding rose from 3,967 in 1999 to 5,380 in 2000 (Metzger 2001a). Venture-funded firms received an average of about $19 million each in 2000 to fuel their growth. The fall 2000 crash of the dot-coms slowed investment but did not stop it. Venture capital investments for the last two quarters of 2002 were more than $4 billion per quarter, according to the National Venture Capital Association (NVCA 2003).

In sum, the explosive growth in equity investment occurred at the same time as the dramatic increases in number and size of women-owned businesses. However, women receive only a very small percentage of equity capital. Why is equity investment in women-led ventures so tiny?

That women are receiving such a small share of equity capital is of concern for both normative and instrumental reasons. From a normative perspective, women should have opportunities equal to those available to men to create wealth and grow their businesses. The system appears at first blush to be unequal. The instrumental argument focuses on competitiveness and innovation. Society is missing out if the benefits of innovations produced by women entrepreneurs are not quickly diffused.[4] eBay, taken public by Meg Whitman, and Exodus Communications, started by Ellen Hancock, are two examples of women-led ventures that contributed significantly to the economy in the 1990s. Venture capitalists, meanwhile, can benefit by reaping high returns from women-led firms. Programs to support venture capital funding may be a logical extension of the scope of women's entrepreneurship policy. Identification of the appropriate interventions in this area requires further analysis, however.

A MODEL OF ACCESS TO VENTURE CAPITAL

Research on venture capital falls into three streams. One deals with the relationship between the investor and the venture capital firm; another, with the operations and decision processes of the venture capital firm, particularly its searching, screening, and evaluation activities; and the third, with the relationship between the entrepreneurial company and the venture capital firm.[5] We used all three streams of work to develop a model (see Figure 7.1) that encompasses the structure of the industry and the activities of the three key actors in the process. Its purpose is to provide insights into the treatment of women entrepreneurs in the venture process, a subject neglected to date.

The first element of the model is the investor, the person or institution that supplies funds. The investor is most concerned about the rate of return and risk protection. The second element is the venture capital firm, which brings investors and recipients of capital together in deals. These firms vary in size, but all participate in a search/screen process, evaluation, and negotiation, and they often provide management advice as well. The third element is the entrepreneurial firm, which is

---

[4] The authors are indebted to James E. Post for his thoughtful comments on this section.

[5] Our academic literature review examined all issues of *Journal of Business Venturing* published between 1997 and 2002, a search that yielded thirty-four studies about venture capital. We also identified four literature reviews published in the *State of the Art of Entrepreneurship* (Bygrave 1992; Timmons and Sapienza 1992) and *Entrepreneurship 2000* (Brophy 1997; Tmmons and Bygrave 1997). All articles except for the literature reviews were empirical studies.

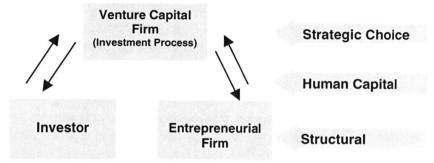

Figure 7.1. Women and venture capital–potential barriers

worried primarily about the value that would be added by the venture capitalists and the conditions and relationships that would accompany any investment.

Potential Barriers to Access

The three categories on the right side of Figure 7.1 comprise barriers that might preclude women entrepreneurs from securing access to venture financing for their businesses. One possibility is that women entrepreneurs may choose for strategic reasons not to seek venture capital. Another is that they lack the knowledge and capabilities to obtain it. Third, they may encounter structural barriers that preclude their access to equity funding. Data from a survey conducted in 2000 by the National Foundation of Women Business Owners (NFWBO) and from the Springboard 2000 Venture Forums (in which women entrepreneurs pitch their ventures to potential investors) were used to explore these hypotheses.

Strategic Choice: Grow or Not?

Growth is a strategic choice for entrepreneurs. Growth is a function of the entrepreneur's aspirations, her product and market strategy, and her context. All these factors are influenced by the economic sector and geographic location targeted by the venture's entry strategy. Because women-owned businesses tend to be smaller than those owned by men and are concentrated in service and retail sectors, women are often seen as choosing to start and grow businesses in economic sectors or geographic locations that are mismatched with the preferences of venture capitalists. Statistics from 1999 show that venture capitalists invested largely in computer software, hardware and services; medical, health, and biotechnology; communications; and consumer goods (Thompson Financial Securities Data 1999).

The applicant pool for the Springboard Forums in 2000 was analyzed to determine the strategic characteristics of the proposed businesses. All 900 applicants were competing in technology sectors, such as telecommunications, internet, software, biotechnology, and medical technology. More than 80 percent of the applicants sought "rapid growth" and indicated that they would consider public or private sale to achieve liquidity. An indicator of the aggressiveness of new ventures is the size of the markets they targeted. More than half the Springboard applicants estimated the size of their target market to be more than $15 billion in scale and international in scope. Approximately 53 percent of all applicants were in beta stage of development, and 47 percent had commercially launched their product or service. These applicants were further along in the development of their businesses than the average early-stage recipient of venture investment found in the NVCA data.

Eighty-four of the 900 Springboard applicants were selected to make presentations to investors. We compared applicants to presenters and found that the latter were more likely to be larger, to have launched a product, and to be business-to-business internet providers (at a time when this category was still attractive to the venture capital community). Presenters sought an average of $10 million for second stage financing and often had patented products.

Although the sample of Springboard applicants is biased because the applicant pool only included technology, life sciences, and new media companies, it is nevertheless representative of the types of businesses most often funded by venture capitalists. Over the two years of Springboard Forums more than 1,700 women have applied, and after several screenings and evaluations, 170 were selected to present (Springboard Enterprises 2000). The evidence from these forums, added to the sizable number of women-led ventures with sales greater than $1 million, suggests that there is a significant population of women entrepreneurs desiring to expand their businesses. Hence, strategic choice probably does not adequately explain the gender disparity of equity investments in entrepreneurial businesses.

Human Capital

Industry pundits and researchers alike have pointed to human capital as the single most important factor for venture capital investment. Human capital includes knowledge and capabilities, such as business experience and appropriate training. Venture-capital-funded businesses typically have experienced management teams, often with technical or scientific graduate degrees, and relevant leadership decision-making experience. It may be that too few women entrepreneurs are qualified to run high-growth, high-technology firms.

The aggregate evidence on educational qualifications of women is mixed. The proportion of women receiving master's degrees in business administration has increased steadily over the years, reaching 37 percent in 1998. At the undergraduate level, nearly 50 percent of students majoring in business are female. Less encouraging is the fact that only 19 percent of graduate engineering students and less than 10.6 percent of employed engineers are female (White, Blaisdell, and Anderson-Rowland 2000). On the other hand, 25 percent of all managers of Fortune 200 companies are female, suggesting that the pool of qualified women managers is adequate to staff rapidly growing ventures (Catalyst 1998).

Our analysis of data collected by the NFWBO in 2000 finds that women owners who have higher levels of financial knowledge, prior experience in starting new ventures, senior management experience, and graduate education are more likely to receive equity funding (Carter, Brush, Greene, Gatewood, and Hart 2001). These findings are corroborated by the Springboard data, which show that only 6 percent of applicants had less than a bachelor's degree; one-third were college graduates and 49 percent had graduate degrees. Further, 18 percent of Springboard applicants had received MBAs, and 31 percent held graduate degrees in science or technology. As a comparison, only 35 percent of *Inc.* 500 founders, the majority of which were male, had advanced degrees or MBAs (Bhide 2000).

Male entrepreneurs leading equity-funded ventures tend to have technical and relevant managerial experience (Shepherd and Douglas 1999). Bhide (2000) notes that, in contrast, most entrepreneurs don't have the experience that venture capitalists believe is necessary to rapidly build and manage large companies. More than 40 percent of *Inc,* 500 founders had no prior experience in the area of their venture

(Bhide 2000). The founding teams of the Springboard applicants (generally two or three people) had an average of 39 years of industry experience. Of the 900 ventures we analyzed, more than 40 percent had teams with previous business start-up experience.

This evidence suggests that the management team composition, experience, and education of women-led firms are not significantly different from those of men leading fast-growth ventures. Women entrepreneurs who wish to start businesses in growth areas appear equally capable in terms of human capital to their male counterparts. The teams they create appear particularly strong in the areas of knowledge and capabilities most desired by venture capitalists. Given Bhide's finding that venture capitalists consider most entrepreneurs to be lacking in the most appropriate human capital for starting and building businesses, the stocks of human capital held by women entrepreneurs should not place them at a disadvantage relative to male entrepreneurs.

Structural Barriers

Our third hypothesis about the equity-funding gap is that structural barriers preclude women's access to venture capital markets. Pundits have speculated that "it's not so much what you know, as who you know." Social networks that allow entrepreneurs to gain access to opportunities and resources, save time, and tap into advice and moral support offered by venture capital firms can be critical in leading to funding access. Aldrich (1989: 112) argues that "venture capitalists are probably as important for their broker role as for the funds they provide to struggling entrepreneurs." The venture capital network is a "knowledge network," bringing together technical experts, management consultants, and financial planners to supplement an entrepreneur's limited knowledge and experience.

This argument raises the question of whether women use the experiences and knowledge of individuals in their social network to augment their own human capital, or whether they are locked out of the critical networks altogether. Bygrave (1992) describes the venture capital industry as a closed network that is geographically concentrated and tightly interconnected. It is widely stated that raising capital is a "non-formal process." Social network theory suggests that people tend to interact with people like themselves. This preference leads to segregated networks (Brass 1985). If the venture capital industry is male-dominated, the likelihood that the networks of women entrepreneurs will overlap with those of venture capitalists who can assist them in securing financing is remote.

To examine this supposition we "mapped" the gender composition of the venture capital industry using *Pratt's Guide to Venture Capital Sources* for 1995 and 2000. Over these five years, the number of women in the industry has risen, but the percentage of women in the industry has remained the same. In 1995, 3,647 people were employed in the industry, of which 276 or 7.8 percent were women. By 2000, the industry had grown significantly, by more than 65 percent, whereas the proportion of women rose only slightly, to 8.8 percent. Among those who typically make investment decisions in venture capital firms (partners, managing directors, and principals), women constituted less than 4 percent. The number of firms listing one woman in a decision-making position increased from 201 to 276 between 1995 and 2000, but the average number of women per firm increased only from 1.37 to 1.49. The number of firms having more than three listed women remains very small.[6]

Our analysis of the Springboard applicant pool for 2000 shows that women seeking venture capital reported extensive use of informal networks. Fifty percent of the applicants stated they spent more than six hours a week talking with advisors, most often business associates, attorneys, or other business owners. More than 60 percent relied on the internet to contact advisors who might prove useful in securing equity investment. Further, women reported personal contacts with up to thirty potential equity providers and making twelve formal presentations. Most interesting, 35 percent reported that it was a female who really opened the door for them, with an additional 20 percent reporting it was both men and women.

In sum, although their representation increased by an impressive percentage, the number of women in the venture capital industry remains small, and their growth in numbers has only maintained pace with overall growth in the industry itself. To the extent that people

---

[6] Some of these increases, especially at the senior executive levels, are the result of a rise in the number of "women-focused" funds, typically directed by women.

prefer to interact with people like themselves, women will be locked out. Less than 10 percent of those in the venture capital industry are women, and less than 5 percent of the decisionmakers are women. Therefore, it is plausible that the makeup of the venture capital industry is an issue in women's access to venture capital.

PUBLIC POLICY RECOMMENDATIONS

We have made the case that gender discrimination in equity financing should be eliminated for both normative and instrumental reasons. Yet, it exists. We find that women are starting and growing businesses that contribute significantly to the U.S. economy, but they receive an extremely small share of the billions of dollars of venture capital invested each year. Women entrepreneurs are limited in scale and scope by a lack of venture capital. Strategic choice and lack of human capital are convenient hypotheses to explain this inequity, but they are not strongly supported by our analysis. On the other hand, structural barriers and limited access to venture capital networks appear to be serious obstacles. Public policies and innovations in governance that aim at eliminating these obstacles would be logical extensions of earlier women's entrepreneurship policy initiatives. We offer three recommendations.

Our first recommendation targets the expansion of networking opportunities. In recent years various groups around the country have coalesced around the issue of women's entrepreneurship, growth, and equity investments. Networking and support organizations are emerging to develop and promote programs to bring together women business owners and investors. Venture fairs, business assistance centers, and technology incubators targeting women are being launched in San Francisco, Seattle, Boston, New York, Chicago, and Washington, D.C. Programs like these should be expanded and replicated across the country. Partnerships of business groups, local development organizations, and educational institutions can play important roles in bringing together women, equity capital providers, and those who "chauffeur" deals (such as lawyers, accountants, and investment bankers). Their funding and sponsorship of such forums will link women with potential investors and engage them in knowledge networks. Increased visibility of strong deals generates awareness and investor interest. Events should encourage venture capital firms and angel networks to devote significant attention to what is sometimes perceived as a niche market – women entrepreneurs.

Our second recommendation deals with research and data collection. The data compiled by the Diana Project from NVCA and Springboard are revealing but not conclusive. Tracking equity investments to determine the distribution by gender is difficult since the leading data bases do not report or analyze the gender composition of management teams and investments. We have launched a panel study of high growth ventures to assemble a database that will allow full gender-based comparisons of the venture capital process. More complete data are needed, however, particularly with regard to screening and investment, as well as management, exit events, and returns.

Relatedly, it is acknowledged that the venture capital industry is highly concentrated, with several large firms controlling the bulk of capital and consistently producing superior returns (BenDaniel, Reyes, and D'Angelo 2000). The main reason given for this concentration is a tendency to risk aversion by limited partners (such as pension funds, endowments, and insurance companies) who encourage venture funds to invest in later stage deals that are less risky. The degree to which risk-averse, large venture capital firms avoid investments in women-led ventures may be a manifestation of behavioral discrimination. If we had a better understanding of the relationships and investment behaviors of limited partners relative to venture capital firms and their investment decisions for women-led ventures, we might be able to discern whether overt discrimination is present.

The federal government, foundations, and entrepreneurship centers should sponsor, fund, and disseminate research that provides a more complete picture of women's pursuit and success in acquiring equity capital compared to men. Investments and performance of investments by gender should be tracked and compared. A complete understanding of the participants and the process of equity investment is hindered by missing data.

Our final proposal concerns education. It might be possible to increase the number of women in the venture capital industry by encouraging and educating women to participate in the investment process, as angels or through corporate venture funds and venture capital firms. It is estimated that fewer than ten equity funds are women-owned, and approximately the same number target women-led ventures as investments. Women are playing a very minor role in the supply side of this multibillion dollar industry. Educating women about angel investing, the investment process, and careers in the industry might serve to lessen the male dominance of the venture capital network. Venture firms, nonprofit foundations, investment banks, educational institutions, and local agencies might sponsor and fund such programs.

Programs must also be developed that prepare women to lead high-growth businesses. The objective is not to encourage all women business owners to seek venture capital, but to encourage women to develop an understanding of the growth process and the role and fit that equity plays in that process. It is through this understanding that informed choices about business ownership and growth would best be made.

CONCLUSION

The answer to the question posed by the title of this chapter is "yes." Gender is an issue in access to venture capital. Women own over 35 percent of U.S. businesses and receive only 5 percent of venture capital funding. The gap is all the more impressive when one considers that 10 percent of all businesses with over $1 million in sales are owned by women.

Structural barriers associated with this gap, especially within the social networks that are so critical for gaining access to resources, ought to be addressed. A continued lack of investment in women-led ventures diminishes the opportunity for women to build wealth and create assets for future generations. Gender inequality in the venture capital process limits the innovations, jobs, and economic contributions that our nation should realize. The extension of women's entrepreneurship policy to the venture capital industry would benefit not just women entrepreneurs and the venture capitalists who invest in them, but the entire society.

According to Amy Millman, President of Springboard Enterprises,

The equity markets are the last frontier for women entrepreneurs. The stories of the women who tried to build their businesses without a map to the gold in these markets were the motivation for launching the Springboard forum series. Now we have more than stories, we have results. The experiences of these women have become the gold mine that will be used to guide the next wave of entrepreneurs through these markets.

8

Minority Business Assistance Programs Are Not Designed to Produce Minority Business Development

Timothy Bates

Minority business enterprises (MBEs) have been expanding rapidly in size and scope in recent years. Public policies seeking to promote MBE development have sometimes contributed to this growth process. Yet government has generally preferred to pursue assistance strategies that generate little entrepreneurship. Lending programs targeting overcrowded, low-profitability lines of business have been particularly widespread. Tiny loans flow to marginally viable firms; consequent high loan-default rates erode the capital available. The U.S. Commission on Minority Business Development put it well: "Minority firms seem to be gaining ground in a system that perpetuates their relegation to areas of business endeavor that are among the most crowded and least profitable" (1992: 24).

The contrast between high MBE growth and misdirected assistance policies is striking. This apparent paradox can be resolved by understanding the dichotomy between low-growth "traditional" MBEs and high-growth "emerging" MBEs. Although the latter generate most of the job creation and economic development, the former receive most of the government assistance. Unfortunately, as this chapter will show, most MBE assistance programs are flawed in intent, design, and implementation; they are designed to fail. There are a few success stories, however. This chapter will identify effective strategies for assisting minority-owned businesses and provide concrete examples that demonstrate that they work.

As long as minority entrepreneurs are thought of as the walking wounded of the small business world, minority entrepreneurship policy will be misdirected. Programs frequently fail because they ignore the factors that determine and shape small business viability. Successful entrepreneurs tend to be highly skilled, experienced, and well educated. In addition to this human capital factor, their ventures require access to financial capital and access to product markets. Minorities possessing the human capital prerequisites to operate viable firms often face discriminatory barriers that restrict their access to financial capital and markets. Effective MBE assistance programs alleviate these barriers.

This chapter begins by tracing the legacy of discrimination that has traditionally thwarted minority business development. Specific barriers have been lowered in recent years, and this loosening of constraints has allowed rapid MBE expansion in fields that had been traditionally closed. Business assistance efforts are placed in this context of constraints and opportunities, and public programs that have generated creation and expansion of viable firms are compared to ineffective assistance strategies.

TRADITIONAL MINORITY ENTREPRENEURSHIP AND THE LEGACY OF DISCRIMINATION

Throughout most of the twentieth century, the typical minority-owned business operated in personal services or small-scale retailing. As late as 1970, most MBEs were mom-and-pop food stores, restaurants, barbershops, beauty parlors, laundries, and shoe-shine firms that served household clienteles (Bates 1973). This form of minority entrepreneurship was not a major route to upward mobility in the United States (Bates 1987). Minority entrepreneurs commonly struggled to make a living running marginal enterprises. Discrimination was an all-encompassing force that gave the minority business community its traditional shape.

From its origins, the black business community was constrained by limited access to credit, limited opportunities for education and training, and white stereotypes about suitable roles for minorities in society (Bates 1993). In 1944, Gunner Myrdal observed, "The Negro businessman encounters greater difficulties than whites in securing credit. This is partially due to the marginal position of Negro business.

It is also partly due to prejudicial opinions among whites concerning business ability and personal reliability of Negroes. In either case a vicious circle is in operation keeping Negro business down" (p. 308). The typical black-owned business of Myrdal's day and for the next couple of decades was concentrated in black residential areas and served a local clientele.

Asian-American entrepreneurs faced similar constraints for similar reasons. In fact, the traditional Asian-American small-business sector was even less diverse than that of the black community. Three lines of small-scale enterprise – laundries, restaurants, and food stores – made up the bulk of Asian-American-owned firms. Hispanics and Native Americans pursuing self-employment presumably faced similar constraints, but their experiences have not been documented by scholars. Self-employed minorities nationwide had, on average, 7.6 years of education and mean self-employment earnings of $1,812 in 1960. Their earnings lagged behind those of minorities working as employees (Bates 1987).

The racial-caste system that shaped the minority business community was particularly confining for college-educated minorities. Difficulties facing Asian-American college graduates were spelled out in 1932 by a Stanford University official: "It is almost impossible to place a Chinese or Japanese of either the first or the second generation in any kind of position, engineering, manufacturing, or business. Most firms have general regulations against employing them" (Ichihashi 1932, in Bonacich and Modell 1981: 86). Denied access to most managerial and professional jobs, self-employment was a common refuge for Asian-American college graduates (Light 1972). Blacks who attended college were similarly hemmed in by social attitudes about which occupations were appropriate for them. Between 1912 and 1938, 73 percent of blacks who had graduated from college nationwide became either teachers or preachers (Holsey 1938). The few entering professions – law, medicine, dentistry – served an all-black clientele. Caterers, shoe shiners – even barbers – might serve a white clientele, but black college graduates did not. College-educated blacks therefore avoided self-employment. Merit still mattered in this caste system, but the range of opportunities open to professionals was narrow. The size of the minority middle class was restricted, and the minority business community was circumscribed.

In retrospect, it is clear that the traditional minority business community entered the 1970s as a fading relic of a declining era. Options for Asian-Americans had begun to open up as early as the late 1940s, and they left the most restrictive entrepreneurial occupations to take up salaried employment. By the late 1960s, blacks also had more options. A new age was dawning, an age not only of growth but also of qualitative improvement for minority entrepreneurship in America.

EMERGING LINES OF BUSINESS: A GENERATION OF PROGRESS

The most dynamic minority enterprises today are in emerging lines of business, which minorities generally could not enter in the past. Areas of particularly rapid growth include skill-intensive services, such as finance, business services, and professional services (Bates 2001). The growth of black-owned firms in the business-services industry typifies the transformation of minority entrepreneurship. Total employment in such firms has grown explosively, from about 12,000 employees in 1982 to over 150,000 employees in 1997 (U.S. Bureau of the Census 1991; U.S. Bureau of the Census 1996; U.S. Bureau of the Census 2001). Over the same period, employment in traditional niches, such as barbershops and food stores, has been stagnant (Bates 1998).

Economic analysis reveals two major causes for the differences between traditional lines of business, in which revenue growth and job creation are weak, and emerging fields, like business services. First, the emerging lines have attracted more highly educated, experienced, and skilled business owners than have the traditional lines. The emerging lines are also more oriented toward serving a racially diverse clientele, including major corporations and other business clients, whereas the traditional neighborhood personal-service and mom-and-pop retail businesses serve a minority clientele. These patterns are not perfectly consistent across all industries and minority groups, but the overall trend is powerful and clear (Boston 1999; Bates 1997).

The median owner in the present-day minority business community is college educated. Average incomes reported by the self-employed nationwide exceed those of minorities working as employees (Bates 1997). Neither of these statements was true in 1960. Gains in higher education in the past several decades are a key factor in the turnaround.

In one generation, the fields of concentration pursued by African-American college students shifted dramatically, a shift that helps to explain subsequent changes in entrepreneurship. Blacks receiving bachelor's degrees in 1965 were heavily concentrated in education departments. In the 1970s and 1980s, the number of education degrees granted began to slip, and interest in studying business and engineering rose substantially (Carter and Wilson 1992; Carter and Wilson 1995). These educational gains took some time to be translated into changes in patterns of entrepreneurship, because new businesses are rarely started by recent college graduates. Entrepreneurship is most common among people in their late thirties and forties with fifteen or more years of work experience (Bates 1997). The graduates of the 1970s and 1980s are now following entrepreneurial paths. We should expect to see continued increases in minority entrepreneurship as the consequences of educational choices continue to be felt.

The Asian-American experience broadly mirrors that of black Americans. Bachelor's degrees awarded in business nationwide to students of Asian ancestry, for instance, rose from 1,829 in 1976 to 10,592 in 1992 (Carter and Wilson 1992; Carter and Wilson 1995). The link between educational achievement and entrepreneurship is somewhat less direct for Asian Americans than for blacks. The Asian-American self-employed universe is dominated by people who were born (and often educated) abroad, particularly in China, Korea, and India (Bates 1997).

For black and Asian-American college graduates, business and technical degrees awarded have outdistanced overall enrollment growth. For both groups, bachelor's degrees in business are more numerous than degrees in any other field, and engineering degrees exhibit the most rapid growth rates. Trends in MBA degrees awarded exhibit phenomenal growth rates (from a low base). Whereas the MBA degree was an extreme rarity among black Americans in the 1960s, more than 4,000 were being awarded annually by the 1990s. Today, nearly 100,000 African Americans hold MBA degrees. Educational gains stand out as a major cause of the ongoing transformation of the minority business community: high-growth fields are those in which college-graduate small-business owners are most numerous (Bates 1997).

In addition, growing numbers of experienced, financially sophisticated minority entrepreneurs are penetrating mainstream corporate markets in the United States. In 1972, *Black Enterprise* magazine published its first listing of the top 100 black-owned firms, ranked according to sales: total revenues for the group were $473 million (Jaynes and Williams 1989: 181). By 1997, aggregate sales for the largest 100 black businesses exceeded $10 billion. The ranks of the largest 100 in 1972 were dominated by firms catering to black households. Of the top 100 black-owned businesses in that year, only two were in business services. By 1997, well over half of the largest 100 were in business services or manufacturing. The business-services subset was dominated, in turn, by firms selling high-tech products, and their clients were commonly other businesses and government agencies, not individuals. The transformation of the minority business community has been dramatic. Unfortunately, the minority business policy of the government had little to do with it (Bates 1995).

DIRECT GOVERNMENT ASSISTANCE TO MINORITY-OWNED BUSINESSES: THE HISTORICAL LEGACY OF EOL

Minority entrepreneurship first emerged as a high priority for policymakers in the mid-1960s. Destructive civil disorders in Los Angeles, Detroit, Cleveland, Chicago, and other cities drew national attention to socioeconomic conditions in inner city minority communities and compelled leaders from government, business, and academia to take action. Skeptics saw promotion of business ownership as little more than a traditional bootstrap solution to poverty and unemployment. The political appeal of the approach was broad, however, and the coalition supporting the resulting policy initiatives was diverse. Black Power spokesman Roy Innis described its appeal in terms that transcended bootstrapping: "A critical weakness has been the lack of control by black people over the institutions that surround them, institutions that not only establish imposed values for them but also control the flow of goods and services in their communities" (1969: 51). Greater minority ownership of community businesses has been an objective of government assistance policies since this time.

Few would disagree with the assessment that, before the mid-1960s, the U.S. Small Business Administration (SBA) was "a bureaucracy that was generally unresponsive, if not specifically hostile, to the needs of minority individuals and groups" (Blaustein and Faux 1972: 119). Government officials who were proponents of minority-business assistance found that the SBA regional office in Philadelphia, for example, had approved seven loans to minority-business borrowers during the 1954–1963 period; the Washington, D.C. regional office had authorized six loans. In January 1964, the SBA launched an experimental program to provide loan assistance to disadvantaged owners of very small urban retail and service enterprises. Offering loans of up to $6,000 and six years in maturity – leading the program to be designated "6 × 6" – SBA officials envisioned that Negro business owners would be the primary beneficiaries (U.S. Small Business Administration 1970: 2; Bates and Bradford 1979). Indeed, they were.

The 6 × 6 program provided the basis for and was superseded by the Economic Opportunity Loan (EOL) program, the pioneering national lending effort that funded tens of thousands of minority business borrowers between 1965 and 1984. EOL lending was part of the "War on Poverty" and was authorized under Title IV of the Economic Opportunity Act in 1965. The SBA-administered EOL program sought solely to assist persons living in poverty. EOL eligibility was determined by the family income of the borrower.

Amendments to Title IV subsequently broadened EOL eligibility to include people with incomes above the poverty level who had been socially and economically "disadvantaged." EOL affected more minority-owned businesses than any other government assistance effort. By the early 1970s, the peak years of MBE assistance, more than 5,000 EOL loans were extended to minority business borrowers nationwide each year (Bates 1984; U.S. Comptroller General 1973).

The minority business assistance efforts of the federal government, particularly the EOL program, have come under attack repeatedly since the 1970s (Bates and Bradford 1979). Critics have noted minimal development of viable businesses, high loan-default rates, and a paucity of evidence regarding the benefits of assistance efforts. The defenders of these programs often find themselves in a paradoxical state: the strongest candidates for government aid tend to be well educated, high-income individuals, traits that make them ineligible for assistance. Truly disadvantaged persons, toward whom assistance is targeted, commonly lack the expertise to establish and operate viable businesses. When loans flow to disadvantaged borrowers, high rates of business failure and loan default predictably follow.

The history of the EOL program supports the critics. A comprehensive study of EOL loans extended to minority business borrowers operating in three central cities – New York, Boston, and

Chicago – uncovered delinquency and default in 67.2 percent of the mature outstanding loans (Bates and Bradford 1979). Few of the EOL borrowers who repaid their loans were actually low-income individuals at the time of loan approval. The eligibility of many who eventually repaid EOL loans to receive them in the first place was questionable. In hindsight, it is clear that the EOL program was designed to produce high rates of loan delinquency and default. SBA, for nearly a decade, successfully covered up the fact that over half of the MBEs receiving EOL loans defaulted on their repayment obligations.

The MBE assistance efforts launched in the 1960s reflected views that highly placed white politicians held toward minorities. President Nixon's Secretary of Commerce, Maurice Stans, was the point man for implementing the President's "Black Capitalism" program to promote minority entrepreneurship. Stans, in 1969, candidly laid out his views on how government would direct its assistance: "We have to be realistic about it. We are not going to create overnight manufacturing companies with 500 employees. The American economy did not build that way. It started out with the corner grocery, and the deliveryman – the group of people who cut lawns or perform services, and so forth, and I think we have to recognize that by and large a very high percentage of the things we do are going to be in the small ma-and-pa area" (quoted in Blaustein and Faux 1972: 155).

Stans and most of his contemporaries in government thought of minorities as people who lacked skills and talents. Removing discriminatory barriers that had retarded MBE development was not a primary concern. Rather, Stans saw government as encouraging entrepreneurship among a group of people (minorities) who were poorly prepared to pursue the entrepreneurial path to upward mobility.

Doomed by design, the EOL program experienced high failure rates that destroyed its credibility. The program was terminated in 1984. Worse, EOL's credibility problems adversely affected the credibility of the entire federal effort to assist minority-owned firms.

AN ALTERNATIVE APPROACH TO GOVERNMENT MINORITY BUSINESS LENDING PROGRAMS

MBE assistance programs that generate successful business creation and expansion must start from a different set of assumptions and pay close attention to the traits of viable small businesses. Entrepreneurs who are likely to succeed are highly educated, experienced workers, and they possess substantial resources. High personal net worth, advanced education, and skills increase one's access to loans from financial institutions, thus increasing the resources available for small-business investment. In addition to human and financial capital, the creation of viable MBEs requires access to product markets. Public policies that seek to generate minority business development are most effective when they aid firms capable of having all three elements in place. The human-capital prerequisite is the fundamental building block; access to financial capital and markets round out the basic list of requirements for building viable small businesses (Bates 1997).

A number of existing programs offer models for turning the minority business community into an economic-development powerhouse. Maryland's Small Business Development Financing Authority (MSBDFA), for instance, generates substantial MBE development and job creation at minimal taxpayer expense. Its lending efforts are guided by a specific economic development rationale. Loans are targeted to high-growth lines of business possessing substantial job creation potential, and they tend to be large enough – over $200,000 on average – to support viable, growing firms. Loan default rates are low, preserving funds so that they may be circulated to other MBEs (Bates 1995).

MSBDFA's largest program targets assistance to MBEs that have received procurement contracts from local, state, or federal government agencies, or from regulated utility companies that operate in Maryland. The Contract Financing Program alleviates one of the barriers – access to credit – that has plagued MBE recipients of large contracts. MSBDFA provides working-capital financing to MBEs that have demonstrated initiative and competence by competing successfully for procurement contracts. MBE borrowers assisted by MSBDFA, in all cases, had been denied loans by commercial banks that looked only at their limited experience. To alleviate MBE vendor liquidity problems, MSBDFA specifically tailors working-capital assistance to both the size and duration of the procurement contract held. MSBDFA realizes a positive cash flow on its Contract Financing Program, in the sense that revenue from borrower interest payments exceeds loan losses.

A major criterion for MSBDFA loan approval is the economic impact of the loan. Targeted loan recipients are to increase the number of jobs created and/or retained, generate incremental tax revenues, and serve the needs of local communities. Operational specifics that enable MSBDFA to meet important MBE vendor credit needs while minimizing loan losses include:

1. Tying financing to MBE receipt of procurement contracts
2. Financing MBEs that are capable, experienced, and have financial controls in place
3. Offering flexible loan terms (such as lines of credit)
4. Having the contracting agency send loan payments directly to MSBDFA
5. Accepting loan requests before a procurement contract has been finalized
6. Processing loan requests on a timely basis
7. Employing staff who possess accounting and auditing skills

Thanks in part to these policies, nearly all Contract Financing Program loan recipients are able to deliver on their contracts.

MBE ASSISTANCE DELIVERED BY PRIVATE-SECTOR PARTNERS: BREAKING WITH THE PAST

In addition to aggressively implementing EOL, the Nixon Administration had a long-lasting impact on MBE assistance efforts by shifting aid decisions increasingly into the hands of private-sector entities acting in concert with government to promote minority business development. Observed Secretary of Commerce Stans in 1969, "I would rather see, and I think the President would much rather see, a private bank make a loan to a minority enterprise with a government guarantee than the government to put out the money" (quoted in Blaustein and Faux 1972: 156).

Even before Nixon came into office, the SBA, through its 7(a) program, had begun to encourage banks to expand their lending to MBEs. The incentive offered to banks was the loan guarantee: in the event of default, banks would recoup 90 percent of the outstanding balance by transferring the nonperforming loan to the SBA. Profits from repaid loans belonged to the bank whereas losses from defaults were shared, with the government partner picking up the majority of the tab. Lending to MBEs thus became a low-risk proposition.

The Nixon Administration vastly increased bank participation in MBE loan guarantee programs by launching Operation Business Mainstream at the SBA. Operation Business Mainstream minimized the paperwork involved in obtaining guarantees for bank loans. By 1970, nearly 40 percent of the SBA loans received by MBEs were guaranteed-bank loans. After 1975, the majority of MBE lending assistance came in the form of such loans (Bates 1984).

Operation Business Mainstream had one enormous advantage over the EOL program. The practice of targeting disadvantaged loan recipients was dropped, and the goal was simply to increase the number of MBEs operating nationwide. Banks active in MBE lending therefore sought out more viable minority borrowers, hoping to attract clients who would become long-term customers. MBEs initially financed with guaranteed loans often continued as regular bank clients, receiving products such as working-capital loans that were not covered by SBA guarantees. The tradition of minimal contact between banks and MBEs was broken; although full equality of access to loans has not been achieved, large increases in MBE bank borrowing have occurred (Bates 1993; Cavalluzzo and Cavalluzzo 1998). Although black business borrowers in the 1990s were less likely to have their loan applications approved than whites having otherwise identical business and owner traits, blacks nonetheless received more of their debt financing from banks than from all other sources combined (Bates 1997; Cavalluzzo, Cavalluzzo, and Wolken 1999).

ADDRESSING THE DILEMMA, ACHIEVING VIABILITY

The Minority Enterprise Small Business Investment Companies (MESBIC) program is an important example of a policy that has delivered assistance to MBEs through private partners over the past three decades. MESBICs are privately owned, for-profit small business investment companies that receive funds at subsidized rates from the SBA (Bates 2002). In their early days in the 1970s, MESBICs behaved like community development banks, focusing on financing small, disadvantaged minority-owned businesses. This emphasis was due, in part, to the fact that large-scale, growth-oriented minority-owned businesses were less numerous then than they are today. This approach, not surprisingly, quickly led to major difficulties, from which there was only one viable way out.

The history of Equico nicely illustrates the point. Equico was one of the nation's original MESBICs, created by a major corporation, Equitable Life, in 1970. In its first decade of existence, it operated like its peers. By 1981, Equico had a cumulative deficit of $5.6 million, in addition to carrying on its balance sheet large unrealized losses on its loans and investments in MBEs. The company lost $2.55 million in that year.

Equico's moment of truth had arrived. Judged by its initial capitalization, Equico was clearly bankrupt. Its corporate parent considered admitting defeat and shutting it down. Instead, however, it decided to inject $3.5 million into the business and hired a new president, Duane Hill, to turn things around. Prior to joining Equico, Hill had worked as a vice president at J. P. Morgan for eight years.

When Hill came on board, Equico resembled the overall MESBIC industry. It had nearly as much money in money market assets like bank certificates of deposit (CDs) as it did in loans to MBEs. Its equity investments were modest, far less than 10 percent of its loans. The big element of Hill's turnaround strategy for Equico was to drop the community-oriented mom-and-pop operations, and focus solely on larger-scale MBEs with growth potential. These firms could put funds to profitable use financing growth. Hill's shift from small operations to growing MBEs competing in the broader marketplace included a shift in Equico's investment strategy from loans to equity investments.

The new strategy was risky. A loan portfolio (not to mention holding CDs) generates a steady cash flow for a MESBIC; repayments of principal and interest pour in each month. New equity investments hurt cash flow; recipient MBEs invest equity dollars for a long-term payoff. Initial dividend payments are unlikely to be forthcoming if the young MBEs successfully generate high growth with their financing. It is difficult to judge what the return will ultimately be to a rapidly growing MBE during the first several years of its lifespan.

By the mid-1980s, Hill's willingness to take the riskier strategy had paid off. He had cleaned up Equico's deficit-laden balance sheet and put the firm on a trajectory of growth and profitable operations. During the 1985 to 1990 period, neither the SBA nor Equitable Life injected additional capital into the company. Equico's new-found financial strength was rooted in the operating strategy Hill had successfully implemented (Bates 1996). Hill and his partner purchased Equico from Equitable Life in 1992, creating TSG Capital.

How does one identify an MBE that is capable of using an equity-capital investment to create firm growth, as well as appreciation in the value of the firm itself? The minimal requirements include, according to TSG, a very strong management team, a proven product and/or service, annual sales exceeding $1 million, and profitable operation in the past year. A firm with these traits would also have to demonstrate strong internal accounting and financial controls, audited financial statements, strong personal credit ratings of the top managers, and a written business plan with three-to-five-year projections. The key element is having a firm run by experienced, successful, highly capable managers. Finally, a firm with the potential to grow tenfold over the next five years is more likely to attract an equity capital investment than one on a slower growth trajectory.

TSG emerged as a premier venture-capital firm in the MESBIC industry after its 1992 management-led buyout of Equico. A comparison of 1981 and 1994 balance sheets indicates that the value of TSG's small-business equity investments increased nearly twentyfold. These were real gains, not merely paper gains. Year-end 1994 balance sheet figures indicated that TSG relied primarily on internally generated earnings from equity investments in MBEs as its source of funds. The important lesson offered by TSG is that a professionally managed venture-capital firm can thrive by serving the equity capital needs of growing minority-owned businesses. By 1999, TSG had grown to become an $800 million plus venture-capital company.

Unfortunately, the rest of the MESBIC industry has not followed the Equico/TSG model. TSG president Duane Hill sees the SBA itself holding down the number of successful MESBICs specializing in venture-capital investing. Top administrators at the SBA, according to Hill, have often been political appointees who cannot move the entrenched SBA career bureaucrats, so they stop trying, which results in poor program management (Bates 2000). The SBA prefers to have MESBICs financing unsophisticated minority business owners, not college graduates with corporate experience. Hill believes that the SBA is gradually pushing the most successful MESBICs out of the government's program. Equico coexisted amicably with its SBA partner while it was drifting toward bankruptcy; TSG and the SBA parted ways when TSG repaid all its SBA funding and left the program in 1999.

DESIGNED FOR FAILURE: MBE ASSISTANCE
IN THE 1990S

The pattern that Hill perceives in the administration of MESBICs is apparent in other elements of the federal government's assistance to MBEs, including the new arrangements that were launched in the 1990s under the Clinton administration. Many of these programs are designed for failure. The clones of SBA's EOL program continue to be widespread today at all levels of government and in the nonprofit sector (Bates 1995).

Among the largest new initiatives of the past decade are microenterprise loan programs. These programs were initially funded by foundations and have been increasingly funded by government. The SBA's Microloan Demonstration Program, begun in 1992, for instance, finances loan programs, rather than individual borrowers. By 1993, sixty-five SBA loans had been extended to microenterprise programs (Servon 1999). In 1992, the Community Development Block Grant (CDBG) program created a special category for microenterprise programs, providing federal dollars that could be directed to microenterprise assistance by state and local governments. HUD's Office of Community Planning and Development provides funding for microenterprise programs, in conjunction with its empowerment zone and enterprise communities programs. Since 1994, the National Community Economic Partnership (NCEP), a program of the Department of Health and Human Services, has targeted the urban and rural poor, providing credit to community development corporations for revolving loan funds to support microenterprises. Even the Office of Refugee Resettlement in the Department of Health and Human Services has launched a Micro-Enterprise Development Project (Servon 1999). This list of programs is illustrative rather than exhaustive.

These MBE assistance efforts typically target a broader clientele of which minorities are a major component. The target may be lower-income communities, welfare recipients, poor people generally, immigrants, or any other group that appears to fit the "disadvantaged" label. Like their EOL predecessors, loan recipients or borrowers assisted by microenterprise programs are targeted *not* because of their strengths, but rather because of some weakness associated with the owner of the firm, the business location, or both. Minorities with MBA degrees and years of corporate experience may be excellent candidates for creating viable small businesses, but they are not recipients of microenterprise loans.

Broadly, the mandate to microenterprise loan programs from government is to invest in high-risk firms, whereas the best strategy for organizational survival is to invest in low-risk firms. Assisting the disadvantaged business borrower is expensive, due to both loan default losses and the high costs of making small loans to poorly prepared borrowers. High costs and loan losses are often serious problems for the private-sector partners that deliver most of the aid that government funnels to disadvantaged minority (and nonminority) firms. Programs operating with the stated intent of assisting the disadvantaged therefore tend to gravitate away from that target group, assisting, instead, an increasingly well-educated and skilled clientele of entrepreneurs. "Although microenterprise programs set out to bring entrepreneurship to the most disadvantaged populations, the portrait that has emerged makes sense, given the demands involved in running a business" (Servon and Bates 1998: 423).

The Aspen Institute's Self-Employment Learning Project (SELP) conducted an assessment of U.S. microenterprise programs, tracking them from 1991 to 1996. Although these programs generally targeted the poor, the client profile uncovered by SELP revealed that typical microentrepreneurs were educated and skilled workers. Early SELP assessments revealed that 57 percent had some college education or a technical degree (Clark and Huston 1993). SELP's next published assessment reported that persons assisted by microenterprise programs had a median annual income of $29,054. Furthermore, nearly half of all SELP respondents own their own homes. Completing this profile, 62 percent were minority and 78 percent were women (Clark and Kays 1995). In her more recent assessment of five well-established microenterprise programs, Servon reaffirmed the SELP findings: "The participants in these programs are at the least highly motivated; they are also often relatively well educated, experienced in their business, and have a support network of family and friends that provide them with a safety net" (1999: 47).

The need to move up market is reinforced by the high lending costs being incurred by microenterprise programs. Costs per loan in a 1996 SELP study averaged $1.47 per dollar loaned (Edgeworth, Klein, and Clark 1996: 37). A Mott Foundation evaluation calculated an average cost per loan of $10,521; average loan size was $3,034 (Charles Stewart Mott Foundation 1994: 5–6). Delinquency and default problems add to the burden of running microenterprise loan programs: Mott's assessment revealed an overall delinquency rate of 19.2 percent (Charles Stewart Mott Foundation 1994: 6).

Working Capital, a well-established microenterprise loan fund in Cambridge, Massachusetts, is perhaps a typical case. Although Working Capital seeks to serve low-income persons, being low-income (or otherwise disadvantaged) is *not* a prerequisite for receiving its financing. Servon's analysis of Working Capital's Boston lending project revealed that the median borrower was both well educated and not low income (Servon 1999).

Equico's strategy for maintaining financial viability prior to 1981 was one of relying on the deep pockets of Equitable Life to cover its operating losses. This, too, is a popular strategy among the current generation of microenterprise loan funds. Absent large, continuous operating subsidies, such lending efforts are unsustainable. Yet, the realization is widespread that subsidies will decline and that microenterprise lenders will have to move toward financial self-sufficiency in the long run.

WHY DO MINORITY BUSINESS DEVELOPMENT PROGRAMS GENERATE SO LITTLE MINORITY BUSINESS DEVELOPMENT?

The fundamental conflict that plagues minority business assistance programs pits redistribution for alleviating poverty against economic development. To date, the redistribution rationale has generally trumped the economic development rationale. Disadvantaged business owners remain the preferred aid recipients for government MBE programs. The poor person running a firm in a depressed urban area is disadvantaged; this disadvantaged trait, in turn, inspires those who plan public-sector MBE assistance programs. Evidence on the effectiveness of such assistance efforts does not necessarily carry much weight. It is true that the EOL program was abolished in 1984, and the high loan default rates of EOL loan recipients were a major reason for the program's termination. Yet the philosophy of targeting aid to the disadvantaged – the heritage of EOL – remains a dominant theme in modern business-assistance programs. The dilemma observed in contemporary microenterprise programs is essentially identical to the paradox observed by scholars who analyzed the 1960s generation of MBE loan programs. Successful loan programs to assist minority (and nonminority) businesses sought out experienced, skilled, well-educated owners who possessed the expertise to run viable business operations. These owners were rarely low-income earners (Bates and Bradford 1979).

However, when government assistance flows to higher income entrepreneurs, an objection invariably arises: why help those who are already successful? The response is straightforward: viable firms generate economic development and create jobs. When the firm owner is minority, the vast majority of the jobs are going to be filled by the minority employees (Boston 1999; Bates 1993). Business profits support investments that permit future expansion and job creation. Viable firms repay their loans, permitting relending of the loan pool funds to other borrowers. The alternative of supporting nonviable firms simply creates mass loan default and business failure (Bates and Bradford 1979; Bates 1993).

If MBE assistance genuinely seeks to create strong firms capable of generating jobs for underemployed minorities, financing must be targeted to entrepreneurs possessing the resources that will allow them to build successful businesses. Most of these entrepreneurs will be well educated and possess above-average incomes. The evidence is strong that this approach makes sense. Among black-owned businesses, the high-end firms that create most of the jobs have been growing much more rapidly than the overall black business community. Among firms operating in 1997, 17,182 black firms (2.1 percent of the total) generated annual sales revenues exceeding $500,000. These 17,182 firms employed 487,076 workers, 67.8 percent of the 718,341 workers employed by all black businesses in 1997. The financial-capital needs of such firms cannot be met by microenterprise programs authorized to make loans up to $10,000. One study of black firms started nationwide between

1979 and 1987 that employed ten or more workers revealed that their average capitalization at startup was $134,753 (Bates 1998). Average annual revenue for these firms was $1,406,997. Business services was the industry most heavily represented in this group.

The college-educated business owner seeking to create a firm in the million-dollar-plus revenue category is not effectively assisted by a microenterprise loan. Firms like TSG Capital finance such businesses; the MSBDFA Contract Financing Program seeks to assist them as well. These are the model programs described in this chapter. If society's aversion to assisting the MBEs most capable of generating jobs and economic development could be alleviated, then MBE assistance could be transformed into a powerful strategy for creating and expanding viable firms.

The thought of helping affluent minorities to establish small businesses is simply too much for the designers of most programs; they prefer to aid failure-prone MBEs. The result is predictable: such efforts produce high levels of business failure, along with little economic development. In futile efforts to avoid this outcome, microenterprise loan programs currently stretch the concept of disadvantage past the point of meaninglessness. Like the EOL program of the 1960s, these programs are designed for failure.

PART FOUR

SECTOR-SPECIFIC ISSUES

9

Understanding Entrepreneurship in the U.S. Biotechnology Industry

Characteristics, Facilitating Factors, and Policy Challenges

Andrew A. Toole

In his famous 1943 lecture "What Is Life," the renowned physicist Erwin Schrödinger described human genes as "law code and executive power – or to use another simile, they are the architect's plan and the builder's code in one" (Zweiger 2001). Fifty-eight years later, in February 2001, both *Nature* and *Science* published draft versions of the complete human genome. This achievement is the latest revolutionary development associated with biotechnology. As an industry, biotechnology has experienced an almost continuous stream of scientific and technological advances creating new methods, tools, and information that have fueled dramatic progress in health care, agriculture, environmental cleanup, and criminal justice. Many policymakers are excited about these developments. They stand ready to assist entrepreneurs to cultivate and harvest the enormous returns that are expected to materialize.

The real challenge facing policymakers is to identify policies that effectively promote entrepreneurship in the biotechnology industry and nurture economic development. For a policy to be effective, it needs to be based on an understanding of the industry and its existing policy environment. However, on closer inspection, it quickly becomes clear that both of these are changing in complex and unpredictable ways. The extent and nature of commercial opportunities emerging

I would like to thank David M. Hart for his very helpful editorial advice.

as a result of the sequencing of the human genome are unknown and unpredictable. Today's policy environment involves a diverse array of institutions and organizations with wide-ranging agendas and divergent incentives, through which biotechnology entrepreneurs must navigate. It is not unusual for an entrepreneur to have to interact with the National Institutes of Health, the U.S. Patent and Trademark Office, the Food and Drug Administration, and other agencies as well before a product can be introduced into the marketplace.

It is worth noting at the outset that the phrase "biotechnology industry" is somewhat misleading. There is no homogeneous group of firms that defines this industry, and no single technology that is used uniformly. At the broadest level, biotechnology refers to the use of micro-organisms to make or modify a product or process. The contemporary industry dates from the invention of the recombinant DNA (rDNA) technique in 1973 by Stanley Cohen of Stanford University and Herbert Boyer of the University of California at San Francisco. This technique lets scientists transfer specific DNA segments from one organism to another. The Cohen-Boyer breakthrough provided the foundation on which a wide range of complementary scientific methods and tools has been developed. To get a sense for the variety of technologies encompassed by the term "biotechnology," one need only consult an industry publication like *Genetic Engineering News* (*GEN*). *GEN*'s industry directory lists thirty-three different technologies currently used either individually or in combination (GEN 1997).

The intent of this chapter is to summarize our understanding of entrepreneurship in biotechnology with the hope that this information will help to identify effective policies. The chapter begins by outlining the major public policy spheres and institutions that influence biotechnology entrepreneurs. Next, the chapter zooms in on the entrepreneurial process to discuss three areas of critical influence: scientific and technical knowledge, financial and human resources, and market applications. I review evidence identifying the underlying factors related to each of these areas, which have permitted a few fortunate regions to develop an advantage in biotechnology entrepreneurship. The final section of the chapter summarizes the challenges to policymakers and researchers. Policymakers need to streamline existing policies, particularly in intellectual property law, and to continue to develop programs that bridge laboratory research and innovation. Researchers need access to data in order to sort out and evaluate the effectiveness of policies already in place.

PUBLIC POLICY INFLUENCES ON BIOTECHNOLOGY ENTREPRENEURSHIP

Entrepreneurs in the biotechnology industry face a challenging public policy environment. Figure 9.1 identifies the broad spheres of policy that define and shape this environment in the United States. Each of these spheres represents a critical set of influences on current and future entrepreneurship in this industry. Given biotechnology's close connection with scientific knowledge and its enormous investments in R&D, the first policy sphere encompasses the science base, commercialization, and tax policy. It includes all federal, state, and local research funding agencies, commercialization programs, and tax incentives. The number and variety of agencies and programs preclude a detailed discussion at this level of abstraction, but the National Institutes of Health (NIH) is the "big gorilla" among public agencies

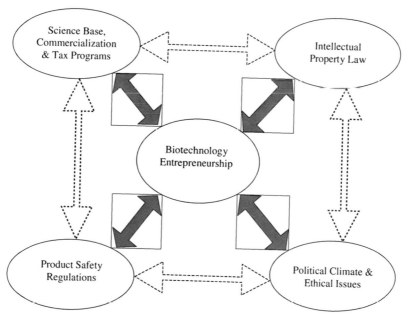

Figure 9.1. Biotechnology's public policy environment.

supporting research and commercialization. Its share of total federal support for biotechnology-related R&D far exceeds that of other agencies. In the mid-1980s, the Office of Technology Assessment estimated the NIH share of biotechnology-specific federal funding at 83 percent of the total (U.S. Congress 1988). Although more recent biotechnology-specific numbers are not available, data from the National Science Foundation for fiscal year 2001 show that the NIH supports over 82 percent of all federal basic research in the life sciences (National Science Foundation 2001). The largest commercialization programs include the Small Business Innovation Research (SBIR) program and the Small Business Technology Transfer (STTR) program. The NIH is again the key agency for biotechnology entrepreneurs. The total value of NIH SBIR and STTR awards in 2001 exceeded $435 million. With respect to tax incentives, a federal research and development tax credit is in place through 2004. This tax credit was first passed into law as part of the Economic Recovery and Tax Act of 1981. Unfortunately, since this law requires regular renewal, it has been subject to many political ebbs and flows and actually lapsed entirely in 1995–1996. Given the importance of research and development to entrepreneurship in biotechnology, it is unfortunate that a more permanent law has not been passed.

The U.S. Patent and Trademark Office (USPTO) sits at the center of the policy sphere for intellectual property law. Patents granted by the USPTO protect inventors from competition for a period of twenty years so that they may commercialize their inventions and recoup their R&D costs. Patents are vital assets for most markets that biotechnology entrepreneurs expect to enter, particularly human therapeutics and diagnostics. In a recent study by Cohen and colleagues (2000), survey data from 1,478 R&D laboratories in thirty-four manufacturing industries were used to compare alternative methods that firms use to appropriate profits from their inventions, including patenting, lead time, secrecy, and investment in complementary marketing and manufacturing capabilities. Patents were found to be the most effective means of protection for therapeutic applications.

Product safety regulation constitutes the third broad sphere of policy influence on biotechnology entrepreneurship. In June 1986, the White House Office of Science and Technology Policy published a "Coordinated Framework for the Regulation of Biotechnology," which is still the governing framework for the industry (U.S. Congress 1991). The framework exempted scientific techniques, such as rDNA, from regulation. Instead, the products derived from these methods were to be regulated within the existing federal regulatory framework (Spohn 1996). Because most biotechnology entrepreneurs target human health care applications, the key regulatory body for the industry is the Food and Drug Administration (FDA). The FDA is responsible for reviewing all evidence of safety for human drugs and biologics, animal health products and feed components, and bioengineered foods. In addition to the FDA, the Animal and Plant Health Inspection Service at the U.S. Department of Agriculture regulates the importation and field testing of genetically modified plants and micro-organisms. Finally, the Environmental Protection Agency regulates the marketing of genetically modified plants resistant to pesticides, bioremediation products, and potentially hazardous research chemicals. In cases where there is overlap, the agencies are supposed to coordinate their efforts.

The fourth sphere of public policy influence on biotechnology entrepreneurship is the political and ethical climate. The novelty of the various biotechnologies and their associated products has created uncertainty, misunderstanding, and distrust in some quarters. As early as February 1975, for example, less than two years after the invention of the rDNA method, an international conference of prominent biologists convened to discuss the potential dangers from new lines of research that rDNA made possible. The group called for a two-year moratorium on rDNA research until proper facilities, procedures, and regulations could be developed (Ruttan 2001). Although these dangers never materialized and no new regulations were developed, the NIH formed a Recombinant DNA Advisory Committee (RAC) that sets guidelines and monitors adverse events. In addition to issues of safety, ethical disagreements about appropriate areas of research also shape biotechnology entrepreneurship. The most recent ethical controversy focuses on the use of human embryonic stem cells in federally supported research. On August 9, 2001, President Bush announced a new federal policy permitting limited use of these cells in research (National Research Council 2001). Political and ethical debates will continue to influence both the development of new scientific knowledge and the ultimate market acceptance of genetically modified products.

It must be kept in mind that the four broad policy spheres presented in Figure 9.1 are not static and isolated from one another. The reality is quite the opposite. Interaction and interdependence among all components of this diagram create an environment that is dynamic and unpredictable. The Supreme Court case of *Diamond v. Chakrabarty*, for example, fundamentally changed not only intellectual property law, but the entire policy environment for biotechnology entrepreneurship as well. Chakrabarty, a scientist working for General Electric, submitted an application for a patent on a genetically modified oil-consuming bacterium for use in cleaning up oil spills. The USPTO rejected his application on the grounds that micro-organisms are the "product of nature" and that living things are not patentable. In 1980, the Supreme Court overturned a lower court decision and ruled that genetically modified organisms can be patented (U.S. Congress 1988). Since this decision, intellectual property policy has continued to shape and be shaped by changes in all the other policy spheres. Public policy and entrepreneurship evolve over time within a mutually interdependent system.

FACTORS THAT FACILITATE BIOTECHNOLOGY ENTREPRENEURSHIP

Entrepreneurship can be viewed as a process that begins with the recognition of a commercial opportunity and ends with the introduction of a new product or service into the marketplace. Although this sketch glosses over the complexities and feedbacks that characterize the actual process, it allows us to group the factors that facilitate entrepreneurship in the biotechnology industry into three areas: scientific and technical knowledge, financial and human resources, and market applications. There is an unusually close connection between the evolution of scientific and technical knowledge and the emergence of entrepreneurial opportunities in biotechnology. This connection, the available evidence suggests, has a strong geographic component rooted in a region's scientific infrastructure, its private sector employment in biotechnology, and its concentration of firms in complementary industries, especially in information technology. With respect to financial and human resources, the key underlying factors are patents, venture capitalists, founders, and specialized labor. The market applications in biotechnology vary widely and these variations imply very different development paths and regulatory hurdles.

Scientific and Technical Knowledge

Entrepreneurial opportunities in biotechnology are driven primarily by "supply side" changes in scientific and technical knowledge rather than changes in "demand side" signals to entrepreneurs. I do not mean that entrepreneurs pay no attention to the expected return on their investments. Of course they do. As noted by Timmons and his coauthors, an entrepreneurial opportunity is critically "anchored in a product or service which creates or adds value for its buyer or end user" (Timmons et al. 1990: 71). Most new biotechnology products and processes, however, are targeted at long-standing needs that have historically proven impossible to meet in the marketplace. This type of entrepreneurship is quite different from "demand driven" innovation that responds to price and quantity signals (Mowery and Rosenberg 1979). For example, consider the explosive growth in new biotechnology-based therapeutics for the treatment of cardiovascular disease and cancer. This growth cannot be explained by changes in the needs of the patient population. Data from the National Center for Health Statistics show that patient needs for cardiovascular and cancer treatments are substantial, but they have also been relatively stable for over two decades. Changes in scientific and technical knowledge in the last two decades have opened up new possibilities for addressing this long-standing demand and have fueled the growth in biotechnology entrepreneurship.

Most of the "supply side" advances in scientific knowledge that facilitate biotechnology entrepreneurship occur in the life sciences, such as molecular biology, biochemistry, and protein chemistry. Among the myriad examples that one could use to illustrate this connection, the case of synthetic insulin stands out. Stern (1995) describes the evolution of scientific understanding and techniques developed by Genentech in the mid to late 1970s before the firm was able to get bacteria to express human insulin. Keiichi Itakura of the City of Hope National Medical Center, working under a contract with Genentech, achieved the critical first step. He refined the existing method for producing synthetic DNA, reducing the time required from years to weeks in the process. Itakura then used this technique to construct the DNA sequence that codes for human somatostatin. This synthetic gene was inserted, using rDNA techniques, into bacteria by a postdoctoral researcher in Herbert Boyer's lab. The expression of somatostatin by bacteria as a result of this experiment was hailed as a "scientific triumph of the first order" by the president of the National Academy of Sciences (Swanson 1986: 429). Genentech then transferred this technique to the insulin gene. The result was the first rDNA-derived human therapeutic, marketed by Eli Lilly as Humalin. The connection between scientific research and biotechnology entrepreneurship is equally vital today. The draft sequence of the human genome reveals the identity and position of over 3.1 billion nucleotides (the building blocks of the genome); thirty to forty thousand genes are thought to be contained in the sequence. By all indications, the advancement of scientific knowledge about the function of the sequence and the proteins it encodes will continue to fuel entrepreneurial opportunities far into the future.

Funding the advance of scientific knowledge is a long-term and indirect way for policymakers to spur entrepreneurship. In the United States, life science research funding is the purview of the NIH. For over fifty years, the NIH has supported undirected basic research designed to advance "scientific opportunities." Scientific opportunities are fundamentally different from entrepreneurial opportunities because they have no market value proposition connected with them. An average of seventeen to nineteen years elapses between the disbursement of NIH research funding and the introduction of new drugs based on that research (Toole 2000). When and if any single line of basic scientific research will turn out to have market value is unpredictable. Herbert Boyer, the co-inventor of rDNA and cofounder of Genentech, states, "Who would have dreamed that my work on how bacteria have sex could combine with other pieces of basic research to help form a new industry?" (Swanson 1986: 430).

A necessary condition to facilitate the advance of knowledge is a strong scientific infrastructure. Scientific infrastructure includes laboratory facilities, research materials and equipment, senior researchers, and the graduate students who carry out much of the lab work. Most observers agree that the uneven regional development in the biotechnology industry reflects the uneven distribution of scientific infrastructure. In a broad analysis of innovation across the United States, Feldman (1994b) finds that states with well-developed infrastructures have greater concentrations of commercial innovation. For a study of the human therapeutic and diagnostic segment of the biotechnology industry, I use the cumulative stock of NIH investment at the regional level as a proxy for scientific infrastructure. My analysis of five California regions over the 1988 to 1997 period reveals that, measured in this fashion, infrastructure has a strong positive effect on biotechnology entrepreneurship (Toole 2001). Zucker and her coauthors argue that the contribution of regional scientific infrastructure to biotechnology entrepreneurship is channeled through an elite group of "star" scientists (Zucker et al. 1997; 1998). They observe that biotechnology discoveries are complex and characterized by "tacit" knowledge that cannot be communicated except through face-to-face contact. Only those who do the work truly understand the opportunities. There is little doubt that this "natural excludability" has played a role in the evolution of the biotechnology industry. It does not exist for all discoveries, however, and even when it does exist, it is likely to last for a relatively short period of time because valuable ideas and methods spread quickly.

Zucker and her coauthors go on to suggest that star scientists are so important that if they are properly measured, neither universities nor federal research funding would be found to be a cause of biotechnology entrepreneurship (Zucker, Darby, and Brewer 1988). This claim implies that star scientists could somehow exist independently of the scientific infrastructure. Quite the opposite is the case; a strong scientific infrastructure is a necessary precondition for the emergence of star scientists. Biotechnology entrepreneurship is facilitated by the availability of laboratory space, sophisticated instrumentation, top-notch students, and other components of the infrastructure beyond its most visible scientists.

Zucker and her coauthors' exclusive emphasis on academic stars also leads them to ignore the contributions of executives with industrial experience to the formation of new biotechnology firms. Their analysis simply fails to distinguish between scientific and entrepreneurial opportunities. In fact, data from the U.S. Census Bureau suggest that growth in biotechnology entrepreneurship is greater in those regions with a strong industry presence. Table 9.1 ranks thirteen U.S. regions from the most entrepreneurial to the least entrepreneurial in this industry, using a normalized measure of the growth between 1988 and

Table 9.1. *Rank of Thirteen Entrepreneurial Regions in the United States*

Biotechnology Regions MSA NAME	(1) "Biotechnology" Small Estab. Growth per Capita 1988–1997	(2) "Biotechnology" Total Estab. Growth per Capita 1988–1997	(3) "Biotechnology" Specialization 1988	(4) "Biotechnology" Specialization 1997	(5) High-Tech Specialization 1988	(6) SIC 283 Employment of Natural Sci.	(7) SIC 283 Employment of Machine Oper.	(8) Change in Employment 1988–1997
Research Triangle, NC	86.0	100.7	3.05	4.10	2.84	5.10	1.30	4,250
Bay Peninsula, CA	74.4	94.9	2.16	2.76	2.77	2.20	0.97	6,368
San Diego, CA	59.6	85.9	1.95	3.85	1.60	1.93	0.79	7,984
Denver-Boulder, CO	52.4	62.8	1.25	1.64	1.28	2.39	0.56	3,123
Washington, DC	45.8	62.3	1.78	2.94	2.23	3.54	0.34	11,293
Boston, MA	42.7	58.5	1.67	1.83	2.15	1.80	0.49	3,019
Ann Arbor, MI	38.1	50.7	0.61	0.95	1.27	0.95	0.79	415
Seattle, WA	36.5	50.0	0.58	0.81	1.14	1.23	0.78	1,695
East Bay, CA	35.8	42.8	1.74	2.29	1.23	2.30	0.69	2,946
Madison, WI	33.7	50.5	1.68	2.36	1.07	1.60	1.14	997
Yolo-Sacramento, CA	22.5	25.4	0.43	0.63	0.90	1.29	0.58	642
Houston, TX	13.1	18.1	0.32	0.52	0.97	2.48	1.25	1,896
LA-Orange-Ventura, CA	12.4	14.5	1.15	1.06	1.13	0.99	1.72	−668

Source: Author's calculations based on U.S. Census and U.S. Bureau of Labor Statistics data.

1997 in the number of new biotechnology establishments with fewer than twenty employees.[1] The first two columns list the change in the number of small establishments and the change in total establishments per one million 1988 population. Columns 3 and 4 show each region's specialization in biotechnology relative to the United States as a whole in 1988 and 1997, respectively.[2] The final column displays the nonnormalized change in employment in each region.

Several interesting observations emerge from Table 9.1. First, the normalized measure identifies Research Triangle, North Carolina, as the most entrepreneurial region and the Los Angeles area as the least entrepreneurial. Bay Peninsula, California, which includes San Francisco, San Mateo, and Santa Clara counties, is second, followed by San Diego. Second, column 3 suggests that the growth in entrepreneurship between 1988 and 1997 was higher in regions where the industry was relatively more concentrated in 1988. As one moves down the column from the most entrepreneurial region to the least, one sees that industry specialization generally falls. This positive association between entrepreneurship and specialization suggests that feedback or "agglomeration" mechanisms are at work within these regions (Glaeser et al. 1992). A third observation emerges from a comparison of columns 3 and 4. All regions, except Los Angeles, have become more specialized relative to the nation over the 1988 to 1997 period. Increased specialization is particularly dramatic for San Diego. By 1997, San Diego was almost four times more specialized in biotechnology employment than the nation as a whole. Finally, looking at column 8, it

---

[1] There is no public data source that cleanly measures the biotechnology industry. One gets reasonably close for the human therapeutic and diagnostic segment by using the standard industrial classifications (SIC) 283 and 8731. This is still not ideal since SIC 283 includes traditional pharmaceutical firms and SIC 8731 includes commercial physical research companies. However, nearly all biotechnology firms formed in this segment fall into these SIC classifications. This assertion has been verified using detailed data on all California firms formed between 1988 and 1997. These categories are also used by Ernst and Young (2000) in their study of the economic impact of the biotechnology industry on the U.S. economy.

[2] All specialization measures represent the region's employment share in biotechnology relative to the nation. It is calculated by dividing the region's proportion of employment in biotechnology by the proportion of U.S. national employment in biotechnology. This measure is called the location quotient. If the location quotient exceeds 1.00, the biotechnology employment in the region is higher than that of the United States as a whole.

appears that the more entrepreneurial regions also experienced greater employment growth. (One must remember, however, that these figures have not been normalized to adjust for the size of regional population.)

A third factor that facilitates biotechnology entrepreneurship is the advance of technological capabilities embodied in new research tools and instruments. As the industry evolved in the late 1980s, particularly in the human therapeutic and diagnostic segment, improvements in instruments and tools precipitated substantial changes in drug discovery and created many entrepreneurial opportunities. The interrelated technological developments include the use of electronic libraries of biological information (like GenBank), the development of polymerase chain reaction (PCR), the discovery of the combinatorial chemistry methodology in high-throughput screening, and the invention and improvement of "lab-on-a-chip" technology.[3] These advances ushered in a new type of biotechnology company that focuses on "supplying" the drug discovery process. Many of these new companies became partners with large pharmaceutical firms with the intention of making small-molecule discovery "faster, better, cheaper." They may target bio-informatics or a broader "technology platform" that integrates many of the technologies listed above. In San Diego, this segment of the industry registered the highest number of new firm births (43) between 1988 and 1997, including Discovery Partners International, Nanogen, CombiChem, Aurora Biosciences, Digital Gene Technologies, and Trega Biosciences.

The trend linking instrumentation, especially information technology, and biotechnology entrepreneurship is likely to continue well into the twenty-first century. The sequencing of the human genome has produced an enormous amount of biological data stored on electronic media. Entrepreneurial ventures in information technology and biotechnology increasingly cluster together. Martha Prevezer has documented the convergence of the two industries. She states, "This intertwining of the evolutionary paths of the different technologies has made it increasingly difficult to distinguish between computing and biotechnology skills, as the blending of specialist skills in the variety of disciplines that are contained under both broad headings becomes

---

[3] Nontechnical descriptions of these technologies can be found at the Biotechnology Industry Organization's website, www.bio.org.

more essential and more commonplace" (Prevezer 1998: 256). Table 9.1 provides further evidence in support of this hypothesis. Biotechnology entrepreneurship is greater in regions that are relatively more specialized in civilian high-technology industries. Column 5 contains the value of the region's specialization index for high-technology employment.[4] Research Triangle, the most entrepreneurial region and the one most specialized in biotechnology employment, is also the region most specialized in high-technology employment. As one would expect, Bay Peninsula, California, which contains Silicon Valley, is at the top as well. Generally, as one moves down column 5 from most entrepreneurial to least entrepreneurial, the index values become smaller. Regional high-technology employment and biotechnology entrepreneurship appear to be closely related.

Financial and Human Resources

After identifying a potential commercial opportunity, entrepreneurs must move to protect that opportunity from competitors and to assemble the necessary financial and human resources to begin developing their idea. To protect ideas, biotechnology entrepreneurs depend heavily on patents. Controversy has peppered the patent process in biotechnology since the early years of the industry. Throughout the 1990s, the debate centered on the patentability of human genes and gene fragments. In 1991 and 1993, two court decisions upheld broad patent protection on the erythropoeitin gene and the beta-interferon gene, respectively. In 1998, the USPTO allowed patents on partial gene sequences known as express sequence tags (ESTs). The next major controversy in the field is likely to focus on gene patents based on database searches using ESTs. In April 2000, the USPTO granted such a patent to Human Genome Sciences. The patented gene was soon shown to be exactly the same gene (called CCR5) that had been discovered and described by two NIH researchers four years earlier. Their publication, which should have rendered CCR5 unpatentable and placed it in the public domain, showed that the gene has a function in the AIDS

---

[4] Specialization is calculated in the same way as in footnote 2. Civilian high technology is defined using the following SIC classifications: 357, 362, 366, 367, 382, 384, 737, and 871 except 8731.

virus. According to one scientist involved in the policy discussion, "In 2000, the USPTO had a backlog of about 30,000 additional gene patent applications of this type [EST and computer database identified], and even before the CCR5 controversy began the patent office was being pressed to alter its policy" (Zweiger 2001: 204). It seems clear that conflicts between scientific research in the public domain and private interests trying to secure market exclusivity are likely to continue.

Raising sufficient financial capital is one of the most difficult challenges facing biotechnology entrepreneurs. Unlike the famous Palo Alto garage where Hewlett-Packard was created or the Internet company getting its start in the founder's living room, entrepreneurs in biotechnology require expensive laboratory space, specialized instruments, and equipment. Based on estimates from Maryland's Montgomery County Department of Economic Development, the set-up costs for an rDNA lab range from $100 to $400 per square foot after obtaining the land and building space. Moreover, laboratories set up to work with live viruses, like the AIDS virus, are even more expensive since they must meet the bio-safety guidelines issued by the NIH. Moving closer to the market, entrepreneurs interested in manufacturing their products must follow current General Manufacturing Process guidelines. Estimates of the cost of bio-manufacturing facilities fall in the range of $20 million to $60 million and require from one to four years before they are operational (Feldman 2001). These heavy laboratory and manufacturing expenses must be sustained over many years as drugs are developed. Hence, biotechnology entrepreneurs have a constant need for funding, particularly in human health care applications.

Venture capitalists are an important source of financial investment for new biotechnology firms.[5] Kenney (1986) provides one of the first and most complete discussions of the interactions between academic founders and venture capitalists in the early years of the industry. Economic research attempting to identify and measure the contribution of venture capital, however, has been quite limited. Empirical work by Zucker, Darby, and Brewer (1998) found that the presence of venture capital in a region decreased biotechnology entrepreneurship,

---

[5] Public equity markets are also an important source of financing for publicly held firms. See Ernst and Young (2000) for a detailed discussion.

as measured by the number of new biotechnology firms, once other factors were controlled for. Employing a different technique, my study of California regions finds that venture capital investment stimulates new firm formation (Toole 2001). Resolving the causality issues in this area of research is tricky because entrepreneurs respond to profit opportunities that cannot be observed by researchers. Much work remains to be done.

A critical part of attracting venture capital and other private investment is the makeup of the founding team. Research has shown that the typical founding team in biotechnology has up to six people, with an average of three (Prevezer 2001). Because of the difference between scientific and entrepreneurial opportunities, members of the founding team often bring different but complementary skill sets to the venture.

Academic scientists are the most widely discussed group of biotechnology entrepreneurs. Kenney (1986) documents the industry's early history and describes some of the underlying motivations. Not surprisingly, financial rewards appear to be the strongest incentive. In a study of the greater Seattle area, Haug (1994) finds that 41 percent of company founders previously worked at academic research institutions. For ten out of the thirty-three firms studied, all founders were previously employed in academic research. Audretsch and Stephan (1999) analyze the backgrounds of 101 scientific founders identified from the prospectuses of 60 firms making an initial public stock offering (IPO) between March 1990 and November 1992. Looking only at the "scientific" portion of the company founding teams, their data suggest that 57 percent of the scientific founders had no formal employment history with private industry prior to starting the firm. Of course, this does not mean they were completely unfamiliar with industry. Kenney (1986) describes the long and "venerable" tradition of consulting between academic faculty and corporations, government, and nonprofit institutions. Equally revealing is that the remaining 43 percent of these scientist-founders had some formal employment connection with industry prior to founding the new firm.

As the industry has matured and entrepreneurial opportunities have become more technology-based, the backgrounds of founders of biotechnology companies have become more industrial and less academic. In the 1970s, over half of the founders came from academic settings, but this proportion had dropped to one-fifth by the mid-1980s and the proportion of founders from industry had increased to two-thirds (Prevezer 2001). Experienced managers bring crucial skills and knowledge to the founding team, which make them better able to evaluate entrepreneurial opportunities than most academic scientists. Alejandro Zaffaroni exemplifies the sort of "serial entrepreneur" who has contributed so much to the industry. Zaffaroni has been instrumental in founding five successful biotechnology companies in the San Francisco Bay Area (Alza, DNAX Research Institute, Affymax Research Institute, Crescendo Pharmaceuticals, and Maxygen) (Day 2000). Venture capitalists often look for such founders and help them to spin off new firms by financing their deals. For instance, the chairman of CoCensys, F. Richard Nichol, took one of his firm's early stage technologies to the venture capital market in April 1998. He raised $10 million and Cytovia, Inc., was born (Van Brunt 1999). Biotechnology spin-offs are a major mechanism of entrepreneurship.

Biotechnology start-ups require specialized labor beyond that of their founders. Their key employees must understand the relevant science and have the skills to carry out lab research. Recently trained graduate students are an important part of the flow of skilled labor into entrepreneurial biotechnology ventures, as are individuals with some experience in the industry. The Bureau of Labor Statistics reports that "natural scientists" and "chemical machine operators" are the two largest groups of skilled labor employed in the human therapeutics and diagnostics industry, comprising 15 and 26 percent of the total employment, respectively.[6] These two groups represent two ends of the innovative process. Natural scientists work primarily in the product discovery stage while machine operators are used more intensively in production. Columns 6 and 7 of Table 9.1 display indicators of regional employment specialization for natural scientists and machine operators in 1997. Column 6 indicates that the most entrepreneurial regions also have greater specialization in scientific employment. Column 7 is ambiguous; there is no apparent trend among machine

---

[6] This figure is for 1997 SIC classification 283, which encompasses human therapeutics and diagnostics, although it is not restricted to biotechnology. See footnote 1. The 5-digit OES occupational codes used to calculate 1997 regional labor specialization are: 24000 for natural scientists; 92935 and 92938 for chemical machine operators.

operators. This finding illustrates the key role of biotechnology start-ups in the research phase of the human therapeutics and diagnostics industry. Abundant regional pools of natural scientists are associated with high rates of biotechnology entrepreneurship.

Market Applications

One of the most distinctive features of entrepreneurship in biotechnology is the diversity of potential market applications. These applications span vastly different sectors of the economy including human and animal health, agriculture, industrial processes, cosmetics, environmental cleanup, marine applications, criminal justice, paternity rights, and more. Unlike the information technology industry where a core product can be tailored to specific application needs across different sectors, biotechnology applications often require completely different products and processes to be developed for each market. Limited flexibility to transfer core product designs across multiple market applications implies that entrepreneurs in biotechnology face greater risks from downstream market movement. Developing products to treat human disease is fundamentally different from developing products for agricultural markets, for instance. The stories of Genentech's success at expressing human insulin in bacteria and Monsanto's success at creating herbicide-resistant soybeans share little in common except for their use of rDNA technology (Stern 1995; Ruttan 2001).

An entrepreneurial firm's particular market application will determine which government agencies must review and approve its product for marketing. Since the approval criteria are specific to each agency, the necessary steps and implied cost for product development will also vary across applications. For human therapeutic and diagnostic applications, the cost and time required can be overwhelming to a small start-up. Robert Swanson, describing the early experience at Genentech (which he served as CEO), summarizes the challenge:

Costs to build a production facility exceeded $80 million, and development expenses were well into the tens of millions of dollars. It required more than 1,000 man-years to bring the product through the various stages of development – beginning with fermentation scale-up and purification, through animal and human testing, and finally obtaining approval for marketing from the Food and Drug Administration. (Swanson 1986: 432)

If anything, these costs have increased over time. The Tufts Center for the Study of Drug Development (2001) estimates the inflation-adjusted average cost to develop a new prescription drug to be $802 million.

Recent research on trends in product development and FDA approval times indicates that biotechnology-based drugs face longer clinical development periods than traditional pharmaceuticals. Using data on biotechnology therapeutics approved by the FDA between 1995 and 1999, Reichert (2000) finds that the total time between first notification of clinical testing and market approval has increased relative to the 1982–1994 period. This total time to market can be further broken into its clinical and FDA approval phases. When this is done, the data suggest that clinical trials are taking longer for biotechnology candidates whereas mean FDA approval delays have decreased. Extended clinical development can have a ripple effect on investor expectations and choke off equity capital.

As significant development hurdles get identified, entrepreneurs respond with new solutions. For instance, some observers note that the emergence of platform technology and other "tool-based" start-ups was a response to the difficulties of becoming a fully integrated drug company (Deger 1997). Moreover, a new variety of start-up has emerged that targets clinical development. This new type of company focuses on either in-licensing or contracting with discovery-focused firms to take promising biotechnology candidates through clinical trials and FDA approval. Further, many researchers point to the emergence of collaborative agreements as a creative response to evolving development challenges. These agreements often involve the exchange of financial capital as well as research, marketing, and production capabilities between younger biotechnology firms and established pharmaceutical companies (Pisano et al. 1988; Arora and Gambardella 1995; Powell et al. 1996; Feldman 2001).

CHALLENGES FACING POLICYMAKERS AND RESEARCHERS

The challenges facing policymakers and researchers in this area of entrepreneurship policy are different. Policymakers must draw on the insights of all concerned parties, make logical connections between cause and effect, and choose the actions that appear to be the best for promoting entrepreneurship and economic development. Researchers, on the other hand, must identify, describe, and evaluate the factors and policies that facilitate entrepreneurship and, further, connect entrepreneurship to indicators of economic development like employment growth. These challenges are difficult because biotechnology and its policy environment are complex, interdependent, and fluid. Moreover, we are just beginning to distinguish the features that make policy effective, and are just starting to build an understanding of the factors that drive biotechnology entrepreneurship. Still, a few modest suggestions are warranted.

At the national level, policymakers need to streamline the patent process. In light of the enormous up-front investments in research and development required in the biotechnology industry, investors demand patent protection for both initial and follow-on rounds of financing. The USPTO, however, has huge backlogs of biotechnology patent applications that take an average of two years to be approved. These delays and the attendant uncertainty jeopardize the financial viability of emerging biotechnology companies.

National policymakers also need to work cooperatively with the social science research community so that current polices can be evaluated. Unfortunately, at a time when biotechnology policy questions are taking on greater importance, federal agencies are becoming less cooperative and, in some cases, are actually pulling critical information out of the public domain. For instance, the NIH, the most important funding agency in the field, no longer publicly reports the financial award amount as part of its grants and contracts database. Needless to say, without access to this information, researchers will be unable to evaluate the effectiveness of the uses to which tax dollars are being put.

At the regional level, policymakers should note that biotechnology entrepreneurship is highest in regions that have a strong scientific infrastructure and venture capital investment. This is the traditional "one-two punch" that sparked the development process in regions like the Bay Peninsula in California and Boston's Route 128 area. Building a strong scientific infrastructure is a long-term process that must include both commercial laboratories and not-for-profit research institutions. Building infrastructure is a necessary first step. Venture capital should be made available as viable opportunities emerge. Venture capital can only be effective when there are quality deals to fund.

Emerging evidence also suggests, however, that regional entrepreneurship policy for biotechnology should be part of a larger "integrated" plan to promote growth in complementary high-technology industries.

Policymakers should continue to consider programs designed to bridge laboratory research and innovation. Scientist-entrepreneurs interested in pursuing ideas for new products require independently owned laboratory space. To help overcome the laboratory cost barrier, many private and public "incubators" are being set up. These incubators provide low-cost laboratory space and other business services. In 1998, for instance, Montgomery County, Maryland, opened a fifty-thousand-square-foot facility housing twenty-four fully equipped modular wet laboratories. Although it is still too early to gauge success, this incubator has a waiting list of interested entrepreneurs and has successfully "graduated" twelve firms to independent facilities. Incubators are only one example of bridging policies. A recent survey sponsored by the Biotechnology Industry Organization looks at a full range of programs being pursued by state and local governments (Biotechnology Industry Organization 2001).

Researchers face the combined problems of limited data and interdependencies in entrepreneurship. Any researcher who hopes to identify the causal effect of biotechnology policy must somehow account for the behavior of academic scientists, venture capitalists, industrial executives, and other relevant factors. Despite the difficulties, such research is urgently needed to understand and enhance the contribution of public R&D funding and commercialization programs like SBIR. Policy would also benefit from case study research describing regional development experiences or firm-specific experiences that help shed light on the path from invention to innovation.

10

E-Commerce, Entrepreneurship, and the Law

Reassessing a Relationship

Viktor Mayer-Schönberger

The commercialization of the Internet in the second half of the 1990s triggered a wave of entrepreneurial activity, as well as a burst of innovation and Schumpeterian "creative destruction" (Schumpeter 1942).[1] Despite the eventual burst of the dot-com bubble, a number of ecommerce brands have become household names, and the services they offer are used by millions around the world.[2] Entrepreneurship in the virtual world has frequently been compared with nineteenth-century gold rushes and land grabs (see Spar 2001: 2–4). As in the mountains and prairies of the Wild West, public policy seems to have no place on the virtual frontier, except to stifle, obstruct, and slow down the new breed of entrepreneurs and innovators.

In this chapter, I argue that this offhand rejection of public policy is mistaken. To make my case, I consider the relationship between law (which I conceive of as a subset of public policy) and entrepreneurship,

---

[1] "Creative destruction" is the process "that revolutionizes the economic structure from within, incessantly destroying the old one, incessantly creating a new one" (Schumpeter 1942: 152).

[2] For example, by 2000 Amazon.com, founded only in 1994, had become the forty-eighth most valuable brand name in the world, and at the end of the second quarter of 2001 had 21 million regular customers.

I thank Lewis M. Branscomb for his criticism and my research assistant Edgar Lee for his tireless help.

using the ecommerce sector as a test case.[3] In particular, I look in some detail at three functions of the law: leveling the playing field for market competition, protecting innovation, and enforcing transactional obligations. My interest lies in how these functions may serve to support ecommerce entrepreneurship, rather than to stifle it. Much more research into the interaction between law and entrepreneurship is needed to understand law's potential costs and benefits, so I proceed to suggest a preliminary agenda for further scholarship. Finally, I take the idea of entrepreneurship and apply it to law-making itself. Contrary to conventional wisdom, I propose that entrepreneurs in some sectors may actually benefit from risk-taking rule makers.

ANTAGONISTIC VIEWS

Entrepreneurship and law have long been seen as naturally antagonistic. Law promises certainty. Entrepreneurship thrives on risk. Entrepreneurs expand the scope of possibility, overcome limitations, break rules. Laws restrict.

Entrepreneurs portray the situation this way. They see themselves as trailblazers, the business world's equivalent of Nobel laureates, renowned artists, and path-breaking societal leaders. The law in this view is a hindrance, constraining their innovative activities. Nothing expresses this "sense of self" better than the award winning, emotional 1997 Apple commercial entitled "Think different."[4] Interspersed between short snippets of Albert Einstein, Pablo Picasso, Mahatma Gandhi, and Alfred Hitchcock, we see entrepreneurs Richard Branson and Ted Turner. A somber voice comments:

Here is to the crazy ones, the misfits, the rebels, the trouble makers, the round pegs in the square holes, the ones who see things differently. They are not fond of rules and they have no respect for the status quo. They change things, they push the human race forward. And while some may see them as the crazy ones, we see genius.

---

[3] I use the term "law" to refer to formal societal rules, created through an agreed-on societal process. "Policies" include a broader set of principles determining what and how things are done.

[4] This ad can be found at the Apple website: http://www.apple.com/thinkdifferent/ad1.html.

Seen from this vantage point, entrepreneurs, the ones who break the rules, must necessarily clash with the law, a structure designed to protect the status quo. Entrepreneurs have found two ways to describe this clash. According to the first, the struggle is one of absolutes. Cyberspace is a legal void, a lawless frontier from which government, the law, needs to be kept away. "Grateful Dead" lyricist and digerati John Perry Barlow is the most articulate representative of this view. In his much-quoted "Declaration of Independence of Cyberspace" he declared cyberspace outside the physical world and its rules (Barlow 1996). For him, extending laws to online activities would be an act of usurpation and the end of creativity, innovation, and entrepreneurship.

A more pragmatic understanding of the situation concedes that law cannot be kept out of cyberspace forever. Internet entrepreneurs holding this point of view, like Barlow, see government intervention mainly as a threat. But in contrast to Barlow, they aim only at slowing the pace of law's entrance into cyberspace, while they move on to another yet unregulated niche, where they can continue to innovate.

Such antagonistic views are not surprising. Over the last decade, legislatures have been busy imposing numerous legal restrictions on ecommerce entrepreneurs. In the United States, a legislative framework dating from the Cold War prohibited the export of software for secure data transfers (see Diffie and Landau 1998; Levy 2001). A law tagged onto the much-awaited Telecommunications Act of 1996 threatened Internet content and access providers with criminal liability and draconian reprisals should they not police the spread of "indecent" information.[5] Killing Napster, large recording and publishing companies secured the passage of a new copyright law making illegal the development and use of technology to share information – even if the sharing itself would be legal (see Litman 2001).[6] And in the European Union, a stringent data protection statute has severely curtailed the data mining

---

[5] The Communications Decency Act (CDA), held unconstitutional in *ACLU v. Reno*; much of the substance of the CDA was enacted again as the Children Online Protection Act (COPA), held unconstitutional in 2000 by the Federal Court of Appeals for the Third Circuit, *ACLU v. Reno II*, No. 99-1324, U.S. Supreme Court granted certiori, decision pending; undeterred, Congress passed a slightly amended version as the Children's Internet Protection Act (CIPA), codified as 20 U.S.C. § 9134 and 47 U.S.C. § 254(h); a complaint filed in Federal Court against CIPA is pending.

[6] The Digital Millennium Copyright Act is not the only recent law strengthening existing owners of intellectual property (see Litman 2001).

of personal information, the very lifeblood of many ecommerce entrepreneurs banking on mass customization of information and services (see also Mayer-Schönberger 1999).[7] No wonder entrepreneurs have seen themselves besieged by the law. Intriguingly, much of this legislative activism restricting entrepreneurial activity in cyberspace stems from a sense of loss of control similar to that felt by entrepreneurs in the face of government intervention. Passing laws is policymakers' crude reaction to what they perceive as the infringement of standards of decency, of privacy, and of property brought about by cyberspace entrepreneurs.

From the perspective of both the entrepreneurs and the legislators, this struggle looks momentous, an eternal ebb and flow between risk and security. Given these circumstances it is understandable that entrepreneurs view the law as their enemy, and that a conventional wisdom has formed not just among the digerati, but among the public at large that the legal system is the enemy of entrepreneurship in cyberspace.

There is some truth in this view. Yet it provides only a limited perspective of a complex relationship, in which the "law" can be as much an enabling as a restrictive force.

LAW AS LEVELER

Law is a potent tool to initiate and sustain competition, and by doing so may transform itself from being an entrepreneur's enemy to becoming an ally. By fostering entrepreneurial niches and enabling new entrants to gain entry to a market space, a new regulatory framework may turn into a powerful enabler for entrepreneurs, overcoming the legacy of the old regulatory regimes, which stifled innovation and entrepreneurship.

Over the last decades, many entrepreneurs have become advocates for the "liberalization" of economic sectors from regulatory control. Their quest has been joined by many others, resulting in an impressive stream of economic "liberalization" in the United States as well as in many other nations around the world. From the airline industry (Boaz

---

[7] Directive 95/46/EC of the European Parliament and of the Council of 24 October 1995 on the protection of individuals with regard to the processing of personal data and on the free movement of such data, 1995 O.J. (L 281) 31.

and Crane 1993) to telecommunications (Spiller and Cardilli 1997) to financial services (Meerschwam 1991) and the provision of energy (Kalt 1996), old-style monopolies that were highly regulated by arcane administrative rules have been replaced with – mostly[8] – vibrant markets offering better goods and services at a fraction[9] of the original prices.

Entrepreneurial companies typically see themselves as potential beneficiaries of such de-regulation. Given the complexity of older regulations, no regulation seems the best of all options. "Before government comes in and regulates," a senior manager from Microsoft remarked, "everything is fine, after that it's chaos" (Heileman 2000).[10] It seems that all government has to do is eradicate regulations, weed out the stifling law, and let the invisible hand of the market take care of the rest.

Yet successful "liberalization," as Stephen Vogel and others have eloquently shown, requires a skillfully crafted and carefully implemented legal framework to guarantee a market's ongoing success (Vogel 1996; Hills 1986; Moran 1991). At first glance, this may sound counterintuitive. But highly regulated sectors are often dominated by powerful monopolies or oligopolies. Merely abolishing the old regulatory framework may leave the new market with an all-powerful incumbent, ready to squash any entrepreneurial new entrant. This is particularly true for sectors like telecommunications, energy, or transport, which require new entrants to invest heavily in infrastructure that incumbents have already put in place and paid for through inflated monopoly prices, and to connect to elements of the incumbents' infrastructure that they cannot duplicate.

Hence such re-regulations regularly define the conditions of "interconnection" for linking the networks of incumbents and new entrants.

---

[8] De-regulation is not a magic potion. It needs to be done right. Not surprisingly, some attempts to introduce markets have failed. The California electricity crisis was one of the more visible failures (see Hogan 2001).

[9] The European Union, for example, has calculated that due to the de-regulation of telecommunications and electricity markets, real term expenditures for a standard household on electricity and telecommunications were reduced by up to 25 percent in EU member states. EU consumers continue to benefit, but reforms must be accelerated.

[10] Microsoft provides an interesting example, as it still retains a very strong entrepreneurial spirit, despite the fact that it has turned into the world's second biggest multinational corporation.

Left to the market, incumbents could extract prohibitively high fees from new entrants, and, given the financial resources at their disposal, could elect to starve out their nascent competition until it has run out of money. Successful "re-regulation" requires more than just reining in large incumbents, however. New entrants must not get too good a deal, either. If they did, they would have less of an incentive to innovate and be efficient, and to create an attractive alternative. The challenge is to find a balance that creates incentives for all market players.

Consequently, a sophisticated replacement of the old regulatory framework must fulfill two distinct tasks. First, it must replace the old noncompetitive setup by opening the sector to entrepreneurial new entrants. Equally important, however, it must also provide a framework that ensures continuing competition. What is termed "de-regulation" is in fact a complex "re-regulation," the replacement of old-style rules with a market-based regulatory framework. Thus Vogel entitled his book *Freer Markets, More Rules* (1996). (See Eli Noam's chapter in this volume as well.)

A wide variety of entrepreneurs have already benefited from these new regulatory frameworks. For example, the de-regulation of financial services in the United States made it possible for ecommerce companies to "go demand-side," to offer a bundle of services not based on artificial regulatory categories but on their customers' comprehensive financial needs. New Internet access providers and network operators exist because of the de-regulation of the telecommunications sector, whereas ecommerce resellers of excess energy are enabled by the re-regulation of energy markets.

There is no certainty that "de-regulation" will be successful in creating and maintaining competitive markets. Building a new legal framework is a complex undertaking. Regulators may err and create the wrong set of incentives. In such ill-designed markets, competition will fail and entrepreneurs won't be better off than they were in closed markets. Yet, re-regulation – if done right – holds significant potential for entrepreneurs.

Law as Protector

Creating and maintaining competitive markets is only one function of the legal system. Another is recognizing and protecting valuable rights. The most obvious example of such a right is the right to own property.

Property has always provided an important incentive for entrepreneurs. During the days of the gold rush individual entrepreneurs invested in prospecting claims. Similarly, whatever land families had staked out and fenced in during the Oklahoma land rush was theirs. In the postindustrial society of the Internet, the power over physical property has been replaced by the power to control information. For example, the astonishing stock market valuation of Microsoft is based not on its holdings of real estate, facilities, inventory, or investment in other firms. It is based almost exclusively on intangibles – most notably intellectual property rights for its best-selling software.

Entrepreneurs should be expected to fully embrace intellectual property rights. Yet many entrepreneurs in the information technology sector, an area in which intellectual property protection is quite important, have become openly skeptical of the intellectual property law's ability to serve their needs.[11] They argue that entrepreneurship depends on the open exchange of information, of innovative ideas and designs. Entrepreneurs, they maintain, combine existing ideas from a vast corpus of human knowledge when seizing new market niches. Destroying this sense of openness and robust informational exchange threatens the very culture in which entrepreneurship thrives.

Moreover, they suggest that intellectual property protection is less important for ecommerce entrepreneurs operating at breakneck speed. At such speed, entrepreneurs can easily let others copy their offerings, because the time it takes for these others to introduce similar services will be used by entrepreneurs to create new innovations. However hard they try, the copycats will always lag behind as the innovators blaze the trail and make money off the lead-time advantage they enjoy over their competitors. Additionally, it is argued, intellectual property rights have been modified over the last decades to benefit the incumbents, the "majors," the large possessors of intellectual property, while new entrants, the start-ups, the true entrepreneurs, are suffering from a stifling climate of overprotection. Finally, they contend, these legal changes have made it harder, more costly, and time-consuming for entrepreneurs to protect their innovations, further eroding their chances in the information markets. In sum, entrepreneurs would, contrary to

---

[11] For example, ecommerce entrepreneur Robert Young (1999), of Red Hat Software, argues that intellectual property protection creates barriers restraining commercial success.

the conventional wisdom, actually benefit from the abolition of intellectual property rights, as their agility, adaptability, and ingenuity provide them with a material advantage over slow-moving traditional competitors.

The critics have a point. To achieve innovation in today's complex markets, entrepreneurs invariably have to build on existing innovations, which are likely to have been patented or copyrighted by others. Jessica Litman and Pamela Samuelson have persuasively argued that in the last three decades intellectual property protection has been strengthened at the behest of large rights holders (Litman 2001; Samuelson 1996; Bettig 1996). And these "majors" now control more of the intellectual property markets than ever before. For example, the five leading media companies control more than 90 percent of the cinema and 80 percent of the home video market. Microsoft maintains more than 90 percent market share not only of the operating systems but also of the office application software and the Internet browser markets. AOL/Time-Warner, Microsoft, and Yahoo provide online services for more than fifty million subscribers, orders of magnitude more than their closest competitors. Moreover, with the questionable recognition of business method patents, dominant companies like Amazon.com can patent parts of their shopping experience (the so-called one-click-shopping)[12] and require royalties from every small ecommerce entrepreneur (Wells 2001).

Against this backdrop, the call to abolish intellectual property laws and to open information vaults and let knowledge and innovation be used freely by others has fallen on surprisingly fertile ground. The operating system Linux is its most prominent poster child. Known as "open source," "open content," or "open code," this system has proponents who claim they are bolstering, not destroying, ecommerce opportunities. Even "majors" like IBM, Sun, and Apple, never timid about enforcing their own intellectual property rights, have jumped on the open source bandwagon.

Yet this perspective provides a lopsided view of the full picture. As Jane Ginsburg argues, intellectual property rights have also been weakened, both by lawmakers responding to calls for more "fair use,"

---

[12] See *Amazon.com, Inc. v. Barnesandnoble.com, Inc.*, 73 F. Supp. 2d 1228, 1232 (W.D. Wash. 1999).

and, much more important, by technological advances that ease illegal copying and distribution (Ginsburg 1999). Attempts to strengthen intellectual property laws are mainly responses to the threat posed by technological change. On a more abstract level, economists have argued that well-crafted intellectual property protection not only benefits rights holders, but provides an incentive framework that maximizes innovation as well as information diffusion. For example, comparing the strength of national intellectual property protection and its relationship to economic growth, Robert J. Barro and Xavier Sala-I-Martin suggest that "poorly defined intellectual property rights imply that leaders have insufficient incentive to invent and followers have excessive incentive to copy" (Barro and Sala-I-Martin 1997).

Furthermore, most infringers are not the highly innovative coders, but competitors out to make a "quick buck." For example, the company complaining loudest that Amazon.com, a successful entrepreneurial start-up, had been granted a questionable business method patent that stifled innovation was not a small entrepreneur, but traditional bookselling incumbent Barnes & Noble. In addition, many of the more dubious intellectual property rights initially granted are, as Amazon had to realize, successfully contested because they lack originality or novelty. It is true that large corporations have drastically stepped up their intellectual property protection activities, but small companies are even more adamant. In 1972, small entrepreneurs only accounted for 5 percent of patent applications. In 1992 their share had grown to a staggering 23 percent. And, as Kevin Rivette and David Kline point out, these entrepreneurial Davids have successfully employed the law to win hundreds of millions of dollars in patent cases against powerful Goliaths like Microsoft or General Electric (Rivette and Kline 2000).

Alternatives to intellectual property come with their own problematic baggage. Limiting intellectual property protection may prompt businesses to protect their intellectual property by using other legal constructs, like trade secrecy, trademark, and unfair competition laws, which tend to overprotect and favor larger players, exactly the opposite of what entrepreneurs would want.

Moreover, despite the claims of open software proponents, speed cannot fully substitute for protection. Massive innovation still requires substantial capital investment, which ultimately must be earned back. Information can be copied in a matter of seconds, much faster than any fast-paced innovation can ever occur. If a return on the initial investment is not assured, it must be financed through different means. IBM gave away its software in the 1970s (although it never gave up its intellectual property rights), because it was bundling it with (proprietary) hardware. Hardware sales were subsidizing software. Such cross-subsidization is, however, usually not an option for a fledgling start-up company, and uncertainty over the ability to recoup its initial investment makes it harder to attract outside capital. It is no surprise then that so far open source initiatives have almost entirely been focused on nonstrategic information. IBM may have embraced Linux, but it certainly has yet to open source its own most valuable software gems. The same is true for Sun and Apple.

On a more conceptual level, experts have argued that the collaborative, piecemeal style of innovation championed by the open source community and epitomized by Linux cannot provide the paradigm-shifting innovative breakthroughs entrepreneurs are pushing for. Hence, from an entrepreneurial perspective intellectual property protection may actually have a concrete conceptual advantage over the open source paradigm.

In sum, intellectual property laws are not faultless. Neither are they perfectly aligned with the interests of the entrepreneurs. Yet, contrary to some entrepreneurial sentiment, on balance they seem to protect rather than stifle entrepreneurial activity.

Law as Enforcer

Law fulfills a third potentially useful function: it enforces contractual obligations. When market participants transact with each other, they need to trust that the other side will fulfill its contractual obligation. Market participants have many different means to establish the necessary trust among them – from frequent, personal interactions to reliance on third party rating systems.[13] They may also find an appropriate

---

[13] This is what online auction site eBay.com and others do by permitting auction participants to rate the reliability and trustworthiness of the other parties in the auction. Over time, reliable buyers and sellers establish a strong positive rating, on which potential business partners rely.

substitute to trust in. This can be another human being, like a guarantor, or a societal contract enforcement and conflict resolution institution. The legal system is the main such institution. It permits buyers and sellers to contract without having to establish complete trust in each other's willingness to execute. Instead they rely on the threat of law's power to coerce the other side to perform (or at least to pay the damages caused by its nonperformance). Law enables us to transact with others whom we do not know, whom we have not met, or who live far away.

The legal system functions as an enforcer of contractual obligations at a societal as well as individual level. Each individual enforcement action sends a signal not only to the parties affected, but also to other observers that noncompliance is costly. This societal signaling device reduces noncompliance, lowering overall transactional risk and thus transaction costs (Coase 1960).

Entrepreneurs generally are engaged in riskier business propositions than established corporations, in the hope of reaping disproportionate rewards. But risk comes at a cost. Although entrepreneurs may not be able to influence external risks such as overall market conditions or interest rates, they certainly desire to lower the risks they can control. Transactional risk is one such controllable component. When the legal system successfully lowers transactional risk, it directly assists entrepreneurs, arguably even more so than traditional businesses. What is true for entrepreneurs in general is even more true for ecommerce entrepreneurs, who typically receive orders from customers they have never met, and with whom they have had no chance to establish mutual trust. According to BizRate.com, the leading provider for ecommerce metrics, on a typical week in 2001 more than 5 million ecommerce transactions took place.[14] Amazon.com, the largest ecommerce retailer, received almost 38 million orders in the six weeks before Christmas 2001 from its 21 million registered customers,[15] and online auctioneer eBay hosted more than 5 million auctions in parallel. Every one of these millions of transactions bears some risk, especially where the seller knows little about the buyers. The power of the legal system to

---

[14] For the first week of October, 2001, less than a month after the terrorist attacks on the World Trade Center and the Pentagon, BizRate.com reported 5.04 million ecommerce transactions, not substantially lower than a month or two earlier, for a total value of 657 million U.S. dollars.

[15] Amazon.com 2001 Annual Report, available at http://www.amazon.com.

enforce contracts and protect bona fide contractual parties helps lower the overall risk, benefiting fledgling ecommerce entrepreneurs.

The legal system as enforcer incorporates another advantage to entrepreneurs. It scales. Unlike building network infrastructure or brand recognition, utilizing the legal system does not require heavy initial investment from the parties. Instead, enforcement costs are mostly a linear function of transaction volume. At least in this limited sense the legal system is a public good. This feature of the law directly benefits ecommerce start-ups in transactional markets, from ecommerce retailing to financial services to travel agencies online. Quite directly, the law is their ally, and in a way they most likely have not thought of.

The legal system is not the only way to lower transaction costs, however. Alternatives to lower transaction costs – like mediation, arbitration, self-regulation, or insurance – exist, yet so far the law has kept its primacy, partly because it is so widely accepted an institution, partly because, ceteris paribus, it has been less costly than other alternatives. But the success of law as a tool to lower transaction costs rests on a number of premises, two of which may be undermined by the very characteristics of Internet-based commerce. The first premise is the strong locational dimension of any legal system. Law functions well as enforcer as long as both parties are within the same jurisdiction, within the law's area of effective enforcement. Things get complicated if the two parties are from two different jurisdictions. The legal system has evolved to resolve such situations by referring to meta-rules, rules to decide whose rules should apply (Scoles and Hay 1992; von Mehren and Trautman 1965; Leflar 1968). But this process is costly and time-consuming.

The second premise is one of relative transaction value. Although enforcement scales with the number of transactions, it does not scale so well with the value of each transaction. Legal enforcement cost for a very high-value transaction is higher than for a low-value transaction, but below a certain threshold enforcement costs are more or less flat. It is about as expensive to enforce a five-hundred-dollar contract as it is to enforce a five-dollar contract. Unfortunately for enforcement by law, ecommerce is all about millions of low-value transactions, regularly crossing jurisdictional boundaries. In a typical week in 2001, for example, the average value of an ecommerce transaction was just $130 according to BizRate.com.

As a result, alternative systems may provide lower transaction costs than the law, thus robbing it of its competitive advantage, at least in economic terms: The legal system is too expensive to provide efficient contract enforcement. Even if no cheaper alternative exists, the increasing costs of using the law relative to the absolute value of the transaction may pose a problem not just for the law, but for the very business proposition: if one cannot enforce one's business transactions, one may not be able to survive as a business.[16]

Ecommerce companies have therefore looked carefully at alternative systems to ensure contractual enforcement. eBay has achieved a very low "fraud" rate of .01 percent through its rating system, which provides risk assessment information for contractual parties, and an optional arbitration system. It has also spurred a cottage industry of companies offering risk minimizing payment and escrow alternatives. On a much larger scale, credit card companies, too, offer a powerful alternative. They guarantee payment – contractual enforcement – for a percentage of the transaction value, thus ensuring excellent scalability, as well as efficiency even at comparably low transaction values.[17]

Does this spell the end of law as enabling and supporting ecommerce entrepreneurship? It is too early to tell. Without doubt, the law is challenged in its role as enforcer by the swell in cross-jurisdictional low value transactions online (Mayer-Schönberger 2001a; Mayer-Schönberger 2001b). Addressing this challenge must be high on the agenda of any serious legislator, as well as on that of any entrepreneur hoping for an affordable system to reduce transactional risk. The legal system remains a powerful player, however, even in the wake of this substantial challenge and the advent of alternative structures. The law is deeply rooted in our society. It retains a strongly visible signaling effect, especially in high-profile cases, causing some to use it despite its economic shortcomings. Furthermore, alternative systems may complement the legal system in reducing transactional risks, rather than

---

[16] Not every business needs legal enforcement. Software shareware, for example, is based on the honor principle: you pay if you decide to keep using it. Enforcement is based on ethical values rather than legal rules. If the transaction value is small, and the ethical values to pay are fairly widespread, such a business model may not only be sustainable but in fact may be more efficient than one based on legal enforcement.

[17] Credit card companies do, however, have a transaction minimum fee regardless of transaction value.

replacing it. Alternative systems often require the law to be in place for them to work. Credit card companies, for instance, can only perform the role of enforcer because they themselves rely on the legal system ultimately to resolve disputes. Without the law, they could not exist.

As we have seen, one of law's functions is to guarantee contractual enforcement. Because it may thus reduce transactional risk it assists ecommerce entrepreneurs. They benefit from its scaling structure, its public good character, and its societal acceptance. Yet low transaction values and cross-jurisdictional transactions reduce its potential usefulness. Legislators must confront this "jurisdictional challenge" but even if alternative systems abound, the law will not be completely displaced. It may become less visible as transactional enforcer, but its existence is no less needed.

MAPPING OUT A RESEARCH AGENDA

Among the law's many functions, the three described above potentially assist and benefit ecommerce entrepreneurs in their activities by

- providing a regulatory framework enabling new entrepreneurial entrants in "liberalized" markets,
- protecting entrepreneurs in their innovative endeavors through intellectual property rights, and
- enforcing transactional contracts.

Law's role as supporting entrepreneurs is not a given for any of these functions. Whether or not law is aligned with and thus supportive of entrepreneurship depends on its substance, on how it is crafted. As we have seen, law holds substantial promise, but wrongly worded it can be what many entrepreneurs intuitively suspect it to be in general: stifling.

Hence, much of the success or failure of the law to support entrepreneurship depends on the concrete effect of legal rules on entrepreneurial activity. Yet neither the exact implications of certain legal designs on entrepreneurship, nor entrepreneurship's demands on the law, have received much academic analysis. A search on Lexis, the comprehensive legal database in the United States, retrieves less than a handful of articles over the last three decades looking at the interface of entrepreneurship and law (Hobbs 1997; Aoki 1996; O'Reilly 2000). The harvest is not much bigger when looking at the teaching side. Researching law schools around the country reveals few programs or centers devoted to "entrepreneurship and the law."[18] Courses that are offered focus mostly on the legal and regulatory requirements to start a business, describing law as a hurdle, not a tool to be used.

Some research parallels may be drawn from work conducted on the role of law in so-called transition economies. Studies in that field looked at the suitability of the legal framework for contract enforcement, intellectual property protection, and the denationalization of certain economic sectors (Hendley 2001; Hendley, Murrell, and Ryterman 2001; Hendrix 2001; Pei 2001; Heller 2001). Although they may provide a solid set of general assumptions, the focus of these studies is different. Their goal is to understand transition dynamics, not the more general interface between entrepreneurs and the legal system.

Additional academic work is therefore necessary to shed light on the subject, and to aid legislators in their difficult task. Different kinds of entrepreneurial activities are linked to different functions of the legal framework. In this chapter, I have focused on ecommerce entrepreneurship and identified three related functions of the law. Furthering our understanding of these three functions and their interaction with entrepreneurship through additional research could provide valuable insights, by, for instance:

- looking at how recent "re-regulations" attempt to rebalance the "playing field" for new entrants and incumbents alike, in order to analyze how this rebalancing was intended by the policymakers, and to what extent the rule structure put in place has resulted in the intended competition (Schipke 2001; Vogel 1996; Mayer-Schönberger and Lazer 2002)
- exploring the concrete needs for intellectual property protection and information sharing for entrepreneurial companies in various sectors, for example with quantitative or case methods, to compare

[18] These few include Pepperdine University School of Law's Center for Entrepreneurship and Technology Law, the Germeshausen Center for the Law of Innovation and Entrepreneurship at Franklin Pierce Law Center, the Program on Law and Entrepreneurship at Oregon Law School, and Chicago-Kent Law School's Information Technology & Entrepreneurship Clinic.

intellectual property protection with open source software and to better understand the linkage between intellectual property protection and necessary start-up funding (Weber 2000)

- determining the (fixed) cost component of legal enforcement for various ecommerce transactions, to examine established alternative enforcement and dispute resolution structures, like credit card companies or online arbitration, their economic benefits and costs, as well as the level of their reliance on existing national legal systems

This functional agenda could be complemented with research on the actors and their perceptions of the law. For example, more detailed research in how entrepreneurs assess the role of law, and the relationship between their activity and the legal system, could clarify what – in the minds of the entrepreneurs – contributes most to law's unattractiveness (Frye 2001).[19]

Entrepreneurship may directly benefit from such research in at least two important ways. First, this research could provide the empirical foundation to argue for a reassessment of law, to see the law less in terms of black and white, of friend or foe, and more as a societal tool potentially beneficial for entrepreneurs if used appropriately. Second and equally important, such research could provide a better understanding of what kinds of legal rules entrepreneurs should ask for. Such a deepened understanding would then permit the political debate to move beyond entrepreneurs' traditional calls for "no regulation" or "no laws" and toward an informed advocacy for rules enhancing and supporting entrepreneurial activity.

REASSESSING THE NEED FOR LAW: A CALL FOR LEGAL ENTREPRENEURSHIP

Law is a set of predefined rules. By providing societal guidance and enforcement against violators, law fosters predictability. Predictability in turn lowers transactional risk. Increasing predictability is particularly welcome in economic sectors with high risks. It is in these sectors that entrepreneurs are most active. Consequently, as a provider of some

---

[19] Here, too, studies from transition economies may provide early indications.

predictability law offers relatively greater utility for entrepreneurs in high-risk areas than for businesses in other economic sectors.

Predictability dictates that legislators not act prematurely, but take their time to "understand" the inner workings of a particular sector before enacting rules. Even after legislators have grasped an understanding of a sector, however, predictability may not be served by a "big bang approach," by passing one comprehensive legislative act. Instead, slowly evolving the legal framework through easily correctable small and deliberate steps will more likely provide overall predictability than an untested comprehensive act. The more cautious, evolutionary approach resonates well with American legal and business culture. The value of pragmatism and the common law tradition point in the same direction. Yet the desire for predictability through legislative caution transcends culture and legal tradition. It is as important in civil as in common law systems for economic actors to be able to anticipate what the law is.

It is unclear, however, whether such a risk-averse stance toward rule making is in fact preferable for entrepreneurs to an early legislative act. As we have seen, re-regulation – opening markets – cannot be done piecemeal, but requires a comprehensive framework. Moreover, for entrepreneurs, the sooner markets are open, the better. Similarly, if intellectual property rights need to be changed to create incentives for innovation, waiting may unduly burden entrepreneurs. And if law can efficiently provide enforcement of ecommerce transactions, failing to extend it swiftly across jurisdictions and to modify it to lower transaction cost may in fact discriminate against start-ups, who do not have an established enforcement system of their own.

Therefore, legislators may be ill advised to adopt legal frameworks reluctantly. This argument applies particularly to economic sectors like ecommerce with a strong first-mover advantage, high fixed and low variable costs. In network and information industries, in which these properties and general network effects create a dynamic business environment, timeliness may be more important than perfection. In essence, predictability – although certainly an important factor in "timing" rule making – does not necessarily trump other considerations.

To be sure, bad rules enacted in a timely fashion will be as much of a hindrance as badly timed but better written rules. It is after weighing these two alternatives and their potential outcomes that most legislators and entrepreneurs alike find themselves advocating a "wait-and-see" approach. But this presupposes that adopting no rules is always preferable to having the "wrong" rules, and that picking the "right" rules is nothing but a gamble, not a process with calculable risks. Such a risk-averse stance may be expected from legislators, but hearing it from entrepreneurs – continuously exposed to risks – is baffling. It also indicates a belief that the rule-making process is a black box, prone to produce unintended results.

Law making in a dynamic area obviously comes with certain risks. Like entrepreneurship, it may require action and decision making without knowing all the facts. And unlike software, there is no straightforward method to "test" a law. Centuries ago, legislators could enact a new legal framework in a remote region of the state. Like a beta-test of software, after some time the "bugs" in the law were discovered, and could be fixed before it was enacted for the rest of the nation. This is an early model of legislative research and development (Hausmaninger 2000).[20] Over time, however, even the remotest regions resisted being turned into legal and societal guinea pigs and lawmakers had to abandon this approach. They replaced it with the evolutionary approach of "real-time" development and evaluation. Should one of the incremental steps taken turn out to be "wrong," it could easily be changed back to the previous "version."

This approach may have worked in the past, but in the highly dynamic, globally integrated economies of today, such a cautious approach loses much of its appeal. Economic windows of opportunity open and close quickly. Lawmakers often find themselves in competition with their colleagues in other jurisdictions. If legislation comes too late, others who acted earlier may have already attracted economic activity.

Legislators need to understand this evolving market of rules, and their role in it. By becoming active, by daring to innovate, to learn from their actions as well as from the actions of others, and to adapt quickly

---

[20] One example of this phenomenon is the enactment in western Galicia of a "beta version" of what later became the civil code of the Austro-Hungarian Empire. In the U.S. Supreme Court, Justice Brandeis called for the states to be "laboratories of democracy" (*New State Ice Co. v. Liebmann* 1932).

to a changing environment, they not only ensure the competitiveness of their jurisdiction, they also greatly assist their entrepreneurs. Instead of endlessly debating the next legislative steps and considering all the interest groups involved, half of which are stalling the process in the hope of gaining from inertia, legislators may want to legislate swiftly, despite the risk. Instead of just paying lip service to supporting entrepreneurship, pro-active legislators demonstrate that they understand the inherent dynamic of economic windows of opportunity. In sum, they may want to turn themselves into entrepreneurs, and take a risk by legislating. They may win or fail, but if they waver and wait in a dynamic environment, they can only lose.

Such a change may require a leap of faith for traditional lawmakers. Like former monopolists they have to shift their mindset toward competition. It will be a difficult transition. Yet entrepreneurs are going to be, I am convinced, most supportive of such a move. They understand that giving up predictability in exchange for a timely legal framework will improve their chances for success.

Entrepreneurial law making is not suitable for every economic sector, or all areas of economic activity. But it may hold great promise for areas of high dynamism, and of strong entrepreneurial activity, where moving swiftly and boldly is more important than waiting to get it right.

The ecommerce sector has helped fuel the entrepreneurial spirit. The legal system is still seen as stifling it. This is a mono-dimensional view, untenable in theory and unsuitable in practice. Instead of battling the law, entrepreneurs are better advised to look for and achieve alignment of the law with their own goals, for example by understanding, appreciating, and lobbying for the strengthening of law's supportive functions. In turn legislators may want to become more entrepreneurial themselves.

11

Entrepreneurship and Government in Telecommunications

Eli M. Noam

INTRODUCTION

Entrepreneurship is usually seen as the solution to the key structural problem bedeviling traditional economies in which large and sluggish firms are protected by a subservient government. Entrepreneurs breach the protective walls erected by government and bring forth innovation and efficiency. Joseph Schumpeter's metaphor of the creative destruction of capitalism has thus become a governing cliché, even though Schumpeter himself did not single out small entrants as the destabilizing agents. In the classic view, government is a tool of established firms, and its laws and regulations favor the entrenched incumbents. If the legal barriers are removed through deregulation, the economic barriers set by the incumbents tumble like the Berlin Wall after the withdrawal of Soviet tanks. This notion of government protecting incumbents from entrepreneurs widely prevails. But is it correct?

The subject of entrepreneurship is too large to fit generalizations. One should look at it on a sectoral level, and this chapter will do so for telecommunications. It concludes that entrepreneurial firms exist in this sector not *despite* government but rather *because* of it. No matter how creative the nation's entrepreneurs, an unregulated market equilibrium in the telecommunications sector would not likely have much room for entrepreneurial firms. It takes continuous support from governmental policy to create and maintain room for viable entrants and participants. Therefore, without entrepreneurship *policy* only a little actual *business* entrepreneurship would occur in telecommunications. This is a conclusion I reach with much reluctance, having supported competition, both as a scholar and as a policymaker. But a realistic view might help protect us from future policy miscalculations that equate deregulation with an easing of entrepreneurial entry, when in fact it might have the opposite effect.

MONOPOLY AND ENTREPRENEURSHIP IN TELECOMMUNICATIONS

The problem of an anti-entrepreneurial market structure in telecommunications goes back a long time. Although Samuel Morse and Alexander Graham Bell were quintessential garage inventors, the terms "entrepreneurship" and "telecommunications" almost immediately parted company for a century after their seminal contributions. Telecommunications became a huge sector, dominated in the United States by the world's largest private company, AT&T. AT&T's patents gave it an early hold on the market. After these patents expired, the company cemented its dominant position by making deals with the emerging small independent local firms that operated mostly in rural areas and did not compete with it. The ensuing system was, to an extraordinary extent, an equilibrium – economically, socially, politically, and technologically. Telephone service was available and affordable from Manhattan to Alaska. Service orientation was strong. Reasonable efficiency prevailed, especially in contrast with the state-owned systems elsewhere in the world. Technological progress was steady, with the Bell Labs a well-funded magnet for talent. Technical standards were the same throughout the country and made interoperability easy. Shareholders were happy, and AT&T stock was a favorite blue chip for orphans, widows, and endowments. Unions were strong and cooperative, their members well paid. The national security establishment, using the Bell system as a key resource, was among AT&T's strongest supporters. The company's undeniable power was moderated by regulation, and the regulators' power was moderated by its decentralization among federal and numerous state jurisdictions. Overall, it is difficult to conceive of another sector in the American economy into the 1970s that, in the public's mind, functioned better and more harmoniously. Whatever problems existed were outside of public view.

One generation later, the telecommunications sector stands transformed. AT&T is a shadow of its former self, after a fourth (or is it the sixth?) divestiture. Its former equipment arm Lucent is barely skirting bankruptcy and foreign ownership. Half the regional Bell companies have disappeared. The survivors have ballooned into entities almost as large as the old AT&T, which had been seen as too unwieldy, yet without that company's full range of services. New companies have fared even worse: Most entrants, whether in long distance or in local service, are on the ropes. Shareholders have absorbed vast losses. Unions are weakened. Standards for equipment have proliferated, especially in new technological areas, such as mobile telephony. Consumers are confused. And government is using telecommunications as a cash cow for its budget deficits through the extraction of huge spectrum fees. Where competition exists (as in the market for broadband Internet services), it is among traditional monopolists (telephone DSL versus cable modems in this case) rather than among entrepreneurial entrants.

In interpreting the change, one should neither be nostalgic nor look at the present through rose-colored glasses nor ferret in closets for dark conspiracies. What happened to upset the equilibrium of yore? In a word, entrepreneurship. Rarely has such a small band had such great effect. But it is not the traditional story. The entrepreneurs did not so much destabilize AT&T in the marketplace. They destabilized it in the policy arena.

All of AT&T's horses and all of its men could not keep the established order together, against the determined onslaught of – whom exactly? Minor companies that were not especially innovative in technology or services. AT&T, the long-standing monopolist, was full of inefficiency, complacency, and arrogance, but those things do not bring a company down unless the competitors are very effective. Among the milestone challengers, the *Carterfone* company opened the equipment market to new entrants; its product was a device that patched radio transmission into telecommunications networks. The company and its product soon returned to economic and technological obscurity, leaving its mark mainly in the law books. Most consumer equipment now hails from Taiwan and Japan. On the long distance network side, *MCI* is better known, although it did not survive as a corporate entity. Its great contribution was in marketing, not in technology. As for local networks, the new carriers *Teleport* and *MFS* were rapidly absorbed into the major companies and have not been heard of again.

If the new firms failed to make a big dent, what then explains the success of these entrepreneurs in bringing the world's largest corporation to its knees? In one word: government. Government policy (including the courts) allied itself, after a few uncertain years, with the new firms. This meant, for example, that AT&T was required to design its network interfaces to interoperate with anybody else's consumer equipment. It had to grant its competitors interconnection into its local and long distance networks and to provide access to its customers, its poles and ducts, and its wholesale lines for retail resale. Then, in 1982, it was dismantled by the government in the largest forced business spin-off in history: the AT&T divestiture. Subsequently, government policy expanded the entrants' rights to access physically the switching facilities of the established successor "Baby Bell" companies, to interconnect into them at favorable prices, to obtain favorable wholesale prices for resale, and to get access to unbundled network elements.

This regulatory process was not without zigs and zags by the federal government, and the states occasionally dragged their feet as well. But it is fair to conclude that without the protective umbrella of government and without regulation, relying instead purely on general commercial and antitrust laws, entrepreneurs in the telecommunications industry would have been in dire straits. Left to itself, AT&T would have either prevented their emergence, denied them access to users and technology, or bear-hugged them into cooperation as it had done with the entrepreneurial ventures of the early twentieth century.

It is interesting to speculate where entrepreneurial entrants might have survived. In the equipment field, it is likely that AT&T would have relented its grip somewhat with the variety of equipment options emerging worldwide, and would have focused on network utilization rather than on full control of all equipment. New companies would have emerged as suppliers of specialized equipment, often with close ties to the computer sector. Consumer electronics companies would have provided mass products such as answering machines or low-end fax appliances. AT&T would have kept control over network equipment, with occasional niches for specialized equipment under its sufferance, since it would have been the standard setter and predominant buyer. AT&T would have dominated the emerging Internet service provider (ISP) market, with Internet connectivity merely another service option. Value-added networks, portals, and e-commerce merchants would have been mildly encouraged by the network monopoly as generators of traffic but these users would likely have been forced to operate under restrictive policies.

When it comes to networks themselves, however, it is hard to imagine any significant rival entrants surviving, including in mobile telephony, without an umbrella of governmental protection. Even for the cable TV companies and their networks, the most likely scenario of a laissez-faire market would have been for them to be swallowed by the national telecommunications monopoly. Why did this scenario of AT&T dominance not happen? Why did government policy side with the weak bands of entrepreneurs instead of with the well-heeled troops of AT&T, which were marching in lockstep with much of America? Why could AT&T not simply capture the regulatory system and then charge consumers for the cost of doing so?

There are several possible explanations. The first is anti-big-business ideology. For much of its history, America has loved competition but disliked its winners. The busting of the Standard Oil trust, the fragmentation of banks and broadcasters, and the regulation of railroads are all products of a political perspective shared by the political left and the small-business right. Being leery of the world's largest corporation was hence natural. The flip side was the hold that entrepreneurship exercised over the American mind. Politicians reveled in it. Academic economists extolled it. The anti-establishment sentiments of the late 1960s merged with the Chicago economics of the 1970s into the Washington politics of the 1980s and beyond.

A second reason was the recognition by regulators that they could improve their position and power by supporting competitors. Facing a monopoly, regulators are in the uncomfortable position of lacking independent leverage to make the monopolist toe the line. With competitors, information is developed by adversary sources, and regulators become judges between rival claimants rather than enforcers out on a limb. Related was the fact that American telecommunications regulation was not a centralized affair. It included, on the federal level, the Federal Communications Commission (FCC), the Justice Department, the Commerce Department, the Pentagon, the courts, and Congress, to name just the major players. On the state level, fifty-one public utility commissions (often directly elected) and legislatures had their own perspectives and powers. Hence, telecommunications policy in the United States has never been a neat battle, but a series of endless skirmishes. It was easier to destabilize such a decentralized system than one where a coherent national legislation would have been required, as was the case in Europe.

The third reason was that the entrepreneurs, though weak themselves, had powerful business allies. These were, to some extent, the new electronic industries associated with computers and mass communications that were outside the orbit of AT&T's telecommunications empire, fearing its expansion and coveting its market. These industries included established players like IBM and RCA, but also newer firms in the ascending Silicon Valley. However, much more important allies to new telecommunications entrepreneurs than equipment rivals were the big *users* of telecommunications services. As the size and scope and reach of users grew, so did the importance of information flows and communication. Telecommunications became a major cost item and subject for managerial attention. Specialized corporate telecommunications staffs emerged, and one thing they noticed quickly was that they were contributing disproportionately to the American telecommunications system. That system kept consumers and rural customers happy by overcharging business and urban customers. Corporate users had accepted their lot in the equilibrium system with a grumble, partly because telecommunications were for a while not a huge budget item, partly because all firms benefited from the widespread reach of telecommunications to every household, and partly because they had no alternative. When MCI and its progeny emerged, their basic value proposition was not that they provided better technology or service, but rather that they would reduce their customers' contribution to redistribution and diversity. Competition also lessened the risk that came with putting all one's telecommunications eggs into one carrier's basket. Entrepreneurs did not so much bust a trust as split a policy coalition. They gave the subsidizing partners in that arrangement the possibility to exit and save money. Large users pressured the government for choice and deregulation, but what they primarily sought was de-redistribution. And this is what happened indeed. Where once businesses paid more than residents for service, they now pay less.

The way to reconcile entrepreneurship and the previously existing social compact – to have one's cake and eat it, too – was to believe that competition-induced efficiency gains would more than offset negative redistributional impacts. This belief hinged on the assumption that economies of scale were not of a magnitude that would lead to a "natural monopoly" but permitted a competitive equilibrium. Of this, more later. The high-water mark of this set of ideas was the 1996 Telecommunications Act. That law was proclaimed by its sponsors and supporters to be the revolutionary opening of the telecommunications business to full competition (which it never was, except in the eyes of a Washington-centric press) and the guarantor and even extender of cheap universal service to rural areas.

Whatever its inconsistencies, the Act stampeded an underinformed stock market into a huge telecommunications rally, on top of the general tech-exuberance. But from there, the drop was fast and furious. The various variants of local exchange companies – so-called CLECs, BLECS, and DLECS – are either out of business or barely alive. In long distance service, all three major carriers are in effect for sale. AT&T is breaking itself up and selling off its parts. Resellers have lost their key role in arbitrage. Independent wireless providers have mostly been absorbed by the major telecommunications carriers.

Wall Street, always quick to spot a trend after the fact, shut down telecommunications financing. Initial public offerings became rare. Junk bond funding, long a mainstay for new networks, disappeared. Venture capitalists moved to the sidelines. Vendor financing, in which companies such as Lucent or Nortel funded new networks in return for orders, declined, along with the health of the vendors themselves. And for existing equities, entrant share prices have dropped sickeningly.

What makes this train of tragedies remarkable is that regulatory policy, as discussed, was firmly on the side of the entrepreneurial entrants. The implementation of the 1996 Act by the FCC and the state PUCs was clearly not only procompetition but also procompetitor. It did not merely open the market to entrants, but it gave them a dose of infant protection. That extra step was a logical one, since without functioning competitors there would be no competition, and government policy would fail. This aid made government helpful to entrants, but also a hostage to their success.

And yet, even with a governmental thumb on the scales, the competitors have so far been routed. The reasons are not hard to find.

1. It is Difficult to Do Competitive Telecommunications

Network operations are complex. Many systems (infrastructure, hardware, software, customer service, payment systems, customization) need to be in place and to be integrated. Service must be operational domestically and often internationally, at lightning speed, with great reliability, with easy scalability and flexibility of configuration. None of this is easy or cheap. It became apparent soon after deregulation that the costs of new networks were higher than expected, from truck rolls to customer acquisition to capacity planning. And the incumbents were not passively accepting their challengers but instead fighting them through market responses, foot-dragging, and regulatory delay. They were helped by the risk-averse attitudes of important customers who wanted to be sure that the new network provider would be around next month.

2. Economies of Scale are Back

On the supply side, the fixed costs of network operations tend to be high, but the variable cost of spreading the service is relatively low – the classic attributes of "natural" monopoly. On the demand side, there are positive "network externalities" of having large user communities. Put these three things together – high fixed costs, low marginal costs, and network externalities – and there are real advantages to being large.

For a while, one could ignore these economies of scale because the inefficiency of the incumbents masked them and provided an umbrella. Network externalities were extended to entrants through requirements to interconnect. But the inefficiency of incumbents declined with the threat of competition, and eventually the advantages of being large re-asserted themselves even though the incumbents were slower moving than small entrants.

3. The New Telecommunications Network Environment Is Not Linear But Cyclical

Cyclicality is not new for infrastructure industries. Early railroads were vastly overbuilt in the United States. A century ago, one could take twelve different private railroad routes between New York and Chicago alone. Most of these lines failed and were absorbed by competitors. One of the functions of cyclical slowdowns is consolidation;

competition and commodification are reduced, whereas profitability is enhanced. After profitability is restored, new entrants emerge, investments in capacity pick up, and a new boom-bust cycle emerges. These cycles, so evident in railroading, are equally common in many other industries. But in telecommunications they are an entirely new phenomenon. Therefore, the industry was unprepared to manage reversals in the patterns of capacity and demand. The various network companies, in the aggregate, projected long distance market shares that added up to about 250 percent of the market. Everybody built capacity to overwhelm competitors and gain size. In consequence, some carriers wound up using as little as 10 percent of their capacity, leaving 90 percent "dark," and prices not surprisingly dropped dramatically. Such fluctuations led to consolidation as a way to stabilize the industry.

THE PROSPECTS OF ENTREPRENEURSHIP

The implications of the analysis thus far are that, far from establishing themselves, new entrants have energized incumbents into displaying the strength of their size and bottleneck powers. We must therefore conclude that entrepreneurship in telecommunications is in a deep structural crisis, even assuming that new ventures are more nimble and innovative than incumbents, and that the viability of such entrepreneurship ultimately depends on government. Given economies of scale and scope, the commodity aspects of many of the services, and the network externalities for users, size matters in networks. Even where smaller networks might be possible, they would have to interconnect with the larger ones, and such interconnection is not likely to be forthcoming without regulatory intervention. Hence, a return to monopoly or at least oligopoly seems the likely result if the telecommunications market is left to itself.

This is true for the actual physical networks, but it also has implications for network applications and for equipment, where the economies of scale tend to be much lower. Research has found that new entrant firms to the telecommunications equipment industry were on average more innovative than the large established firms, partly due to innovative reconfiguration of existing components (Dowling and McGee 1994).

These products and services are dependent, however, on using or interconnecting with the networks. They are therefore at the mercy of the network providers, which can, absent clear antitrust constraints, set conditions, favor affiliated and vertically integrated firms, and otherwise hamper innovative entrants.

There is no reason to believe that these economies are only temporary. To the contrary, one reason for the reassertion of economies of scale is the trend toward the broadbanding of networks. Communications become largely distance and time insensitive, flat-priced, ubiquitous, and always on. More of the intelligent processing has been moving to the periphery, to users and specialized value-added providers, and away from the network providers. Networks are thus in danger of becoming commodity transport facilities.

All this has implications for public policy. We are now at a crossroads. Should policymakers tip the scales further in the direction of the entrepreneurs? Or should they let market forces take over, which will lead to ever larger established companies? Under the George W. Bush Administration, the FCC chairman has proposed to end his agency's review of mergers, and the Justice Department is likely to be friendlier to them. Incumbent Baby Bells have or are close to receiving approval to offer long distance service for customers of their home markets. And the Wall Street community has shifted its financial bets and political weight from the entrants to the incumbents.

This shift creates a window of opportunity for major mergers. We might therefore soon reach a national market structure of only three or four telecommunications companies, vertically integrated into long distance, owning the major long distance companies, plus most wireless and ISP backbones. Thus, the core of telecommunications – the network industry, a sector of some $150 billion – will not be hospitable territory for entrepreneurs for the next few years, even as demand for the networks' services continue to expand.

The problem is not one of a temporary downturn on Wall Street that will correct itself soon. The problems in telecommunications are more fundamental, and investor behavior is merely a reflection of this reality. Basic telecommunications transmission has shown itself to be a commodity business. That is why we have less vigorous competition today than two or three years ago. Thus, it is not clear at all that all that is needed is time and patience. Economies of scale and scope are strong. And entrants need the cooperation of the incumbents. Add the three together and it is very hard for entrants to survive.

Such a pessimistic scenario should not obscure the fact that we have just gone through a significant period of rejuvenation and innovation, arguably the most creative period in telecommunications business history. The telecommunications entrepreneurs might not be successful at present, but they have created an important legacy.

1. They have forced the incumbents to shape up and become more efficient.
2. They initiated the creation of a regulatory environment that will permit them to try a comeback.
3. They have created a mechanism for the financing of entry, which will enable a second round of entry in the future.
4. They have created a different mindset and style.

Given the contributions of entrepreneurs, it will be useful for governments to protect their entry or at least their potential future entry. This end might be achieved, in the classic way of government-supported entrepreneurship, through policy tools such as subsidies, free trade zones, tax breaks, education, and so on. But in the telecommunications sector, all these tools pale before the need to create a regulatory environment in which network competition becomes possible, which can then be extended to the other parts of the sector, while at the same time not guaranteeing the survival of inefficient entrants. This is a tall order.

With such an umbrella, there will be plenty of opportunity for telecommunications innovators to supply new tools and ideas. As the market keeps growing, niches open. Entrants could bundle and integrate services, find opportunities in arbitrage, or become suppliers of specialized inputs bundled by incumbents.

Thus, new entrants will find opportunities again. But given that they are riding on the coattails of government, and that government is not normally in the business of revolution, entrepreneurship will be a domesticated process, possibly creative, but not likely destructive.

For this chapter, the author referenced Abernathy and Clark 1985; Baldwin and Clark 1997; Birley 1985, Butler and Carney 1986; Crockett and Elstrom 1998; Dowling and Ruefli 1992; Dowling and McGee 1994; Friar and Horwitch 1986; Hambrick 1983; Hambrick, Nadler, and Tushman 1998; Harrigan 1988; Haveman 1992; Hubbard and Gentry 2000; Kamien and Schwartz 1975; Kelly 1997; Low and MacMillan 1988; Maddy 2000; Mosakowski 1983; Noam 2001; Pages 2001; Schumpeter 1942; Shapiro and Varian 1998; Stein 1997; Tapscott 1995; Triendl 1999; Tushman and O'Reilly III 1997; and West and Ivie 2001.

PART FIVE

IMPLEMENTING ENTREPRENEURSHIP POLICY

12

Knowledge, Power, and Entrepreneurs

A First Pass at the Politics of Entrepreneurship Policy

David M. Hart

The politics of entrepreneurship policy are underdeveloped. Entrepreneurs have their hands full building businesses and typically ignore, if not disdain, collective action aimed at the public good. Yet entrepreneurial success depends critically on good governance, which can only emerge through collective action of some sort. Policymakers, on the other hand, are acutely aware that their terms in office depend heavily on the vitality of the economy and the industries that drive its growth, but they often lack the knowledge and power to devise and implement policies that would enhance economic growth by fostering entrepreneurship.

The entrepreneurial and policy communities have much to offer one another. The involvement of entrepreneurs in designing and supporting entrepreneurship policy could make the efforts of policymakers more politically viable and economically effective. The links between them are thin at best, however, and sometimes nonexistent. Skeptics on both sides of the entrepreneur/policymaker divide have reasonable grounds for their doubts. Entrepreneurship policy advocates must build institutions and change ingrained beliefs if they want to construct durable coalitions that bridge the divide and produce good policy outcomes.

This chapter explores the problems and promise of coalition building between entrepreneurs and policymakers. The argument is largely theoretical and hypothesis-framing, since little empirical work has been done in this area. I begin by making the case for the importance of this coalition, arguing that there is no adequate substitute for the power and knowledge that a politically engaged entrepreneurial community can bring to the policy process. I then turn to the barriers that impede such engagement and mechanisms that might overcome them. The last major section of the chapter addresses the concerns of policymakers, particularly the fear that entrepreneurs will attempt to use their involvement in the policy process to secure public resources for private gain.

KNOWLEDGE AND POWER IN THE ENTREPRENEURSHIP POLICY PROCESS

As other chapters of this volume argue in considerable detail, public policy has emerged as an increasingly significant element in the context for entrepreneurship in the contemporary United States. The development of the knowledge economy is one of the key factors behind this trend. Knowledge-based businesses are more dependent on public goods and on regulatory systems, broadly construed, than their counterparts in earlier economic epochs. Governance processes at all levels, from local to national (and even beyond), determine, for instance, whether educated people are available to start up and work in knowledge-based businesses and whether suppliers, producers, and customers can exchange confidential information securely and inexpensively. Research on the appropriate content of entrepreneurship policy, that is, what governments and other partners in governance ought to do to facilitate the start-up and scale-up of firms, has grown rapidly in recent years, although there is still much work left to do.

Much less attention has been paid by scholars to the process of developing and implementing entrepreneurship policy. This gap in our understanding matters because the policy process always influences the content of policy. No matter how good their intentions, participants in the policy process inevitably have limited time and information. And no matter how hard they try to be objective, they cannot fully shed preconceptions built over a lifetime of experience and training. Knowledge about and conceptions of the public interest inherited from the past, filtered through the confusion of the present, inevitably shape the future (March and Olsen 1984; Simon 1957).

Moreover, many participants in the policy process will be pursuing specific interests, rather than the public interest. Bargains must usually be made to gain support from some of these interests. Such bargains not only shape the distribution of immediate gains from policy implementation, but also the politics of any future rounds of policy-making. They may establish, for instance, which interests have a voice in implementing or modifying policy. The structure of power today may therefore be reproduced in tomorrow's decision-making, even if it has changed in the meantime (Lowi 1964).

The knowledge and power linkages between policy process and policy content are likely to be particularly strong in the making of entrepreneurship policy. Entrepreneurship policymakers must be knowledgeable about an extremely complex environment. A close understanding of market conditions in particular sectors of the economy, for instance, is likely to be relevant to their efforts. In many knowledge-intensive sectors, an accurate assessment of technological opportunities is equally essential. Moreover, both markets and technologies are changing, sometimes quickly, and policymakers must try to look forward to gauge trends. More than a modicum of knowledge about markets, technologies, and trends is required even if the minimal objective of doing no harm is adopted by policymakers, and much more is required if creative interventions in the environment for entrepreneurship are envisioned.

Effective entrepreneurship policy-making makes heavy demands on power resources as well as knowledge resources. Entrepreneurial firms are by definition doing something new and different. Customers, these firms hope, will find their activities valuable, but competitors might not. If these competitors are in the same jurisdiction as their potential rivals, they may attempt to block policies that facilitate entrepreneurship. This form of protectionism is less familiar and visible than protectionism in international trade, but quite widespread, particularly at the state level in the United States (Atkinson 2001). In addition, entrepreneurship policy should be constantly shifting toward ever-emerging opportunities. Current beneficiaries may try to lock in any advantages they gain from a policy regime and prevent it from evolving. Finally, in many cases, entrepreneurship policy presents an ideological challenge to the status quo. The application of power may be the only way to break through the cognitive filters and political resistance tied to ideology.

In a nutshell, "creative destruction," as Joseph Schumpeter would have it, makes for challenging politics. Entrepreneurship policymakers need a lot of knowledge and a lot of power to do their jobs right. In the American context, with its weak civil service and decentralized institutions, such policymakers are constitutionally denied ready access to these resources. In any case, even if a "strong" government solution to the challenges of entrepreneurship policy-making could be tried, it would not work. Too much vital knowledge, and perhaps some essential forms of power as well, reside only in the private sector. That is not to say that government should be "weak" (Katznelson 1992). As I discuss below, government agencies need substantial capacity to analyze and implement entrepreneurship policy. But they simply cannot govern effectively without partners.

THE POLITICAL RESOURCES OF ENTREPRENEURS

Just whose knowledge and power, beyond those of government, ought to be drawn upon in making entrepreneurship policy is not a question with a simple answer. The specific members of any support coalition will depend on many factors, including the level of governance, the composition of the economy, and the political situation. At the local level, for instance, the classic participants in the "urban growth machine," such as real estate developers, bankers, and retailers, may have important roles to play in adding an entrepreneurship thrust to the economic development policy portfolio (Logan and Molotch 1987; Logan, Whaley, and Crowder 1997; Miranda and Rosdil 1995). Universities, which are increasingly relied on by state and local governments to be catalysts of economic growth, in part by fostering start-ups, might bring valuable insights as well as clout to the process (Feller 1990a). Entrepreneurs possess a unique set of political resources, however, that makes their presence more necessary in entrepreneurship policy-making than any other potential participant. Their knowledge and their power may not be enough to ensure a winning coalition, but their absence raises the probability of failed initiatives and flawed policies.

Knowledge about markets and technologies, and about opportunities where the two come together, is the most vital asset that entrepreneurs possess. At the outset of the entrepreneurial process, before any investments are made, it is the only asset they have. The only other actors who might possess the relevant knowledge are the incumbent businesses who are potential targets for entrepreneurial entry. Other potential participants in the policy process are likely to lack either the interest to discover what entrepreneurs know or the expertise to interpret that information. Knowledge of both the status quo and opportunities for change permits the identification of points of leverage where policy can play a constructive role. Such knowledge is necessary but not sufficient for policy-making. It must be verified in some fashion and linked to a realistic understanding of the capacity of government and other entities that may be carrying out public policy, issues that are addressed below.

The political power of entrepreneurs is less evident and less essential for policy-making than their knowledge, but nonetheless is potentially very valuable. It is important to note that entrepreneurs typically do not possess many of the political resources that are often associated with business, especially big business. For instance, they cannot effectively wield "structural power," the implicit threat to invest elsewhere or not at all in exchange for concessions, a form of power sometimes attributed to large firms, especially those that dominate a jurisdiction's economy (Lindblom 1977). Entrepreneurs usually do not have much "instrumental power" either, that is, conventional political assets like lobbyists and campaign contributions that can be dedicated to pushing a specific agenda, although such assets can be developed over time.

What entrepreneurs do have, though, is credibility and legitimacy in the eyes of the public and its elected representatives. Entrepreneurs are respected more than most other groups in American society. They capture media attention, particularly in political contexts, where their presence is usually unexpected. The high status of entrepreneurs is deeply inscribed in American political culture and will survive even the punctured dreams of the Internet boom era.

The knowledge and power of the entrepreneurial community have not often been brought to bear in the policy-making process. Firm size remains one of the most powerful determinants of measurable involvement in national politics. Entrepreneurial firms may be found in the membership of some national trade associations, but such participation is more likely to signify interest in nonpolitical activities like standard setting and trade shows than in the associations' public policy efforts, which tend to be dominated by larger members. At the state and local level, too, nonparticipation in policy-making is the norm. IBM, for example, is far more likely to be represented in the membership and leadership of policy-relevant business organizations at these levels than its entrepreneurial rivals (Rae 1994; Hart 2001b). This norm is one plausible explanation for the "shallow foundations" (as Peter Eisinger, 1995, puts it) of entrepreneurship policy, as it has emerged to date.

MOBILIZING ENTREPRENEURS

The absence of entrepreneurs from the policy process is not a moral failing on their part. They have no particular duty to participate in policy-making above and beyond that of other citizens. However, entrepreneurs may have a special *interest* in shaping governance – improvement in the environment for entrepreneurship – that they fail to recognize or are unable to act on. The barriers to participation are diverse.

Perhaps the biggest and most intractable barrier is lack of time and energy. Entrepreneurship is, by all accounts, an exhausting and all-consuming process. (See Ferguson 1999, for one such account.) Entrepreneurs plunge into business – body, mind, and bank account – and block out all distractions, sometimes including family, all the more so public policy. A sort of tunnel vision often sets in, drastically limiting the scope of information to which entrepreneurs pay attention and activities in which they take part.

Lack of information compounds time pressure. Even if an entrepreneur considers whether it would be worthwhile to get involved in policy-making, she must be convinced that the required investment of time and energy will yield a commensurate payoff. Such information is not usually readily available and may not even exist. Although broad relationships between certain forms of governance and the entrepreneurial vigor of places and societies can be established (as other chapters in this volume attest), specific benefits to specific firms or individuals are much more difficult to demonstrate. At best, public policies may slightly better the long odds for all entrepreneurial ventures. An entrepreneur who has to supply to an investor (or spouse) a bottom-line justification for spending time at policy-related meetings may reasonably choose to skip them on the principle of "better safe than sorry" in the face of ignorance.

The politically rational entrepreneur has other reasons to abstain from participation. He may simply choose to let others do the work of the community. If those others fail to devise a good policy, at least the entrepreneur has not wasted his time and energy in the effort. If they succeed, he shares in the benefits anyway (Olson 1965). In addition, the rational entrepreneur may reasonably doubt whether any policy can be enacted and implemented quickly enough to make a difference to the fate of his business. And he may doubt whether such a policy will be sustained through multiple election cycles and changes of government.

Entrepreneurs aren't necessarily rational, however. If they were, they probably wouldn't be entrepreneurs, since the odds of a start-up succeeding are so low. But the type of person who is drawn to the entrepreneurial gamble is not very likely to be drawn to the challenge of governance, which is a different kind of gamble. The entrepreneurial calling, particularly in the United States, selects for those who have faith in the efficacy of individual action. This faith may translate into ideological conservatism or political apathy, neither of which is conducive to participating in an entrepreneurship policy coalition. The famous "cyber-libertarianism" of many in the information technology industry illustrates the point. Any cognitive dissonance created by acknowledgment of the federal government's important role in establishing and sustaining the industry (Flamm 1988; Langlois and Mowery 1996) is rarely sufficient to undermine the cyber-libertarian belief that government can play anything but a constructive role in the economy (Borsook 2000).

These barriers to the mobilization of entrepreneurs are formidable. They encompass good reasons and bad ones and no reason at all. Given their scale and scope, the participation of a large fraction of entrepreneurs in policy-making is not a realistic objective. Such a mobilization would not be desirable, in any case, if it took much time and energy away from the entrepreneurial process itself. Fortunately, an effective entrepreneurship policy coalition does not necessarily need more than a few entrepreneurs.

Institutions may be imagined that would lower some of the barriers somewhat. Institutions, particularly formal organizations, can serve to legitimate previous deviant norms, build trust among suspicious parties, and routinize activities that were once expensive. Representative groups of entrepreneurs mobilized through new institutions have the potential to bring relevant knowledge and requisite power to bear on the making of entrepreneurship policy.

One sort of institution for mobilizing entrepreneurs concentrates on changing their cultural milieu. The appeal made in this context is oriented to a sense of duty, perhaps, or the promise of fame, rather than to a rational calculation of costs and benefits. Some entrepreneurs may find engagement in policy-making psychologically gratifying, if not financially remunerative, especially if they receive recognition for their investment of time and energy.

The Technology Network (TechNet) is an example, albeit imperfect, of this kind of institution. TechNet's signature activity has been bringing CEOs of Silicon Valley start-ups together with leading politicians. The CEOs enjoy the excitement of rubbing shoulders with their visitors from Washington, D.C. and savor the appreciation of TechNet's organizers, who include some of the best regarded venture capitalists in the Valley. At the peak of the Internet boom, TechNet events drew enthusiastic crowds and credulous notices in the political press (Miles 2001). How much of a cultural change TechNet has achieved and whether its momentum can be sustained are open questions, now that the boom is over. The organization has endured substantial turnover in its staff, and its membership is not so much of a magnet for politicians as it was a couple of years ago when members' capital gains were very large.

A second approach to mobilizing entrepreneurs focuses on cutting the costs of involvement. Although entrepreneurship policy advocates cannot add hours to the entrepreneur's day, they may be able to reduce the time commitment of involvement in public policy and enhance the sense of efficacy felt by those who choose to get involved. The public-private partnership is a popular vehicle for pursuing this approach. Such partnerships come in many forms and have many objectives, but all seek to reduce bureaucratic impediments in policy design and implementation, in part by taking advantage of the capacities of the private partners instead of red tape-encumbered public agencies.

The Arizona Governor's Strategic Partnership for Economic Development demonstrates this process at work. As Mary Jo Waits (2000) describes it, this partnership has been a particularly effective mechanism for engaging representatives of such emerging industries as environmental technology, software, and optics in policy-making. "Many [optics industry executives] began to firmly believe that, by contributing time to developing the state's capacity to support optics companies, they could turn Arizona into an international center of excellence"

(45). Effective public-private partnerships are not easy to build and maintain, however, especially when the partners are unequal. They often degenerate into – or are designed to be – merely symbolic entities.

Improving the quality and credibility of information about entrepreneurship policy and facilitating access to it by entrepreneurs constitutes a third mechanism for mobilizing entrepreneurs. Information will not overcome cultural and ideological barriers, since these beliefs and values tend to filter out anything that might contradict them. On the other hand, for entrepreneurs who are less set in their views, the findings of research that relates policy outcomes to entrepreneurial outcomes may provide sufficient motivation to spur involvement.

The National Commission on Entrepreneurship (NCOE) is one organization that takes this approach.[1] Based in Washington, D.C., and sponsored by the Kauffman Center for Entrepreneurial Leadership (KCEL), the NCOE bills itself as a resource for anyone interested in entrepreneurship and public policy. NCOE staff, for instance, ran a series of focus groups of entrepreneurs around the country in 2000. The meetings served the dual purpose of gathering policy-relevant knowledge and building a constituency for NCOE's advocacy. KCEL's patronage (an arrangement not uncommon among public interest groups (Walker 1991)) and the Commission's membership of successful entrepreneurs and venture capitalists add credibility to the effort, but do not ensure a positive reception. Crafting messages that break out of the noise in Washington, D.C. and translate effectively on both sides of the entrepreneur/policymaker divide remains a major challenge for the organization.

Any approach to mobilization, including the three outlined above, can at best draw in only a few entrepreneurs who are predisposed, for some reason or other, to get involved in policy-making. The newly mobilized may have a taste for fame or public service or be those who are most likely to benefit individually from a change in policy. The mobilizing institutions have strong incentives to make such selection biases even more powerful, possibly to the point of undermining their

---

[1] Full disclosure: The National Commission on Entrepreneurship and Kauffman Center for Entrepreneurial Leadership sponsored the conference that led to this volume. This volume itself, to the extent that it reaches entrepreneurs as well as academics and policymakers, might be considered an element in the informational approach to mobilization.

claims to represent entrepreneurs and their capacity to bring to bear the entrepreneurial community's unique political resources. TechNet, for instance, depends on its members to sustain itself and has been inevitably drawn to admit executives of mature and stable (and thus less entrepreneurial) firms, like Microsoft and Intel, into its leadership ranks. NCOE's commissioners have strong track records, but many are no longer active entrepreneurs; one worries whether they have the most relevant knowledge to contribute to entrepreneurship policy-making.

Such concerns, although legitimate, ought not necessarily lead to the conclusion that mobilizing entrepreneurs is a hopeless endeavor. The mobilization cannot be perfectly representative, but it might be good enough. Judging whether it meets this standard, and thus whether groups and individuals claiming to represent entrepreneurs bring the right kind of knowledge and power to the policy process, is the responsibility of policymakers.

CHECKS AND BALANCES

Andrew Grove's famous dictum, "only the paranoid survive," applies to policymakers equally as well as to the entrepreneurs to whom it was originally directed. Suspicion is the natural condition of both groups, despite the optimistic face they present to the outside world. Policymakers are particularly suspicious of those who equate their special interest with the public interest. Although this equation is sometimes valid, specious claims to the public purse and public authority are the norm. Entrepreneurs interested in entrepreneurship policy, like farmers interested in agricultural policy or defense contractors interested in national security policy, will inevitably try to make the equation and must endure close scrutiny of their claims.

Entrepreneurial motivation is an important basis for this suspicion. Entrepreneurs usually want to get rich (although they may also have other motivations, such as self-fulfillment). Some entrepreneurs will say or do virtually anything to achieve their goal, as any venture capitalist or loan officer will attest. Policymakers want to feel confident that any policies that aim to help entrepreneurs make money also contribute to the well-being of the larger society, rather than merely redistribute revenue from the public to a few well-placed private beneficiaries. They may even want to be assured that helping entrepreneurs get rich is a better way to advance societal goals than the available alternatives.

Even if one assumes that the desire to get rich does not lead entrepreneurs to intentionally mislead policymakers, there are grounds for concern about the quality of information that they bring into the policy process. Most start-ups fail, a fact that implies that many entrepreneurs make incorrect judgments or rely on inaccurate information. Transference of even the best-intended "irrational exuberance" from private decision-making to the policy process is a recipe for failure. Not every region can become the next Silicon Valley, no matter how dearly its local boosters may desire it (Leslie 2001). Policymakers need to be able to sort the wheat from the chaff.

To these worries about the knowledge provided by entrepreneurs who are drawn into policy deliberations must be added a concern about their claim to legitimacy, which is a key source of their power, as I argue above. This legitimacy stems in part from popular enthusiasm for the underdog. Although executives from large firms may seek (and sometimes even deserve) to be labeled "entrepreneurial," that image is difficult for them to maintain in the fishbowl of public attention. At least some of the business participants in entrepreneurship policy-making must be genuine small fry. Paradoxically, though, some measure of success also contributes to the political legitimacy of entrepreneurs. The most politically desirable entrepreneurs, then, are those who are successful, but not too successful. The "serial" entrepreneur, who has a track record of building companies but regularly renews her underdog credentials by starting new ones, may be the most desirable participant of all.

A well-structured entrepreneurship policy process ought to have the capacity to weed out lies, misrepresentations, and unintentionally distorted information, whether pertaining to entrepreneurs, markets, or technologies. This capacity might be vested, at least in part, in government agencies. Although civil servants may be unable to generate knowledge about entrepreneurial opportunities, they can check out information provided by private sector participants in policy-making. These efforts cannot eliminate risk and should not try to do so; risk is inherent in entrepreneurship and thus in entrepreneurship policy as well. Instead, this kind of check should eliminate the most foolhardy ideas on the one hand and the safest bets on the other, while providing an unvarnished assessment of those in between.

Technical competence, rooted in formal education, is an essential element of the capacity to assess the claims of entrepreneurs. But this capacity is also something that cumulates over time through learning by doing among both individuals and organizations. Research suggests that an organization's experience with entrepreneurship policy improves the quality of outcomes and raises the likelihood that the policy will be maintained and expanded (Clarke and Gaile 1989). The emergence of entrepreneurship policy, then, does not mean that the state should be hollowed out or become a virtual organization, assembled on a task-by-task basis (Porter 1990). The public partners in policy-making must be robust and stable to play their roles effectively.

Another obvious way to enhance the entrepreneurship policy process is to encompass within it multiple private viewpoints. If there were not differing assessments of opportunities among private actors, there would be no entrepreneurship. By bringing these differences out and debating them, policymakers can understand the factors that underlie them. The purpose of these debates is not necessarily to produce a policy that is a compromise among the views expressed. Markets often show that one assessment was right, and another was wrong, and policymakers should not shy from concluding that such is the case.

The development of substantial bureaucratic capacity and the inclusion of multiple perspectives are commonsense checks and balances in the entrepreneurship policy process. They reduce the chances that the process will be captured by special interests whose betterment contributes little to the society around them. They help to prevent the starry-eyed leader from chasing every new thing that catches his fancy. These checks and balances make the process more deliberate and also more sustainable over the long term.

CONCLUSION

In the entrepreneurship policy process, as in any other policy process, both knowledge and power are important. This chapter argues that entrepreneurs themselves can provide these political resources and that they should be mobilized to participate in policy-making, subject to a set of checks and balances. There are many pitfalls along the path to creating an effective coalition between entrepreneurs and policymakers, many opportunities for the process to be captured, led astray, or torpedoed. The process requires patience, which, unlike suspicion, is not a quality usually associated with either partner in the coalition (Eisinger 1995).

This analysis is admittedly provisional. The study of the politics of entrepreneurship policy, a sprawling and complex domain of governance, has only just begun. Empirical research on support coalitions is sorely lacking. Further distinctions must be made among the levels of governance, which are blurred together here. The particularities of regions, states, and localities must be borne in mind. Yet, if the reader takes seriously the linkages between process and content discussed early in this chapter, then he must conclude that such research merits as much effort as conventional policy analysis and evaluation.

13

Entrepreneurship as a State and Local Economic Development Strategy

Erik R. Pages, Doris Freedman, and Patrick Von Bargen

Throughout the 1980s and 1990s, the rise of the entrepreneur was widely reported in the business press. New firms, led by previously unknown entrepreneurs like Michael Dell, Bill Gates, and Steve Case, came to dominate their respective industries, leading young people from all walks of life to want to start their own businesses instead of joining large companies. New magazines like *Inc.*, *Fast Company*, and *Entrepreneur* emerged to educate budding moguls on how they could get into the entrepreneurship game. Entrepreneurship was "The New New Thing," to borrow the title of Michael Lewis's popular study of the rise of Netscape (Lewis 2000).

As popular culture embraced the entrepreneur,[1] economic development policy largely hewed to business as usual. Despite some rhetorical posturing about the "new economy," neither entrepreneurs nor high-growth companies have received serious attention or funding from state and local policymakers. A 1998 survey found that entrepreneurial development programs accounted for less than 1 percent of the more than $2 billion in annual state economic development investments (National Association of State Development Agencies 1998). Given the growing importance of entrepreneurship and the clear bottom-line

---

[1] A 1998 Ernst & Young survey of influential Americans found that 78 percent believed that entrepreneurialism will be "the defining trend of the business world in the next century." Survey results available at www.accountingweb.co.uk.

economic benefits generated by high-growth companies, this lack of interest is puzzling.

Fortunately the divide between business trends and the responses of economic development policymakers may be closing. Over the past two to three years, a boomlet of interest in public policy that supports entrepreneurship has developed. Policymakers have begun to gain a greater understanding of the needs of high-growth companies, and new models of economic development policy are emerging in response.[2]

This chapter examines the emergence of entrepreneurship as an economic development strategy at the state and local level in the United States. It addresses several questions. First, what took so long? We review why many economic development policies remain focused on traditional strategies of "smokestack chasing" despite strong evidence that such approaches yield limited returns. Second, we review the key characteristics and programmatic initiatives that are being used to support entrepreneurship at the state and local levels. Finally, we explore several future challenges. By definition, entrepreneurship is a high-risk activity in which failure is frequent, and this characteristic makes it particularly difficult to design and implement an effective policy in support of entrepreneurs. We conclude by offering some ideas about how the challenges to entrepreneurship policy can be overcome.

THE DEVELOPMENT OF DEVELOPMENT

Public officials have sought to sponsor "economic development" for centuries, but the establishment of an economic development profession in the United States is a twentieth-century phenomenon.

Table 13.1 displays four waves of economic development thinking, dating back to the 1930s (Ross and Friedman 1990). The first wave was centered in the Southern states, where public officials sought to jump-start economic development through aggressive recruitment of branch manufacturing plants from the Northeast. Mississippi's Balance Agriculture with Industry Program set the paradigm for the

---

[2] A recent survey of ten Southern states identified more than a thousand organizations and associations in the region that support entrepreneurship. Corporation for Enterprise Development, *Infrastructure for Entrepreneurial Development: A Scan of Ten Southern States for the Mary Reynolds Babcock Foundation*, April 2, 2001.

Table 13.1. *Four Waves of State and Local Economic Development Thinking*

	First Wave 1930s–1940s	Second Wave 1980s	Third Wave 1980s–1990s	Entrepreneurship 1990s–2000s
Challenge	Lagging regions	Structural change	Declining firm competitiveness	Transforming ideas into commercial opportunities
Goal	Attract plants	Create jobs	Improve firm competitiveness	Build base for successful new firms
Targets of Policy	Relocation or new plants of large corporations	New or expanding businesses	Groups or clusters of firms	Active and aspiring entrepreneurs
Means	Marketing subsidies	Separate government programs	Provision of industrial services	Build local support systems
Mode of Intervention	Smokestack chasing	Respond to firm requests	Lead firms in new directions	Training (education)
Organization	State departments of commerce	Multiple state organizations	State-funded local or sectoral organizations	Regional networks
Success Measures	Number of firms attracted	Number of jobs created	Increased firm competitiveness	Business starts / Firm growth

first wave (Cobb 1993). Under this model, state development agency officials engaged in what one called "a buffalo hunt." They publicized their region's low labor costs in more expensive parts of the country and dangled subsidies and incentives to enhance the appeal of relocation. This approach, also known pejoratively as "smokestack chasing," worked as long as states could maintain low-cost labor environments. It also set the tone for much of the emerging profession of economic development. Industrial recruitment remains the primary activity of many economic development organizations today.

The attraction of low-cost labor centers began eroding in the 1970s when new and cheaper foreign competition emerged. As the benefits of smokestack chasing declined, a second wave of economic development thinking came to the fore. Economic restructuring was the dominant challenge facing the second wave. With old manufacturing industries imploding, economic development officials sought new ways to create jobs and diversify local economies by supporting new and existing home-grown businesses. State and local economies strengthened by these measures, it was hoped, would be better able to respond to growing foreign competition from Asia and Western Europe.

Second wave programs focused on offering services that made it easier to do business. When small firms had trouble getting bank loans, capital access programs were created. As new companies needed office space, business incubation boomed. Businesses could not afford training, so training subsidies were developed. These initiatives helped create an infrastructure of business services around the nation. The target of the economic development system changed in the second wave, but the ultimate purpose of these initiatives – lower costs – did not really change. In the first wave, developers created low-cost environments for branch plants of outside businesses. In the second wave, they created a similar environment for existing and new indigenous firms. The policies of Massachusetts under Governor Michael Dukakis exemplify the second wave. Seeking to stem the decline of major industrial centers in the state, the Dukakis administration created a host of new state-funded institutions, such as the Massachusetts Technology Development Corporation, a venture capital fund, and the Bay State Skills Corporation, which focused on workforce development (Nakajima and Smith 2001). The initial success of these efforts, which contributed to the so-called Massachusetts Miracle, helped vault Dukakis to national prominence.

The second wave produced dividends for many communities, but this approach had inherent limitations. The price of improving local capacity was programmatic sprawl, as every new need was met with a new government program. A plethora of new programs created confusion. Worse, the second wave was simply unable to address the major trauma being experienced by regions that had been dependent on forest products, steel, or other manufacturing industries for decades. A more comprehensive approach was required.

Responding to these limitations, a group of analysts developed a new approach, which they dubbed the "Third Wave."[3] The third wave, which began in the 1980s and continued into the 1990s, called for shifts in both the delivery mechanisms and the content of economic development policy. The new approach sought to shift delivery of development assistance away from the public sector. Instead, nonprofits and private organizations were assumed to have a better grasp of business needs and to be able to provide services more effectively. Programs shifted from a provider-driven to a customer-driven model. The content of the third wave went well beyond reducing the cost of doing business in a given community. It moved inside the firm to assist businesses with manufacturing modernization, technology investments, and the like.

As David Audretsch describes in his chapter, globalization and rapid technological change added to the pressure for a more dynamic approach to economic development. Regions grew in importance as organizing units for economic activity, and customary distinctions between federal, state, and local jurisdictions declined in significance. At the same time, the job of economic development grew more complex. Simply creating new jobs and responding to business needs were no longer sufficient. Communities also needed the capacity to innovate. This approach led to a much more comprehensive vision of economic development. No longer would economic development departments "do economic development" alone. Instead, a range of government

---

[3] This movement included many players, but much of the early thinking was associated with Robert Friedman and other analysts from the Corporation for Enterprise Development (CFED). CFED's approach was widely disseminated through the organization's annual Development Report Card of the States. For more information, see http://www.cfed.org.

agencies, along with partners in governance outside of government, would act together to build local and regional competitiveness.

THE THIRD WAVE IN ACTION

Although many of those involved with third wave economic development thinking wrote as if they were members of an isolated minority, the number of states and localities that adopted some version of this approach was quite large.[4] Oregon was widely viewed as a model "third-wave" state (Mattoon 1993); it based its entire statewide strategic plan on the new approach. The plan included 155 quantifiable benchmarks tracking virtually every government agency. And, unlike second wave programs, this effort was not designed to benefit specific companies. It sought to strengthen the overall foundation of Oregon's economy.

Oregon's initiative was characterized by programs like the Wood Products Competitiveness Corporation (WPCC). This quasi-public organization brought together all the key players in Oregon's wood products sector to identify challenges and opportunities for the region. The WPCC and programs like it represented early efforts to support industry clusters, geographic concentrations of firms and industries that have common needs for talent, technology, and infrastructure.

States and localities were not alone in this effort. The Federal government also aggressively adopted the tenets of third wave thinking. The Commerce Department's Manufacturing Extension Partnership (MEP) served as the centerpiece of this effort (Shapira 1998). MEP, first authorized in 1988 and expanded throughout the 1990s, sought to promote the deployment of new technologies and improvement of business practices among small- and medium-sized manufacturers. It did so through local centers, run by a variety of public and private organizations. MEP provided training and other services directly and also served as a gateway to other sources of assistance for its target group of firms.

MEP succeeded in creating an extensive network of manufacturing extension services. More than sixty centers now exist in all fifty

---

[4] Coburn (1995) reviews 392 separate state programs in the area of cooperative technology development alone. The issue of whether third wave approaches have been fully adopted is controversial. For example, Eisinger (1995) has argued that few states placed significant resources in support of these initiatives.

states, and evaluations of the program have been generally positive (Shapira 2000). Despite its achievements, however, MEP, too, clearly suffered from limitations. The program's emphasis on serving manufacturing firms automatically limited its customer base. In addition, MEP quickly discovered that it had misconceived the needs of these customers. Rather than just embracing new technologies, most of its customers needed to get training or to improve their business practices. Nonetheless, the emphasis on technology continued to dominate the program.

Thus, although third wave thinking represented a step forward over its predecessors, it failed to solve essential problems of economic development. Communities facing severe economic distress and those without major home-grown technology or manufacturing resources often failed to embrace the new strategies. At the same time, third-wave-based programs did not offer much guidance or assistance to America's growing service sector or to the growing numbers of self-employed individuals and start-up firms that might offer hope to these communities. Finally, the vast majority of these programs did not build capacity for future growth by creating new businesses; they tended to focus on enhancing the competitiveness of existing firms. Castells and Hall provide a gloomy summary of the results:

A hasty, hurried study by an opportunistic consultant... to provide the magic formula: a small dose of venture capital, a university..., fiscal and institutional incentives to attract high-technology firms, and a degree of support for small business. All this, wrapped within the covers of a glossy brochure, and illustrated by a sylvan landscape with a futuristic name, would create the right conditions to outperform the neighbors, to become the locus of the new major global industrial centre. The world is now littered with the ruins of all too many such dreams that have failed, or have yielded meager results at far too high a cost. (Castells and Hall 1994:8)

In an effort to create innovation clusters at home, economic development officials aggressively sought to emulate and replicate leading technology centers like Silicon Valley and Route 128. Among the best known initiatives that have produced mixed records to date are Silicon Hills (Austin), Silicon Prairie (Kansas), Silicon Forest (Oregon), Silicon Glen (Scotland), Silicon Dominion (Virginia), and Silicon Fen (Cambridge, England).

ENTREPRENEURSHIP IN ECONOMIC DEVELOPMENT
POLICY: KEY TRENDS

In the early 1990s, a different economic development model – based on the concept of entrepreneurship – began to emerge. This approach is still evolving, but its basic outline has become clear. The goal of this approach diverges from the traditional economic development emphasis on job creation. Instead, entrepreneurial economic development strategies seek to encourage individuals to start new businesses and to grow businesses that can exploit major new opportunities. The focus of economic development policy-making has begun to shift away from the enterprise as the basic unit of analysis to the entrepreneur (or aspiring entrepreneur). With appropriate support and encouragement, these home-grown and high-growth entrepreneurs would generate significant economic benefits for the region and become community leaders as well.

The idea of using entrepreneurship to drive economic development is not new. For years, the economic development profession paid lip service to the importance of entrepreneurs in the local economy (see Schweke 1985, 3–6; Shapero 1981, 19–23). Yet little was done to convert these sentiments into actual practice. Most state and local economic development programs still devoted most of their resources to first and second wave approaches based on industrial recruitment and business finance. In fact, the National Association of State Development Agencies (NASDA) 1998 survey found that less than 1 percent of funds supported entrepreneurial development, whereas 22 percent supported loans and other financing programs (NASDA 1998). Not until 1999 did the Corporation for Enterprise Development's (CFED) widely read Development Report Card for the States, a leading venue for third wave development thinking, include a separate measurement category for entrepreneurial energy (CFED 1999).

Several linked trends contributed to the rise of interest in entrepreneurship as an economic development strategy. First, and most important, the number of small businesses skyrocketed in the 1980s and 1990s. Between 1990 and 1996, for example, the number of U.S. corporations and partnerships grew from 5.2 million to 6.6 million. Meanwhile, sole proprietorships grew from 14.7 million to 16.6 million (Acs 1999: 2). Not surprisingly, high-growth entrepreneurial businesses came to be viewed as a primary engine of new job creation. The increased presence of small firms generated research interest, much of it funded by Federal agencies like the Small Business Administration, on the impact of such companies. The work of David Birch likely had the greatest effect on public perceptions (Birch 1987). In a series of well-publicized studies, Birch concluded that small firms were primarily responsible for most new job creation. Birch's findings faced numerous methodological criticisms, yet they resonated in economic development circles (see Davis, Haltiwanger, and Schuh 1996). As a result, the link between small business and economic development became more widely accepted. The profession responded with a greater openness to entrepreneurial approaches to economic development.

Second, a series of new management approaches and models emerged thanks to the rise of new technologies, especially those linked to the Internet (Evans and Wurmser 2000). The dot-com phenomenon was part of a wider restructuring of the American economy that began in the 1970s and continues today. Downsizing and corporate restructuring changed the nature of the employer/employee relationship (Cappelli 1999). Lifetime employment with a single company is no longer the norm; younger workers assume they will likely pursue jobs with numerous employers and perhaps even have multiple careers during a lifetime. Coupled with this mental shift is an openness to considering starting a new business of one's own. Polls of high school youth in the late 1990s showed that roughly two-thirds were interested in starting their own businesses (Kourilsky and Walstad 2000).

As these perceptions about entrepreneurship evolved, new technologies made it easier to get started in business. New information technologies reduced the barriers to entry for many who sought to start new firms. They also created new business opportunities. Popular books and journals lauded those who "took the leap" and went into business on their own (Pink 2001; Reinhold 2001). These new entrepreneurs, dubbed the "free agent nation" or bands of "lone eagles," thought they could start their businesses anywhere in the United States and would transform communities around the nation.

As business strategies and career patterns took new shapes, the marketplace of ideas also evolved. Responding to student demands for entrepreneurial training, the study of entrepreneurship in America's colleges and universities boomed. The growth in graduate entrepreneurship programs over the past two decades has been astounding. No business school academic concentration has ever grown faster. In the 1980s, a small handful of business schools taught entrepreneurship. Today, more than 550 universities offer courses in entrepreneurship. Programs offering entrepreneurship as an area of concentration number 142, and 49 schools offer an entrepreneurship degree (Solomon, Duffy, and Tarabishy 2002). Funding for these programs has emerged via contributions from leading entrepreneurs as well as from the Kauffman, Lowe, and Coleman foundations.

Coincident with entrepreneurship's new place in business school curricula was a growing wave of research examining the importance of social capital and social entrepreneurship.[5] This strand of research emphasized the role of social trust, local networks, and community connectedness as central to a community's social and economic health. The social capital literature included a wide variety of policy prescriptions, ranging from the strengthening of local business networks to supporting anchor public institutions such as schools and civic organizations. Along with these suggestions, this research also stressed the importance of civic or social entrepreneurs as key players in building community capacity. Much like traditional business entrepreneurs, these individuals are risk-takers and innovators. Yet their initiatives generally focus on community and social benefits as opposed to the purely financial benefits of most new businesses. The significance of this thinking for economic development professionals was that it again emphasized the linkage between entrepreneurship and a community's social and economic health.

A NEW APPROACH

These trends have all merged to fuel a growing interest in supporting entrepreneurship as an economic development strategy. Most economic development programs seek to deliver services. Entrepreneurship programs seek to create more and better entrepreneurs. They do so by adhering to several broad principles.

---

[5] The literature on social capital is huge and diverse. For an introduction to key themes in the field, see Putnam 2001.

1. Focus on an Entrepreneurial Eco-System

Creating an entrepreneurial climate or eco-system is the primary objective of most approaches to entrepreneurship development. Advocates of the entrepreneurial strategy encourage policymakers to see their local economies as "complex adaptive systems" (Axelrod and Cohen 1999). Beyond looking at a local economy's supply of "tools" (financial capital, workforce, access to new technology, infrastructure, etc.), recent scholarship suggests that how a local economy addresses three key questions determines its success:

1. Has the local system worked to increase the *variety* of players in the system, achieving a balance between the exploitation of current opportunities and the exploration of new ones?
2. Has the local system built *networks of reciprocal interaction* that foster trust and cooperation among all the players in the system?
3. Has the local system used its networks to support the spread of *criteria of selection* that produce adaptation and economic growth – criteria by which "successful" players and strategies are honored and held up to be replicated by other players in the system?

Looking through this "eco-system" or "complex adaptive system" lens, we can see why many past economic development programs missed the mark. Most important, creating a "habitat" for an entrepreneurial economy (in the words of Mayor Kirk Watson of Austin, Texas) requires more than providing better "tools." It involves a profound cultural shift: Community leaders and citizens must come not only to welcome economic change, but also to reward those who "adapt" to change. By encouraging youth and adults to consider entrepreneurship as a viable career path, regional leaders not only expand the pool of potential entrepreneurs but also help trigger wider interest in and support for those seeking to start and grow new companies. As Richard Florida's chapter shows, such opinion shifts have occurred in many regions, but this transformation is still far from universal across all regions.

2. Promoting Cultural Change

Education and training about entrepreneurship are critical to achieving this objective. Entrepreneurship curricula exist for grades K-12, and many model programs, such as those sponsored by the National Foundation for Teaching Entrepreneurship and the Ewing Marion Kauffman Foundation (Mini-Society, EntrePrep), encourage young people to view entrepreneurship as a career path worthy of consideration. Youth training should be further supplemented with adult training in the knowledge and skills to become entrepreneurs. Some promising models already exist. For example, FastTrac, a training program created by the Kauffman Center for Entrepreneurial Leadership, is offered at numerous locations across the United States. Studies show that such training not only inspires people to become entrepreneurs but also improves the business performance of the new ventures that are actually launched.[6]

Entrepreneurial education and training initiatives go beyond simply improving the quality and quantity of labor inputs into start-up firms. Entrepreneurship policy introduces a new twist into workforce development. Whereas traditional workforce development programs seek to train, recruit, and attract new workers, scientists, and technologists, entrepreneurship programs seek to encourage people to start their own enterprises. An example of this approach is the movement to attract "lone eagles" to rural areas. This effort, which first emerged in several Western states in the 1990s,[7] targets entrepreneurs and freelance professionals who take advantage of new technologies to become "amenity migrants." Thanks to information technology, such highly skilled individuals can now locate in small towns and rural areas, building community and business leadership in these regions. A number of rural regions around the United States have made attracting lone eagles a core element of their economic development strategies.

Expanding the pool of entrepreneurs in a locality or state has the added benefit of creating a base of expertise in the process of building

---

[6] These findings have been confirmed in evaluations of the FastTrac program. See Kauffman Center for Entrepreneurial Leadership, 2000; 2001.

[7] This effort grew partly out of research by the Center for the New West. Information on the Center's Lone Eagle Project is available at http://www.newwest.org.

and supporting new and emerging companies. This base of service providers makes it easier for subsequent generations of entrepreneurs to access the specialized knowledge and skills involved in starting a new business. As this local base of expertise grows, a virtuous cycle of more entrepreneurs and more successful entrepreneurs can develop (Kenney and von Burg 2000).

3.   Serving Individuals, Not Firms

Entrepreneurship-oriented economic development strategies serve a new customer: the aspiring entrepreneur. Prior approaches to economic development have all viewed the firm, not the individual, as the core customer. Thus, second wave strategies sought to lower costs for business through tax incentives, training, and other support. Third wave programs sought to improve the competitiveness of firms through integrated industrial services. Entrepreneurship strategies emphasize the creation of learning opportunities for individuals running new enterprises or those who aspire to do so.

A review of policy toward networking helps underscore these differences. The interest in social capital that began in the 1980s led many policymakers to embrace the benefits of cooperation and alliances between businesses. New programs, like the Federal MEP initiative, were set up, at least in part, to achieve these benefits. The rationale for these investments was that firms would soon discover the economic benefits of cooperation, and that managers would internalize such behavior. At the same time, cooperation helped aggregate demand and ease delivery of services to small firms.

Most of these earlier collaborations sought to create what some observers have called "hard networks," groups of firms that unite to achieve specific business objectives like entering new markets, co-production, or co-marketing (Rosenfeld 2001: 7–8). Hard networks have a clearly defined focus on the bottom line, and the benefits of such networks are measured in typical performance metrics like new jobs and increased revenues.

Entrepreneurship-oriented economic development strategies, in contrast, focus on soft networks. These networks emphasize opportunities for sharing information and learning from peers and others. Most entrepreneurial networks do not have a primary goal of creating interfirm alliances. Rather, they are networks of individuals, some of whom are the heads of firms and some of whom seek to head their own firms, who share ideas, learn from one another, and do business together. Membership in entrepreneurship networks can vary, but such groups tend to include entrepreneurs, aspiring entrepreneurs, professional service providers, local development officials, and investors. Relationship building is such a network's primary purpose. Through it, entrepreneurs seek to build linkages to others involved with starting and growing new businesses. In effect, networks serve to link entrepreneurs to the entrepreneurial life support system. Each individual enters the network for idiosyncratic reasons, but primarily from a desire to learn from peers and to gain access to local expertise about how to succeed in business.

Northern Virginia's Netpreneur program was a paradigmatic example of an entrepreneurship network focused on people, not firms. First set up in the late 1990s, Netpreneur served individuals involved with Internet-related businesses in the Washington, D.C. metropolitan area. The group was privately funded and operated, and boasted more than ten thousand participants at its peak. Although Netpreneur hosted events and operated a number of specialized on-line networks, its founders did not view themselves as service providers. The program has now spun off most of its activities to private and public partners who operate various components (for example, email list management, mentoring networks) of the original Netpreneur network. The initial single network has now evolved into a diverse range of networks supporting the region's technology start-ups.

4. New Delivery Mechanisms

Local entrepreneurship support systems are based on a decentralized network model. Service delivery occurs via networks, with much of the direct outreach to entrepreneurs occurring through private sector consultants and service providers. In second and third wave writings, analysts regularly spoke of public-private partnerships. The entrepreneurial model often eschews these direct partnerships and instead views government as a facilitator or as simply one cog in a wider regional network.

Under this scenario, private support networks predominate. They include law firms, specialized real estate developers, accounting firms, marketing experts, and executive search firms as well as entrepreneurs. The dominance of the private sector reflects the experience of Silicon Valley and other entrepreneurial "hot spots" around the country. Such support networks can be both formal and informal. Entrepreneurs can be nurtured via the local entrepreneur's club or simply over a meal at popular clubs and restaurants.

Not all regions boast strong local service provider networks, so the mix of public and private service provision may vary according to local needs. Nevertheless, in all cases, public sector investments focus on filling gaps and supporting private sector service delivery (NCOE 2001). For example, local government agencies typically take the lead in support of microenterprise programs. These initiatives require significant investment of time and resources, and such investments may not be cost-effective for some private service providers. In these cases, public sector services or more traditional forms of public-private partnership are common.

The contrast between traditional and new approaches may be most stark in the area of technical assistance. Creating a national network of technical assistance centers was one of the major accomplishments of second wave economic development approaches. Hundreds of Small Business Development Centers (SBDCs), Service Corps of Retired Executives (SCORE) chapters, and University Technical Assistance Centers now exist across the United States. These government-funded centers help aspiring entrepreneurs to write business plans and achieve other specific goals. In contrast, entrepreneurial development strategies normally opt to let others, such as private consultants, provide such services, or simply use classroom training and other techniques to guide entrepreneurs at early stages. For example, North Carolina's Council for Entrepreneurial Development, one of the nation's largest entrepreneurship networks, provides no direct technical assistance to its members. Instead, it has created a series of peer and mentor networks where members can learn from one another. As development organizations begin outsourcing technical assistance services, resources can then be devoted to the provision of higher end services such as business networking and access to new markets and sources of capital.

5.   Focus on High Growth

In contrast to traditional economic development strategies that tend to be "open for business" to all comers, entrepreneurship strategies seek to make clear distinctions about different types of customers. The primary target and ultimate goal is to nurture "high-growth" entrepreneurs. The firms created by these entrepreneurs, sometimes referred to as "gazelles," grow at an annual rate of 15 to 20 percent in revenue and/or jobs (NCOE 2001). Such firms are rare; they account for less than 5 percent of all U.S. businesses. Yet they create a majority of net new jobs in the American economy and generate a high proportion of major innovations (see Timmons 1998; Atkinson and Court 1998). Rare as they are, gazelles can nonetheless be found throughout the United States and in nearly every industrial sector. Thus, all communities can benefit from an emphasis on supporting the creation of high-growth firms.

For better or worse, it is nearly impossible, as with any complex system, to identify gazelles in advance. Two attributes of potential gazelles can, however, narrow the range of targets (Bhide 2000). First, these company founders seek to grow companies quickly. They do not simply seek an employment opportunity for themselves and their families. Second, these firms provide products, services, or manage distribution schemes that embody major productivity gains. For this reason, technology-based businesses tend to be good candidates for fast growth. This combination of the founder's desire for fast growth and latent productivity improvements in the firm's products or services are the primary factors that separate gazelles from the vast majority of businesses, those that start small and stay small.

Because high-growth firms in an economic eco-system can only be identified in hindsight, entrepreneurial development programs are generally not limited to high-growth entrepreneurs. Two other categories of entrepreneurs therefore also benefit from these initiatives. One is aspiring entrepreneurs, who have the desire and have made plans to create new ventures, but have not yet made the jump. The other is lifestyle entrepreneurs, who represent the vast majority of U.S. small businesses, including the classic "Mom and Pop" small business. In these cases, the owners' main intention is simply to earn an income for themselves and their families.

Other types of businesses may benefit from support for "gazelles," but program designs and offerings tend to be heavily skewed toward the needs of high-growth firms. For example, debt financing programs – a hardy staple of business development – are rare in entrepreneurship initiatives. Instead, equity financing is the norm. Similarly, local entrepreneurship networks often include sub-groupings that focus on new technologies, such as biotechnology or nanotechnology, that offer the prospect of massive productivity gains and huge growth opportunities.

CHALLENGES

Interest in entrepreneurship as an economic development strategy emerged in tandem with the 1990s boom in Internet and other technology start-ups. The subsequent dot-com crash may have dampened enthusiasm for entrepreneurship as a quick fix, but the movement embracing these principles is growing and beginning to become institutionalized. The Kauffman Center for Entrepreneurial Leadership and several other leading organizations have created national learning networks that include entrepreneurs, educators, public officials, and economic development professionals. As these networks take hold, new entrepreneurship programs are springing up across the United States.

The jury is still out, however, as to whether entrepreneurship can become a core component of local economic development strategies. A number of challenges may emerge and affect how services are delivered, how progress is measured, and whether entrepreneurship initiatives can maintain political backing and financial support.

Program-itis

Economic development is often plagued by "program-itis." When a new economic challenge emerges, public organizations scramble to create a new government program to meet it. In contrast, building an entrepreneurial environment requires a holistic approach. Numerous government agencies, private sector leaders, and non-profits must come together to build a network that provides education, learning opportunities, and other services for local entrepreneurs.

Creating new government-sponsored and -managed entrepreneurship programs can be a recipe for failure. Some new services and programs, such as new sources of equity finance, may be needed, especially in areas lacking networks of private service providers. But new programs that are not part of a comprehensive entrepreneurship strategy will simply repeat the problems of redundancy and ineffectiveness that plagued earlier economic development strategies. More important, they will do little to foster the culture that lies at the heart of an entrepreneurial climate.

Performance Evaluation

As programs diverge from traditional models of public sector funding and service delivery, performance measurement becomes a significant challenge. Business assistance programs generate quantifiable output, such as the number of firms assisted, the number and value of loans provided, and the number of jobs created. Input measures are even simpler: government dollars invested, matching funds invested, and the like. These measures can be used to assess program quality and service.

Because entrepreneurship programs seek to generate both business and community outcomes, relevant performance measures are more difficult to find. Various research and consulting organizations have created new indices to measure local entrepreneurship, but agreement on what is appropriate does not yet exist (see CFED 1999; PPI 2001). Counting new businesses and entrepreneurs is relatively simple, but finding reliable and valid indicators of an "entrepreneurial climate" is problematic. Even the simple task of measuring inputs can be challenging when programs are co-managed or run by private sector partners, and when investments include both cash and non-cash-based contributions. Creating a consensus set of performance measures and indices must become a priority in the field.

Political Cycle versus Business Cycle

Because they seek to foster long-term changes in both local business culture and the supporting infrastructure, entrepreneurship strategies do not offer a quick fix to bring new jobs and business to a region. Effective programs require a commitment of at least four years and even longer time frames are the norm. For example, the Council for Entrepreneurial Development, a private entrepreneurs' network based in North Carolina, began operations in 1984, but did not witness major expansion and a concomitant growth in local entrepreneurship until the mid-1990s.

These long time frames create political dilemmas for communities considering new entrepreneurship initiatives, as David Hart touches on in his chapter in this volume. Political leaders may demand quick victories that let them take credit for creating new jobs for their constituents. One of the greatest benefits of smokestack chasing is that it creates highly visible ribbon cuttings and similar ceremonies. Entrepreneurship creates jobs, but at a slower pace and in smaller increments. Thus, the short-term benefits of such programs may offer little attraction to political leaders with a shortsighted focus on the next election.

Overcoming these obstacles requires creative thinking and extra attention to building political capital. Regular publicity around new small business starts may not trump a new Toyota plant, but it does create venues for shared recognition by both entrepreneurs and political leaders. Other programs, like annual awards ceremonies, have also proved to be helpful in this regard. For example, Ernst & Young's Entrepreneur of the Year Award has become one of the major business events in many communities around the nation. These events offer excellent recognition opportunities for public officials, even as they serve to honor and reward local entrepreneurs.

CONCLUSION

As entrepreneurship becomes a more widely utilized economic development strategy, policymakers must continue to concentrate time and resources on the individual entrepreneur, who serves as the target and delivery vehicle, and whose success is the desired outcome of this model. No entrepreneurship program will thrive without the commitment of local entrepreneurs. This commitment takes the form of time and resources devoted to supporting fellow entrepreneurs. It should also include active engagement in the formulation and implementation of local economic development initiatives. Whereas entrepreneurs have embraced the objective of helping each other, they have often opted out of involvement in economic development. The mantra of "get the government off my back" must be replaced by a new, more cooperative approach.

Policymakers can help support this new approach through programmatic initiatives such as funding for networking organizations, efforts to improve equity capital access, and the like. But a new perspective may prove more compelling than new programs alone. The old approaches of government as service provider and business as customer often do little to foster close cooperation and empathy. In contrast, the concept of an entrepreneurial eco-system generates a more inclusive and optimistic perspective on the prospects for closer public-private cooperation. As interest in and support for fostering entrepreneurship grow, the prospects for true partnerships in economic development will continue to expand.

Afterword

Michael E. Porter

This volume represents a further step in the debate about U.S. competitiveness that began in the 1980s. Scholars and policymakers who have taken part in this debate too often have failed to accept the crucial role that entrepreneurship plays in generating prosperity and competitive advantage. As this volume suggests, that failure has now begun to be corrected.

The world has not stood still since the 1980s. New elements have been added to the puzzle facing policymakers concerned with entrepreneurship, even as they have grappled with challenges inherited from the past. Although the American economy is structurally sound and, indeed, rather robust from a competitiveness perspective in the medium term, some very serious issues face us over the long term. Many of these issues have to do with innovation and entrepreneurship. In the following pages, I describe these issues and I invite the reader of this volume to bear them in mind.

The first major challenge facing the United States is inequality. Despite historically low rates of unemployment in the 1990s, the gains of the extraordinary economic growth of that decade have been unevenly distributed, in ways that are heavily based on differences in education

These remarks draw on a substantial study I completed in conjunction with the Council on Competitiveness. This study, published as *U.S. Competitiveness 2001*, examines the long-term trajectory of the U.S. economy, the underpinnings of the remarkable prosperity of the 1990s, and the challenges that lie ahead.

and skill. Over the last five or ten years, an individual without a college education has not gained much in terms of real weekly earnings. Even an individual with some college but no degree has lost ground. Those with less than a high school diploma have lost more ground. It is important to realize that only 26 percent of the American workforce has a college education. Yet we know that job requirements are rising. Overall, the problem of inequality is very closely tied to the problems with the K-12 education system in the United States.

The second challenge is lagging national R&D investment. There was a flurry of entrepreneurial activity in the 1990s, but it was fueled by thirty or forty years of prior sustained investment in basic R&D, much of it by the Federal government. The Cold War drove a technology strategy that was well accepted, centered in the Department of Defense. Why do we have the Internet? The roots are in the Department of Defense. Why do we have navigation systems in cars? The roots are in the Department of Defense. The United States has a long history of investing heavily in basic R&D, R&D that produced foundational technologies ultimately commercialized by the private sector.

Unfortunately, R&D investment has fallen significantly as a percentage of U.S. gross domestic product. Our national R&D portfolio has also been badly skewed. Life sciences R&D is growing very rapidly, while many other fields have been starved. Investment has slowed in physics, chemistry, engineering, mathematics, and other disciplines that underpinned the boom in entrepreneurship. More than 70 percent of all industry patents cite publicly financed papers, a truly staggering statistic. Unless we make public investments in R&D in the future on a scale comparable to that of the past, technological innovation and entrepreneurship will lag.

The problems in R&D funding are exacerbated by shortages of human capital. The number of scientists and engineers being graduated in the United States every year is shrinking, at a time when it is increasing in many other parts of the world. Fewer engineers graduated in 2001 than in 2000. Apart from life sciences, there is a shrinking pool of people available to become innovators and high-technology entrepreneurs. We cannot have an entrepreneurially based, innovation-driven economy without a growing pool of well-trained and highly motivated people. The old strategy of encouraging foreigners to study in America and to remain here is no longer as viable as it once was.

There are still lots of non-Americans coming here to study, but the opportunities in the rest of the world are improving and more foreigners are returning home. Part of the crisis in the number of American scientists and engineers is due to underrepresentation of women and minorities in those fields. More effective policies need to be enacted to regenerate the flow of human resources that drive entrepreneurship and innovation.

The fourth challenge facing the United States is a slowdown in workforce growth due to demographic shifts. The robust labor force growth of the recent past, which benefited all groups in America, was based on an unsustainable expansion in workforce participation. Fifteen years from now the growth of the workforce will be approaching zero, unless there is some discontinuity. The people who are and will be retiring are, by and large, better educated than new entrants to the workforce, especially in science and engineering. It will be difficult to sustain economic growth without a growing workforce. Rather than raising workforce participation levels as in the past, the challenge of the future will be to raise the productivity of the workforce if the economy is to continue to grow.

In dealing with this challenge, the United States is confronting a long-term trend of people retiring earlier. Close to 50 percent of men sixty-five and older were still in the workforce in 1950. By 1999 the percentage had fallen to less than 20 percent. At a time when we need more workers to keep the economy growing, people are retiring earlier. This trend is creating the need for a whole new strategy to address the notion of retirement and the role of older workers.

The final major challenge facing the United States is the large asymmetries across states and regions in economic performance and entrepreneurial activity. The intensity of patenting activity, new business formation, entrepreneurial success, and venture capital funding is highly skewed across geographic locations. Regional economies are specialized in different groups that I call industry clusters. Increasingly, it will be necessary to introduce a strong regional dimension in economic policy and see less of the solution in Washington. Otherwise, some regions will continue to fall behind and foster even greater inequality.

As we look at how public policy can affect entrepreneurship and innovation in the American economy, these five areas strike me as the ones that will be central to moving the nation forward. They are all interrelated in many ways, but each requires a clear strategy that is sustained over the long term. These areas create threats, but also raise opportunities. The United States could lead a new period of technological advancement that would make a fundamental contribution to world health and prosperity. The greater opportunities for older citizens, and the potential to attract more women and minorities to science and technology, could provide unprecedented opportunities for reducing inequality and allowing America to lead in new ways in the twenty-first century.

I think we can and will seize the opportunities and allay the threats. The growing attention in the academic and policy communities to the microeconomic roots of competitiveness and prosperity, reflected in this volume and in activity around the country, is laying the foundation for constructive collective action – within, outside, and in conjunction with government.

References

Abernathy, W. J., and K. Clark. 1985. Innovation: Mapping the Winds of Creative Destruction. *Research Policy* 14:3–22.

ACLU v. Reno. 521 U.S. 844 (1997).

ACLU v. Reno II. No. 99-1324, U.S. Supreme Court granted certiori, decision pending.

Acs, Zoltan J. 1999. The New American Evolution. In Zoltan J. Acs, ed., *Are Small Firms Important?* Boston: Kluwer.

Acs, Zoltan J., and David B. Audretsch. 1990a. *Innovation and Small Firms.* Cambridge, MA: MIT Press.

Acs, Zoltan, and David Audretsch, eds. 1990b. *Innovation and Technological Change.* London: Harvester Wheatsheaf.

Acs, Zoltan, David Audretsch, and Maryann P. Feldman. 1994. R&D Spillovers and Recipient Firm Size. *Review of Economics and Statistics* 76:336–340.

Aghion, Philippe, Nicholas Bloom, Richard Blundell, Rachel Griffth, and Peter Howitt. 2002. Competition and Innovation: An Inverted U Relationship. Unpublished manuscript. Available at: http://post.economics. harvard.edu/faculty/aghion/papers.html.

Aldrich, Howard E. 1989. Networking Among Women Entrepreneurs. In O. Hagan, C. Rivchun, and D. Sexton, eds., *Women-Owned Businesses.* New York: Praeger.

Aldrich, Howard E., and C. Marlene Fiol. 1994. Fools Rush In? The Institutional Context of Industry Creation. *Academy of Management Review* 19:645–670.

Aldrich, Howard E., and Martha A. Martinez. 2001. Many Are Called but Few Are Chosen: An Evolutionary Perspective for the Study of Entrepreneurship. *Entrepreneurship Theory and Practice*, Summer, 4.

Aldrich, Howard E., and Gabriele Wiedenmayer. 1993. From Traits to Rates: An Ecological Perspective on Organizational Foundings. *Advances in Entrepreneurship, Firm Emergence, and Growth* 1:145–195.

Almeida, P., and B. Kogut. 1997. The Exploration of Technological Diversity and the Geographic Localization of Innovation. *Small Business Economics* 9:21–31.

Aoki, Keith. 1996. Innovation and the Information Environment. 75 *Oregon Law Review* 1.

Apple, Rima D. 1989. Patenting University Research. *Isis* 80:375–394.

Arora, Ashish, and Alfonso Gambardella. 1995. The Division of Inventive Labor in Biotechnology. In Nathan Rosenberg, Annetine C. Gelijns, and Holly Dawkins, eds., *Sources of Medical Technology*. Washington, D.C.: National Academy Press.

Arora, Ashish, and Alfonso Gambardella. 1998. Evolution of Industry Structure in the Chemical Industry. In Ashish Arora, Ralph Landau, and Nathan Rosenberg, eds., *Chemicals and Long-Term Economic Growth*. New York: Wiley.

Arrow, K. 1962. Economic Welfare and the Allocation of Resources for Invention. In R. Nelson, ed., *The Rate and Direction of Inventive Activity*. Princeton: Princeton University Press.

Association of American Universities. 1986. *Trends in Technology Transfer at Universities*. Washington, D.C.: Association of American Universities.

Association of University Technology Managers (AUTM). *Licensing Survey, 1991–1995; 1996, 1997, 1998, 1999*. Northbrook, IL: AUTM.

Atkinson, Robert D. 2001. Revenge of the Disintermediated: How the Middleman is Fighting E-Commerce and Hurting Consumers. Washington, D.C.: Progressive Policy Institute.

Atkinson, Robert D., and Randolph H. Court. 1998. *The New Economy Index*. Washington, D.C.: Progressive Policy Institute.

Audretsch, D. 1995. *Innovation and Industry Evolution*. Cambridge, MA: MIT Press.

Audretsch, D. 1998. Agglomeration and the Location of Innovative Activity. *Oxford Review of Economic Policy* 14:18–29.

Audretsch, David B. 2001. The Role of Small Firms in U.S. Biotechnology Clusters. *Small Business Economics* 17:3–15.

Audretsch, D., and M. P. Feldman. 1996. R&D Spillovers and the Geography of Innovation and Production. *American Economic Review* 86:630–640.

Audretsch, D., and P. Stephan. 1996. Company-Scientist Locational Links: The Case of Biotechnology. *American Economic Review* 86:641–652.

Audretsch, David, and Paula Stephan. 1999. How and Why Does Knowledge Spill Over in Biotechnology. In David B. Audretsch and A. Roy Thurik, eds., *Innovation, Industry Evolution, and Employment*. New York: Cambridge University Press.

Audretsch, D., and A. Thurik, eds. 1999. *Innovation, Industry, Evolution, and Employment* New York: Cambridge University Press.

Audretsch, David B., and A. Roy Thurik. 2001. Capitalism and Democracy in the 21st Century: From the Managed to the Entrepreneurial Economy. *Journal of Evolutionary Economics* 10:17–34.

Axelrod, Robert, and Michael D. Cohen. 1999. *Harnessing Complexity*. New York: Free Press.

Baldwin, C., and K. B. Clark. 1997. Managing in an Age of Modularity. *Harvard Business Review*, September–October, 84–93.

Barlow, John P. 1996. A Declaration of Independence of Cyberspace. *The Humanist*, May/June, 18–19.

Barnes, M., D. C. Mowery, and A. A. Ziedonis. 1997. The Geographic Reach of Market and Nonmarket Channels of Technology Transfer. Paper presented at the Academy of Management annual meeting, Boston, MA, August 10–13.

Barro, Robert J., and Xavier Sala-I-Martin. 1997. Technological Diffusion, Convergence, and Growth. *Journal of Economic Geography* 2:1–26.

Bartik, Timothy J. 1991. *Who Benefits from State and Local Economic Development Policies?* Kalamazoo, MI: W. E. Upjohn Institute.

Bates, Timothy. 1973. *Black Capitalism*. New York: Praeger.

Bates, Timothy. 1984. Small Business Administration Loan Programs. In Paul Horvitz and R. Richardson Pettit, eds., *Sources of Financing for Small Business*. Greenwich, CT: JAI Press.

Bates, Timothy. 1987. Self-Employed Minorities: Traits and Trends. *Social Science Quarterly* 68:539–551.

Bates, Timothy. 1993. *Banking on Black Enterprise*. Washington, D.C.: Joint Center for Political and Economic Studies.

Bates, Timothy. 1995. Why Do Minority Business Development Programs Generate So Little Minority Business Development? *Economic Development Quarterly* 9:3–14.

Bates, Timothy. 1996. An Analysis of the SSBIC Program: Problems and Prospects. Washington, D.C.: U.S. Small Business Administration.

Bates, Timothy. 1997. *Race, Self-Employment, and Upward Mobility*. Baltimore: Johns Hopkins University Press.

Bates, Timothy. 1998. Job Creation Through Improved Access to Markets for Minority-Owned Businesses. In Wilhelmina Leigh and Margaret Simms, eds., *The Black Worker in the 21st Century: Job Creation Prospects and Strategies*. Washington, D.C.: Joint Center for Political and Economic Studies.

Bates, Timothy. 2000. Financing the Development of Urban Minority Communities: Lessons from History. *Economic Development Quarterly* 14: 227–241.

Bates, Timothy. 2001. Minority Business Access to Mainstream Markets. *Journal of Urban Affairs* 23:41–56.

Bates, Timothy. 2002. Government as Venture Capital Catalyst: Pitfalls and Promising Approaches. *Economic Development Quarterly* 16:49–59.

Bates, Timothy, and William Bradford. 1979. *Financing Black Economic Development*. New York: Academic Press.

Beeson, P., and E. Montgomery. 1992. The Effects of Colleges and Universities on Local Labor Markets. *Review of Economics and Statistics* 75:753–776.

Bell, Tom, and Solveig Singleton, eds. 1998. *Regulator's Revenge*. Washington, D.C.: Cato Institute.

BenDaniel, D., J. Reyes, and M. D'Angelo. 2000. Concentration in the Venture Capital Industry. *Journal of Private Equity*, Summer, 7–13.

Bercovitz, J. E. L., M. P. Feldman, I. Feller, and R. M. Burton. 2001. Organizational Structure as a Determinant of Academic Patent and Licensing Behavior. *Journal of Technology Transfer* 26:21–35.

Berman, Eli, John Bound, and Stephen Machin. 1997. Implications of Skill-Biased Technological Change: International Evidence. Working Paper #6166. Cambridge, MA: National Bureau of Economic Research.

Bettig, Ronald V. 1996. *Copyrighting Culture*. Boulder, CO: Westview Press.

Bhide, Amar. 2000. *The Origin and Evolution of New Businesses*. New York: Oxford University Press.

Biotechnology Industry Organization. 2001. *State Government Initiatives in Biotechnology 2001*. Washington, D.C.: BIO.

Birch, David. 1987. *Job Creation in America*. New York: Free Press.

Birley, S. 1985. The Role of Networks in the Entrepreneurial Process. *Journal of Business Venturing* 1:107–117.

Black, D., Gates, G., Sanders, S., and Taylor, L. 2000. Demographics of the Gay and Lesbian Population in the United States: Evidence from Available Systematic Data Sources. *Demography* 37:139–154.

Blake, D. A. 1993. The University's Role in Marketing Research Discoveries. *Chronicle of Higher Education*, May 12, A52.

Blaustein, Arthur, and Geoffrey Faux. 1972. *The Star-Spangled Hustle*. Garden City, NY: Doubleday.

Blumenstyk, G. 2001. Turning Royalty Patents into a Sure Thing. *The Chronicle of Higher Education*, October 5, A26–28.

Boaz, David, and Edward H. Crane, eds. 1993. *Market Liberalism*. Washington, D.C.: Cato Institute.

Bonacich, Edna, and John Modell. 1981. *The Economic Basis for Ethnic Solidarity*. Berkeley: University of California Press.

Bork, Robert H. 1978. *The Antitrust Paradox: A Policy at War with Itself*. New York: Basic Books.

Borsook, Paulina. 2000. *Cyberselfish: A Critical Romp Through the Terribly Libertarian Culture of High-Tech*. New York: Public Affairs Books.

Boston, Thomas. 1999. *Affirmative Action and Black Entrepreneurship*. London: Routledge.

Branscomb, Lewis M., and Philip E. Auerswald, eds. 2001. *Taking Technical Risks: How Innovators, Executives and Investors Manage High-Tech Risks.* Cambridge, MA: MIT Press.

Branscomb, Lewis M., and Philip E. Auerswald. 2002. *Between Invention and Innovation: An Analysis of Funding for Early Stage Technology Development.* Report prepared for Advanced Technology Program, National Institute for Standards and Technology, U.S. Department of Commerce.

Branscomb, Lewis M., and James Keller, eds. 1998. *Investing in Innovation: Creating a Research and Innovation Policy that Works.* Cambridge, MA: MIT Press.

Brass, D. J. 1985. Men's And Women's Networks. A Study of Interaction Patterns and Influence in an Organization. *Academy of Management Journal* 28:327–343.

Braun, Ernest, and Stuart Macdonald. 1978. *Revolution in Miniature: The History and Impact of Semiconductor Electronics.* New York: Cambridge University Press.

Braunerhjelm, Pontus, and Bo Carlsson. 1999. Industry Clusters in Ohio and Sweden, 1975–1995. *Small Business Economics* 12:279–293.

Bresnahan, T., and F. Malerba. 1999. Industrial Dynamics and the Evolution of Firms' and Nations' Competitive Capabilities in the World Computer Industry. In D. C. Mowery and R. R. Nelson, eds., *Sources of Industrial Leadership.* New York: Cambridge University Press.

Brophy, D. 1997. Financing the Growth of Entrepreneurial Firms. In D. L. Sexton and R. Smilor, eds., *Entrepreneurship 2000.* Chicago, IL: Upstart Publishing, 5–28.

Bruderl, J., P. Preisendorfoer, and R. Ziegler. 1992. Survival Chances of Newly Founded Business Organizations. *American Sociological Review* 57:227–242.

Bundesministerium fuer Bildung und Forschung. 2000. *Zur Technologischen Leistungsfaehigkeit Deutschlands* [On the Technological Capabilities of Germany]. Bonn: Bundesministerium fuer Bildung und Forschung.

Butler, R. J., and M. Carney. 1986. Strategy and Strategic Choice: The Case of Telecommunications. *Strategic Management Journal* 7:161–177.

Buttner, E. H., and B. H. Rosen. 1988. Bank Loan Officers' Perceptions of Characteristics of Men, Women and Successful Entrepreneurs. *Journal of Business Venturing* 3:249–258.

Bygrave, W. D. 1992. Venture Capital Returns in the 1980's. In D. L. Sexton and J. Kasarda, eds., *The State of the Art of Entrepreneurship.* Boston: PWS Kent.

Cappelli, Peter. 1999. *The New Deal at Work.* Cambridge, MA: Harvard Business School Press.

Carlsson, B., and P. Braunerhjelm. 1999. Industry Clusters: Biotechnology/Biomedicine and Polymers in Ohio and Sweden. In D. B. Audretsch and

A. R. Thurik, eds. *Innovation, Industry Evolution, and Employment.* New York: Cambridge University Press.

Carree, M. A. 2002. Does Unemployment Affect the Number of Establishments? *Regional Studies* 36:389–398.

Carree. M. A., and A. R. Thurik. 1999. Industrial Structure and Economic Growth. In D. B. Audretsch and A. R. Thurik, eds., *Innovation, Industry Evolution, and Employment.* New York: Cambridge University Press.

Carree, M. A., A. van Stel, A. R. Thurik, and S. Wennekers. 2000. Economic Development and Business Ownership: An Analysis Using Data of 23 OECD Countries in the Period 1976–1996. Institute for Development Strategies Discussion Paper 00-6. Bloomington: University of Indiana.

Carroll, G. 1983. A Stochastic Model of Organizational Mortality. *Social Science Research* 12:309–329.

Carter, D., and R. Wilson. 1992. *Minorities in Higher Education.* Washington, D.C.: American Council on Higher Education.

Carter, D., and R. Wilson. 1995. *Minorities in Higher Education.* Washington, D.C.: American Council on Higher Education.

Carter, N. M., and K. R. Allen. 1997. Size Determinants of Women-Owned Businesses: Choice or Barriers to Resources? *Entrepreneurship and Regional Development* 9:211–220.

Carter, N. M., C. G. Brush, P. G. Greene, E. Gatewood, and M. Hart. 2001. Women Entrepreneurs Breaking Through to Equity Markets: The Influence of Human, Social and Financial Capital. Working paper. Minneapolis: St. Thomas University.

Carter, N. M., M. Williams, and P. D. Reynolds. 1997. Discontinuance Among New Firms in Retail: The Influence of Initial Resources, Strategy and Gender. *Journal of Business Venturing* 12:125–146.

Castells, Manuel, and Peter Hall. 1994. *Technopoles of the World.* New York: Routledge.

Catalyst. 1998. *Census of Women Corporate Officers and Top Earners.* New York: Catalyst.

Cavalluzzo, Ken, and Linda Cavalluzzo. 1998. Market Structure and Discrimination: The Case of Small Businesses. *Journal of Money, Credit, and Banking* 30:771–792.

Cavalluzzo, Ken, Linda Cavalluzzo, and John Wolken. 1999. Competition, Small Business Financing, and Discrimination. In Jackson Blanton, Alicia Williams, and Sherri Rhine, eds., *Business Access to Capital and Credit.* Washington, D.C.: Federal Reserve System.

Center for Women's Business Research. 2001. Breaking the Boundaries: The Continued Progress and Achievement of Women-Owned Enterprises. Washington, D.C.: CWBR.

Chandler, Alfred D., Jr. 1977. *The Visible Hand: The Managerial Revolution in American Business*. Cambridge, MA: Harvard University Press.

Charles Stewart Mott Foundation. 1994. *Small Steps Toward Big Dreams: 1994 Update*. Flint, MI.

Chesbrough, Henry, and R. S. Rosenbloom. 2001. The Dual-Edged Role of the Business Model in Leveraging Corporate Technology Investments. In Lewis M. Branscomb and Philip E. Auerswald, eds., *Taking Technical Risks*. Cambridge, MA: MIT Press.

Children Online Protection Act (COPA), codified at 47 U.S.C. § 231; held unconstitutional in 2000 by the Federal Court of Appeals for the Third Circuit.

Children's Internet Protection Act (CIPA), codified as 20 U.S.C. § 9134 and 47 U.S.C. § 254(h).

Christensen, Clayton M. 1997. *The Innovator's Dilemma: When New Technologies Cause Great Firms to Fail*. Boston: Harvard Business School Press.

Clark, Burton R. 1998. *Creating Entrepreneurial Universities*. New York: IAU Press.

Clark, Peggy, and Tracy Huston. 1993. *Assisting the Smallest Businesses: Assessing Microenterprise Development as a Strategy for Boosting Poor Communities*. Washington, D.C.: Aspen Institute.

Clark, Peggy, and Amy Kays. 1995. *Enabling Entrepreneurship: Microenterprise Development in the United States*. Washington, D.C.: Aspen Institute.

Clarke, Susan E., and Gary L. Gaile. 1989. Moving Toward Entrepreneurial Economic Development Policies: Opportunities and Barriers. *Policy Studies Journal* 17:574–598.

Coase, Ronald. 1960. The Problem of Social Cost. 2 *Journal of Law and Economics* 1.

Cobb, James. 1993. *The Selling of the South*. Baton Rouge: Louisiana State University Press.

Coburn, Christopher, ed. 1995. *Partnerships*. Columbus, OH: Battelle.

Cockburn, Iain, Rebecca Henderson, Luigi Orsenigo, and Gary P. Pisano. 1999. Pharmaceuticals and Biotechnology. In David C. Mowery, ed., *U.S. Industry in 2000*. Washington, D.C.: National Academy Press.

Cohen, W., and D. Levinthal. 1989. Innovation and Learning. *Economic Journal* 99:569–596.

Cohen, Wesley M., Richard R. Nelson, and John P. Walsh. 2000. Protecting Their Intellectual Assets. Working Paper #7552. Cambridge, MA: National Bureau of Economic Research.

Coleman, S. 2000. Access to Capital and Terms of Credit: A Comparison of Men- and Women-owned Small Businesses. *Journal of Small Business Management* 38:48–52.

Communications Decency Act (CDA), codified as 47 U.S.C. § 609 (1996).

Computer Science and Telecommunications Board. 1999. *Funding a Revolution*. Washington, D.C.: National Academy Press.

Cooke, Philip, and David Wills. 1999. Small Firms, Social Capital and the Enhancement of Business Performance through Innovation Programmes. *Small Business Economics* 13:219–234.

Cooper, R. S. 2003. Purpose and Performance of the Small Business Innovation Research (SBIR) Program. *Small Business Economics* 20(2): 137–151.

Corporation for Enterprise Development. 1999. *1999 Development Report Card for the States*. Washington, D.C.: CFED.

Corporation for Enterprise Development. 2001. *Infrastructure for Entrepreneurial Development: A Scan of Ten Southern States for the Mary Reynolds Babcock Foundation*. Washington, D.C.: CFED.

Council on Competitiveness. 1996. *Endless Frontier, Limited Resources: U.S. R&D Policy for Competitiveness*. Washington, D.C.: Council on Competitiveness.

Crockett, R. O., and P. Elstrom. 1998. How Motorola Lost Its Way. *Business Week*, May 4, 140–148.

Davis, Steven J., John Haltiwanger, and Scott Schuh. 1996. *Job Creation and Destruction*. Cambridge, MA: MIT Press.

Day, Sue Markland. 2000. The Bay Area: The Best Place in the World to Do Biotech. Unpublished position paper. South San Francisco: Bay Area Bioscience Center. Available at: <http://www.bayareabioscience.org/ppmonogram.html>.

Deger, Renee. 1997. 'Tool Time' for Venture Capital's New Guard Brings Thaw to the Three-Year-Old 'Biotechnology Winter.' *Signals Magazine* (online), November 6. Available at: <http://www.signalsmag.com/signalsmag.nsf/0/A42B0BCED7D42B608825654B006F3BBD>.

De Vol, Ross. 1999. *America's High Technology Economy: Growth, Development, and Risks for Metropolitan Areas*. Los Angeles: The Milken Institute.

Dewar, Margaret E. 1998. Why State and Local Economic Development Programs Cause So Little Economic Development. *Economic Development Quarterly* 12:68–87.

Diffie, Whitfield, and Susan Landau. 1998. *Privacy on the Line*. Cambridge, MA: MIT Press.

Dowling, Michael J., and Jeffrey E. McGee. 1994. Business and Technology Strategies and New Venture Performance: A Study of the Telecommunications Equipment Industry. *Management Science* 40:1663–1677.

Dowling, M. J., and T. W. Ruefli. 1992. Technological Innovation as a Gateway to Entry: The Case of the Telecommunications Equipment Industry. *Research Policy* 21:63–77.

Duch, Raymond. 1991. *Privatizing the Economy*. Ann Arbor: University of Michigan Press.

Dunning, J. H. 1996. The Geographical Sources of Competitiveness of Firms. *Transnational Corporations* 5:1–30.

Dunning, J. H. 1998. The Changing Geography of Foreign Direct Investment. In K. Kumar, ed., *Internationalization, Foreign Direct Investment and Technology Transfer*. London: Routledge.

Edgeworth, Elaine, Joyce Klein, and Peggy Clark. 1996. *The Practice of Microenterprise in the U.S.* Washington, D.C.: Aspen Institute.

Eisinger, Peter K. 1988. *The Rise of the Entrepreneurial State*. Madison: University of Wisconsin Press.

Eisinger, Peter. 1995. State Economic Development Policy in the 1990s. *Economic Development Quarterly* 9:146–158.

Ellison, G., and E. Glaeser. 1997. Geographic Concentration in U.S. Manufacturing Industries: A Dartboard Approach. *Journal of Political Economy* 105:889–927.

Ernst and Young. 2000. The Economic Contributions of the Biotechnology Industry to the U.S. Economy. Washington, D.C.: Biotechnology Industry Organization.

Etzkowitz, Henry. 1989. The Second Academic Revolution: The Role of the Research University in Economic Development. In Susan E. Cozzens, Peter Healey, Arie Rip, and John Ziman, eds., *The Research System in Transition*. Dordrecht: Kluwer.

European Commission. 2003. Green Paper: Entrepreneurship in Europe. Brussels: European Commission.

Evans, Philip, and Thomas S. Wurmser. 2000. *Blown to Bits*. Cambridge, MA: Harvard Business School Press.

Fabowale, L., B. Orser, and A. Riding. 1995. Gender, Structural Factors and Credit Terms between Canadian Small Businesses and Financial Institutions. *Entrepreneurship Theory and Practice* 19:41–65.

Feldman, M. 1994a. Knowledge Complementarity and Innovation. *Small Business Economics* 6:363–372.

Feldman, M. 1994b. *The Geography of Innovation*. Boston: Kluwer.

Feldman, Maryann P. 1994c. The University and Economic Development: The Case of Johns Hopkins University and Baltimore. *Economic Development Quarterly* 8:67–76.

Feldman, Maryann P. 2000. Location and Innovation: The New Economic Geography of Innovation, Spillovers, and Agglomeration. In Gordon Clark, Meric Gertler, and Maryann Feldman, eds., *The Oxford Handbook of Economic Geography*. Oxford: Oxford University Press.

Feldman, Maryann P. 2001. Where Science Comes to Life. *Journal of Comparative Policy Analysis: Research and Practice* 2:345–361.

Feldman, M., and D. Audretsch. 1999. Science-Based Diversity, Specialization, Localized Competition and Innovation. *European Economic Review* 43:409–429.

Feldman, Maryann P., and P. Desrochers. Forthcoming. Truth for Its Own Sake: Academic Culture and Technology Transfer at the Johns Hopkins University. *Minerva*.

Feldman, Maryann P., Irwin Feller, Janet Bercovitz, and Richard Burton. 2002. Equity and the Technology Transfer Strategies of American Research Universities. *Management Science* 48:105–121.

Feldman, Maryann P., and Richard Florida. 1994. The Geographic Sources of Innovation. *Annals of the Association of American Geographers* 84:210–229.

Feldman, Maryann P., and Johanna Francis. 2002. The Entrepreneurial Spark: Individual Agents and the Formation of Innovative Clusters. In Alberto Q. Curzio and Marco Fortis, eds., *Complexity and Industrial Clusters*. New York: Physica-Verlag.

Feldman, Maryann P., and Maryellen R. Kelley. 2002. How States Augment the Capabilities of Technology-Pioneering Firms. *Growth and Change* 33:173–195.

Feldman, Maryann P., and Cynthia R. Ronzio. 2001. Closing the Innovative Loop. *Entrepreneurship and Regional Development* 13:1–16.

Feller, I. 1990a. Universities as Engines of R&D-Based Economic Growth. *Research Policy* 19:335–348.

Feller, I. 1990b. University-Industry R&D Relationships. In J. Schmandt and R. Wilson, eds., *Growth Policy in the Age of High Technology*. Boston: Unwin Hyman.

Feller, I. 1997. Federal and State Government Roles in Science and Technology. *Economic Development Quarterly* 11:283–296.

Feller, I., M. Feldman, J. Bercovitz, and R. Burton. 2002. The State of Practice for University Technology Transfer Activities. *Research Management Review Online*. Available at: http://www.ncura.edu/rmr/feature16.htm.

Ferguson, Charles H. 1999. *High Stakes, No Prisoners: A Winner's Tale of Greed and Glory in the Internet Wars*. New York: Times Business.

Flamm, Kenneth. 1988. *Creating the Computer*. Washington, D.C.: Brookings Institution Press.

Florida, Richard. 2002. *The Rise of the Creative Class: And How It's Transforming Work, Leisure, Community and Everyday Life*. New York: Basic Books.

Friar, J., and M. Horwitch. 1986. The Emergence of Technology Strategy: A New Dimension of Strategic Management. In M. Horwitch, ed., *Technology in the Modern Corporation: A Strategic Perspective*. New York: Pergamon.

Fritsch, M. 1997. New Firms and Regional Employment Change. *Small Business Economics* 9:437–448.

Frye, Timothy. 2001. Keeping Shop. In Peter Murrell, ed., *Assessing the Value of Law in Transition Economies*. Ann Arbor: University of Michigan Press.

Galbraith, John K. 1956. *American Capitalism*. Rev. ed. Boston: Houghton Mifflin.

Gelijns, Annetine, and Nathan Rosenberg. 1999. Diagnostic Devices: An Analysis of Comparative Advantages. In David C. Mowery and Richard R. Nelson, eds., *Sources of Industrial Leadership*. New York: Cambridge University Press.

GEN Directory. 1997. *Genetic Engineering News Guide to Biotechnology Companies*. New York: Mary Ann Liebert, Inc.

George Washington University School of Business and Public Management. 2000. National Entrepreneurship Survey. Washington, D.C.: George Washington University.

Georgia Research Alliance. 1999. Background and History. Available at: http://www.gra.org/background.html.

Geuna, Aldo. 1999. *The Economics of Knowledge Production: Funding and the Structure of University Research*. Cheltenham, U.K.: Edward Elgar.

Ginsburg, Jane C. 1999. Copyright Legislation for the 'Digital Millennium.' 23 *Columbia-VLA Journal of Law and the Arts* 137.

Glaeser, Edward. 1998. Are Cities Dying? *Journal of Economic Perspectives* 12:139–160.

Glaeser, Edward. 2000. The New Economics of Urban and Regional Growth. In Gordon Clark, Meric Gertler, and Maryann Feldman, eds., *The Oxford Handbook of Economic Geography*. Oxford: Oxford University Press.

Glaeser, E., H. Kallal, J. Scheinkman, and A. Shleifer. 1992. Growth of Cities. *Journal of Political Economy* 100:1126–1152.

Glaeser, Edward L., Jed Kolko, and Albert Saiz. 2001. Consumer City. *Journal of Economic Geography* 1:27–50.

Glasmeier, Amy. 1991. Technological Discontinuities and Flexible Production Networks. *Research Policy* 20:469–485.

Glendon, Spencer. 1998. Urban Life Cycles. Unpublished working paper. Cambridge, MA: Harvard University, Department of Economics.

Gompers, P., and J. Lerner. 1999. *The Venture Capital Cycle*. Cambridge, MA: MIT Press.

Gompers, Paul A., and Joshua Lerner. 2002. Short-Term America Revisited? Boom and Bust in the Venture Capital Industry and the Impact on Innovation. In Adam Jaffe, Joshua Lerner, and Scott Stern, eds., *Innovation Policy and the Economy, Volume 3*. Cambridge, MA: National Bureau of Economic Research.

Good, Mary L. 2001. New Alliance Targets Funding Shortfall. *Research Technology Management*, July–August, 9–10.

Griliches, Z. 1979. Issues in Assessing the Contribution of R&D to Productivity Growth. *Bell Journal of Economics* 10:92–116.

Griliches, Zvi. 1992. The Search for R&D Spillovers. *Scandinavian Journal of Economics* 94 (supplement):29–47.

Hale & Dorr LLP. 2001. *IPO Report 2001*. Boston: Hale & Dorr LLP.

Hall, Bronwyn H. 2002. The Financing of Research and Development. Working Paper #8773. Cambridge, MA: National Bureau of Economic Research.

Hambrick, D. C. 1983. High Profit Strategies in Mature Capital Goods Industries: A Contingency Approach. *Academy of Management Journal* 26:687–707.

Hambrick, D. C., D. A. Nadler, and M. L. Tushman, eds. 1998. *Navigating Change: How CEOs, Top Teams, and Boards Steer Transformation*. Boston: Harvard Business School Press.

Hannan, M. T., and J. H. Freeman. 1989. *Organizational Ecology*. Cambridge, MA: Harvard University Press.

Harayama, Yuko. 1998. The Relationship between Stanford University and Silicon Valley Industry. Unpublished manuscript. Geneva: University of Geneva.

Harrigan, Kathryn. 1988. Joint Ventures and Competitive Strategy. *Strategic Management Journal* 9:141–158.

Hart, David M. 2001a. Antitrust and Technological Innovation. *Research Policy* 30:923–936.

Hart, David M. 2001b. New Economy, Old Politics: The Evolving Role of the High-Technology Industry in Washington, D.C. In John Donahue and Joseph Nye, eds., *Governance Among Bigger, Better Markets*. Washington, D.C.: Brookings Institution Press.

Haug, P. 1994. Formation of Biotechnology Firms in the Greater Seattle Region. *Environment and Planning* A 27:249–267.

Hausmaninger, Herbert. 2000. *The Austrian Legal System*, 2nd ed. Boston: Kluwer Law International.

Haveman, H. 1992. Between a Rock and a Hard Place: Organizational Change and Performance under Conditions of Fundamental Environmental Transformation. *Administrative Science Quarterly* 37:48–75.

Heileman, John. 2000. *Pride Before the Fall*. New York: Harper Collins.

Heller, Michael A. 2001. A Property Theory Perspective on Russian Enterprise Reform. In Peter Murrell, ed., *Assessing the Value of Law in Transition Economies*. Ann Arbor: University of Michigan Press.

Hellmann, Thomas. 1998. The Allocation of Control Rights in Venture Capital Contracts. *RAND Journal of Economics* 29:57–76.

Henderson, R., et al. 1999. The Pharmaceutical Industry and the Revolution in Molecular Biology. In D. Mowery and R. Nelson, eds., *Sources of Industrial Leadership*. New York: Cambridge University Press.

Henderson, V. 1986. Efficiency of Resource Usage and City Size. *Journal of Urban Economics* 19:47–70.

Henderson, Vernon. 1994. Externalities and Industrial Development. Working Paper #4730. Cambridge, MA: National Bureau of Economic Research.

Henderson, Vernon, Ari Kuncoro, and Matt Turner. 1995. Industrial Development in Cities. *Journal of Political Economy* 103:1067–1090.

Hendley, Kathryn. 2001. Beyond the Tip of the Iceberg. In Peter Murrell, ed., *Assessing the Value of Law in Transition Economies*. Ann Arbor: University of Michigan Press.

Hendley, Kathryn, Peter Murrell, and Randi Ryterman. 2001. Law Works in Russia. In Peter Murrell, ed., *Assessing the Value of Law in Transition Economies*. Ann Arbor: University of Michigan Press.

Hendrix, Glenn P. 2001. The Experience of Foreign Litigants in Russia's Commercial Courts. In Peter Murrell, ed., *Assessing the Value of Law in Transition Economies*. Ann Arbor: University of Michigan Press.

Herzenberg, Stephen A., John A. Alic, and Howard Wial. 1998. *New Rules for a New Economy*. Ithaca: Cornell University Press.

Hills, Jill. 1986. *Deregulating Telecoms*. London: F. Pinter.

Hirschman, Albert O. 1970. *Exit, Voice, and Loyalty*. Cambridge, MA: Harvard University Press.

Hobbs, Steven H. 1997. Toward a Theory of Law and Entrepreneurship. 26 *Capitol University Law Review* 241.

Hogan, William. 2001. The California Meltdown. *Harvard Magazine*, September–October.

Holbrook, D. 1995. Government Support of the Semiconductor Industry. *Business and Economic History* 24:133–168.

Holbrook, D., W. M. Cohen, D. A. Hounshell, and S. Klepper. 2000. The Nature, Sources, and Consequences of Firm Differences in the Early History of the Semiconductor Industry. *Strategic Management Journal* 21:1017–1041.

Hosley, Albon. 1938. Seventy-Five Years of Negro Business. *Crisis* 45:241–242.

Hubbard, Robert Glenn, and W. M. Gentry. 2000. Tax Policy and Entrepreneurial Entry. *American Economic Review* 90:283–287.

Innis, Roy. 1969. Separatist Economics: A New Social Contract. In G. Douglas Pugh and William Haddad, eds., *Black Economic Development*. Englewood Cliffs, NJ: Prentice-Hall.

Irvine, John, Ben R. Martin, and Phoebe Isard. 1990. *Investing in the Future*. Hants, U.K.: E. Elgar Aldershot.

Isserman, Andrew M. 1994. State Economic Development Policy and Practice in the U.S.: A Survey Article. *International Regional Science Review* 16:49–100.

Jacobs, Jane. 1961. *The Death and Life of Great American Cities*. New York: Random House.

Jacobs, Jane. 1969. *The Economy of Cities.* New York: Random House.

Jacobs, Jane. 1984. *Cities and the Wealth of Nations.* New York: Random House.

Jaffe, A. 1989. The Real Effects of Academic Research. *American Economic Review* 79:957–970.

Jaffe, A., M. Trajtenberg, and R. Henderson. 1993. Geographic Localization of Knowledge Spillovers as Evidenced by Patent Citations. *Quarterly Journal of Economics* 63:577–598.

Jaynes, Gerald, and Robin Williams. 1989. *A Common Destiny: Blacks in American Society.* Washington, D.C.: National Academy Press.

Jones, Charles I., and John C. Williams. 1998. Measuring the Social Returns to R&D. *Quarterly Journal of Economics* 113:1119–1135.

Journal of Technology Transfer. 2001. Special Issue on Organizational Issues in University-Industry Technology Transfer. 26, Issue 1–2, January.

Judd, Kenneth, Karl Schmedders, and Sevin Yeltekin. 2002. Optimal Policies for Patent Races. Paper presented to the Harvard/MIT Industrial Organization Seminar, April 8.

Judson, Horace. 1979. *The Eighth Day of Creation.* New York: Simon and Schuster.

Kalt, Joseph P., ed. 1996. *New Horizons in Natural Gas Deregulation.* Westport, CT: Praeger.

Kamien, M., and N. Schwartz. 1975. Market Structure and Innovation: A Survey. *Journal of Economic Literature* 13:1–7.

Katznelson, Ira. 1992. The State to the Rescue? Political Science and History Reconnect. *Social Research* 59:719–737.

Kauffman Center for Entrepreneurial Leadership. 2000. *FastTrac Follow-Up Survey.* Kansas City, MO: KCEL.

Kauffman Center for Entrepreneurial Leadership. 2001. *FastTrac New Venture and FastTrac Planning Follow-Up Survey, Fall 1998 through Spring 1999 Classes.* Kansas City, MO: KCEL.

Kelly, K. 1997. New Rules for the New Economy: Twelve Dependable Principles for Thriving in a Turbulent World. *Wired*, September, 140–197.

Kenney, Martin. 1986. *Biotechnology.* New Haven: Yale University Press.

Kenney, Martin, and Urs von Burg. 2000. Institutions and Economies. In Martin Kenney, ed., *Understanding Silicon Valley.* Stanford: Stanford University Press.

Kindleberger, C. P., and D. B. Audretsch. 1983. *The Multinational Corporation in the 1980s.* Cambridge, MA: MIT Press.

Klepper, S. 1996. Entry, Exit, Growth, and Innovation over the Product Life Cycle. *American Economic Review* 86:562–583.

Klepper, Steven, and Sally Sleeper. 2000. Entry by spinoffs. Unpublished manuscript.

Kortum, S., and J. Lerner. 1997. Stronger Protection or Technological Revolution. Working Paper #6204. Cambridge, MA: National Bureau of Economic Research.

Kotkin, Joel. 2000. *The New Economic Geography: How the Digital Revolution Is Reshaping the American Landscape.* New York: Random House.

Kourilsky, Marilyn L., and William B. Walstad. 2000. *The E Generation.* Dubuque, IA: Kendall-Hunt.

Krugman, P. 1991a. Increasing Returns and Economic Geography. *Journal of Political Economy* 99:483–499.

Krugman, P. 1991b. *Geography and Trade.* Cambridge, MA: MIT Press.

Lane, Joseph P. 1999. Understanding Technology Transfer. *Assistive Technology* 11:1–19.

Langlois, Richard, and David C. Mowery. 1996. The Federal Government Role in the Development of the U.S. Software Industry. In David C. Mowery, ed., *The International Computer Software Industry.* New York: Oxford University Press.

Langlois, Richard, and Ed Steinmueller. 1999. The Evolution of Competitive Advantage in the Worldwide Semiconductor Industry, 1947–1996. In David C. Mowery and Richard R. Nelson, eds., *Sources of Industrial Leadership.* New York: Cambridge University Press.

Leflar, Robert A. 1968. *American Conflicts Law.* Indianapolis: Bobbs-Merrill Company.

Leonard, Dorothy, and Walter Swap. 2000. Gurus in the Garage. *Harvard Business Review*, November–December, 5–12.

Lerner, J. 1999a. The Government As Venture Capitalist. *Journal of Business* 72: 285–297.

Lerner, Josh. 1999b. Venture Capital and the Commercialization of Academic Technology: Symbiosis and Paradox. In Lewis M. Branscomb, Fumio Kodama, and Richard Florida, eds., *Industrializing Knowledge: University-Industry Linkages in Japan and the United States.* Cambridge, MA: MIT Press.

Lerner, J., and C. Kegler. 2000. Evaluating the Small Business Innovation Research Program: A Literature Review. In C. Wessner, ed., *The Small Business Innovation Research Program.* Washington, D.C.: National Academy Press.

Leslie, Stuart. 1993. *The Cold War and American Science.* New York: Columbia University Press.

Leslie, Stuart, and Robert H. Kargon. 1996. Selling Silicon Valley. *Business History Review* 70:435–472.

Leslie, Stuart W. 2001. Regional Disadvantage: Replicating Silicon Valley in New York's Capital Region. *Technology and Culture* 42:236–264.

Lessig, Lawrence. 2001. *The Future of Ideas: The Fate of the Commons in a Connected World*. New York: Random House.

Levin, S. G., and P. E. Stephan. 1991. Research Productivity over the Life Cycle. *American Economic Review* 81:114–132.

Levy, Steven. 2001. *Crypto*. New York: Viking.

Lewis, Michael. 2000. *The New New Thing*. New York: W. W. Norton and Company.

Light, Ivan. 1972. *Ethnic Enterprise in America*. Berkeley: University of California Press.

Lindblom, Charles E. 1977. *Politics and Markets*. New York: Basic Books.

Link, A. N. 1995. *A Generosity of Spirit*. Durham, NC: Duke University Press.

Link, A. N., and J. T. Scott. 2003. The Growth of Research Triangle Park. *Small Business Economics*.

Litman, Jessica. 2001. *Digital Copyright*. Amherst, NY: Prometheus Books.

Lloyd, Richard, and Terry Nichols Clark. 2001. The City as an Entertainment Machine. In Kevin Fox Gotham, ed., *Critical Perspectives on Urban Redevelopment*. Oxford, U.K.: JAI Press/Elsevier.

Logan, John R., Rachel B. Whaley, and Kyle Crowder. 1997. The Character and Consequences of Growth Machines: An Assessment of Twenty Years of Research. *Urban Affairs Review* 32:603–630.

Logan, John R., and Harvey L. Molotch. 1987. *Urban Fortunes: The Political Economy of Place*. Berkeley: University of California Press.

Low, M. B., and I. C. MacMillan. 1988. Entrepreneurship: Past Research and Future Challenges. *Journal of Management* 14:139–161.

Lowen, Rebecca. 1997. *Creating the Cold War University*. Berkeley: University of California Press.

Lowi, Theodore. 1964. American Business, Public Policy, Case-Studies, and Political Theory. *World Politics* 16:677–716.

Lucas, Robert, Jr. 1988. On the Mechanics of Economic Development. *Journal of Monetary Economics* 22:3–42.

Lugar, M. 2001. The Research Triangle Experience. In C. Wessner, ed., *Industry-Laboratory Partnerships*. Washington, D.C.: National Academy Press.

Lugar, M., and H. Goldstein. 1991. *Technology in the Garden*. Chapel Hill: The University of North Carolina Press.

Lundstrom, Anders, and Lois Stevenson. 2001. *Entrepreneurship Policy for the Future*. Stockholm: Swedish Foundation for Small Business Research.

Maddy, Monique. 2000. Dream Deferred: The Story of a High-Tech Entrepreneur in a Low-Tech World. *Harvard Business Review*, May–June, 149–156.

Mansfield, Ed. 1991. Academic Research and Industrial Innovation. *Research Policy* 20:1–12.

March, James G., and Johan P. Olsen. 1984. The New Institutionalism: Organizational Factors in Political Life. *American Political Science Review* 78:734–749.

Markusen, A. 1996. Sticky Places in Slippery Space. *Economic Geography* 72:293–313.

Marx, Karl. 1959. *Das Capital*, vol III. Moscow: Foreign Languages Publishing House.

Mattoon, Richard H. 1993. Economic Development Policy in the 1990s – Are State Economic Development Agencies Ready? In *Economic Perspectives*. Chicago: Federal Reserve Bank of Chicago.

Mayer-Schönberger, Viktor. 1999. Operator, Please Give Me Information. In Sharon E. Gillett and Ingo Vogelsang, eds., *Competition, Regulation, and Convergence*. Mahwah, NJ: Lawrence Erlbaum.

Mayer-Schönberger, Viktor. 2001a. Information Law Amid Bigger, Better Markets. In Joseph S. Nye and John D. Donahue, eds., *Governance Amid Bigger, Better Markets*. Washington, D.C.: Brookings Institution Press.

Mayer-Schönberger, Viktor. 2001b. The International Lawyer in Times of Cyberspace. In Jens Drolshammer and Michael Pfeifer, eds., *The Internationalization of the Practice of Law*. Boston: Kluwer Law International.

Mayer-Schönberger, Viktor, and David Lazer. 2002. Governing Networks: Telecommunication Deregulation in Europe and the U.S. 27 *Brooklyn Journal of International Law* 819.

Mayer-Schönberger, Viktor, and Mathias Strasser. 1999. A Closer Look at Telecom Deregulation. 12 *Harvard Journal of Law and Technology* 561.

McGroddy, James. 2001. Raising Mice In The Elephants' Cage. In Lewis M. Branscomb and Philip E. Auerswald, eds., *Taking Technical Risks: How Innovators, Executives and Investors Manage High-Tech Risks*. Cambridge, MA: MIT Press.

Medearis, John. 2001. *Joseph Schumpeter's Two Theories of Democracy*. Cambridge, MA: Harvard University Press.

Meerschwam, David. 1991. *Breaking Financial Boundaries*. Cambridge, MA: Harvard Business School Press.

Metzger, Jeanne. 2001. Venture Capital Investments Achieve Record Levels in 2000, Torrid Pace Relaxed in Fourth Quarter. National Venture Capital Association website. Available at: www.nvca.org/VEpress01_29_01>.

Micklethwait, John. 1997. Silicon Valley: The Valley of Money's Delight. *The Economist*, March 29, 5–21.

Miles, Sara. 2001. *How to Hack a Party Line: The Democrats and Silicon Valley*. New York: Farrar, Straus & Giroux.

Miner, Anne S., Dale T. Eesley, Michael Devaughn, and Thekla Rura-Polley. 2001. The Magic Beanstalk Vision. In Claudia Bird Schoonhoven and

Elaine Romanelli, eds., *The Entrepreneurial Dynamic*. Stanford: Stanford University Press.

Miranda, Rowan, and Donald Rosdil. 1995. From Boosterism to Qualitative Growth: Classifying Economic Development Strategies. *Urban Affairs Review* 30:868–879.

Mokyr, Joel. 1990. *The Lever of Riches*. New York: Oxford University Press.

Moore, Gordon. 1996. Some Personal Perspectives on Research in the Semiconductor Industry. In R. Rosenbloom and W. Spencer, eds., *Engines of Innovation*. Cambridge, MA: Harvard Business School Press.

Moore, Gordon, and Kevin Davis. 2000. Learning the Silicon Valley Way. Unpublished manuscript prepared for the CREEG Conference on Silicon Valley and its Imitators, Stanford University, July 28.

Moran, Michael. 1991. *The Politics of the Financial Services Revolution*. Houndmills, Basingstoke, Hampshire, U.K.: Macmillan.

Morange, M. 1998. *A History of Molecular Biology*. Cambridge, MA: Harvard University Press.

Morgenthaler, David. 2000. Assessing Technical Risk. In Lewis M. Branscomb and Kenneth P. Morse, eds., *Managing Technical Risk: Understanding Private Sector Decision Making on Early Stage, Technology-based Projects*. Report No. GCR 00-787. Gaithersburg, MD: National Institute of Standards.

Mosakowski, E. 1983. Organizational Boundaries and Economic Performance: An Empirical Study of Entrepreneurial Computer Firms. *Strategic Management Journal* 12:115–134.

Mowery, David. 1996. *The International Computer Software Industry*. New York: Oxford University Press.

Mowery, D. C., R. R. Nelson, B. N. Sampat, and A. A. Ziedonis. 1999. The Effects of the Bayh-Dole Act on U.S. University Research and Technology Transfer. In L. Branscomb, F. Kodama, and R. Florida, eds., *Industrializing Knowledge*. Cambridge, MA: MIT Press.

Mowery, David C., and Nathan Rosenberg. 1979. The Influence of Market Demand Upon Innovation. *Research Policy* 8:102–153.

Mowery, David, and Nathan Rosenberg. 1998. *Paths of Innovation*. New York: Cambridge University Press.

Mowery, David, and T. Simcoe. 2001. Is the Internet a U.S. Invention? Unpublished manuscript. Berkeley: Haas School of Business.

Myrdal, Gunnar. 1944. *An American Dilemma*. New York: Harper and Brothers.

Nakajima, Eric, and Robert Smith. 2001. *State Economic Development Policy in Massachusetts 1983–1991*. Unpublished working paper. Boston: Northeastern University Center for Urban and Regional Policy.

National Association of State Development Agencies. 1998. *State Economic Development Expenditure Survey*. Washington, D.C.: NASDA.

National Commission on Entrepreneurship. 2001a. *Building Entrepreneurial Networks*. Washington, D.C.: National Commission on Entrepreneurship.

National Commission on Entrepreneurship. 2001b. *High-Growth Companies*. Washington, D.C.: NCOE.

National Foundation for Women Business Owners. 1998a. *Capital, Credit and Financing: An Update*. Silver Spring, MD: NFWBO.

National Foundation for Women Business Owners. 1998b. *Paths to Entrepreneurship: New Directions for Women in Business*. Silver Spring, MD: NFWBO.

National Foundation for Women Business Owners. 2001. *Entrepreneurial Vision in Action: Exploring Growth Among Women- and Men-Owned Firms*. Silver Spring, MD: NFWBO.

National Institutes of Health. 1997. *Setting Research Priorities at the National Institutes of Health*. Bethesda, MD: NIH.

National Research Council. 2001a. *Capitalizing on New Needs and New Opportunities: Government-Industry Partnerships in Biotechnology and Information Technologies*. Washington, D.C.: National Academy Press.

National Research Council. 2001b. *Stem Cells and the Future of Regenerative Medicine*. Washington, D.C.: National Academy Press.

National Science Board. 1996. *Science and Engineering Indicators 1996*. Washington, D.C.: NSB.

National Science Board. 2000. *Science and Engineering Indicators 2000*. Washington, D.C.: NSB.

National Science Board. 2002. *Science and Engineering Indicators 2002*. Washington, D.C.: NSB.

National Science Foundation, Division of Science Resources Studies. 2001. *Federal Funds for Research and Development: Fiscal Years 1999, 2000, and 2001*. Arlington, VA: NSF.

National Venture Capital Association. 2003. Venture Capital Investing Flat in Q4 2002. Available at: http://www.pwcmoneytree.com/moneytree/pdfs/02_Q4_Survey_Highlights.pdf.

Nature. 2001. The Human Genome. *Nature*. 409:745–964.

Nelson, Richard R. 1959. The Simple Economics Of Basic Scientific Research. *Journal of Political Economy* 67:297–306.

Nelson, Richard R. 1990. Capitalism as an Engine of Progress. *Research Policy* 19:193–214.

Nelson, Richard R., ed. 1993. *National Innovation Systems: A Comparative Analysis*. New York: Oxford University Press.

Nelson, Richard. 2001. Observations on the Post Bayh-Dole Rise in Patenting at American Universities. *Journal of Technology Transfer* 16:13–19.

Nelson, Richard, and Nathan Rosenberg. 1993. Technical Innovation and National Systems. In Richard Nelson, ed., *National Innovation Systems.* Oxford, U.K.: Oxford University Press.

New State Ice Co. v. Liebmann, 285 U.S. 262 (1932).

Noam, Eli M. 2001. *Interconnecting the Network of Networks.* Cambridge, MA: MIT Press.

Norberg, A., and J. O'Neill. 1996. *Transforming Computer Technology.* Baltimore: Johns Hopkins University Press.

North, Douglass C. 1994. Economic Performance Through Time. *American Economic Review* 84:359–367.

Olson, Mancur. 1965. *The Logic of Collective Action.* Cambridge, MA: Harvard University Press.

O'Reilly, James T. 2000. Entrepreneurs and Regulators. 10 *Cornell Journal of Law and Public Policy* 63.

Osnabrugge, Mark van, and Robert J. Robinson. 2000. *Angel Investing: Matching Start-up Funds with Start-up Companies.* Cambridge, MA: Harvard Business School Press.

Pages, Erik R. 2001. The Telecom Crash: A Meltdown or a Healthy Pause? Available at: www.entreprenuer.com, May 30.

Park, Robert, E. Burgess, and R. McKenzie. 1925. *The City.* Chicago: University of Chicago Press.

Pei, Minxin. 2001. Does Legal Reform Protect Economic Transactions? In Peter Murrell, ed., *Assessing the Value of Law in Transition Economies.* Ann Arbor: University of Michigan Press.

Pink, Daniel. 2001. *Free Agent Nation.* New York: Warner Books.

Piore, Michael J., and Charles F. Sabel. 1984. *The Second Industrial Divide.* New York: Basic Books.

Pisano, G. P., W. Shan, and D. J. Teece. 1988. Joint Ventures and Collaboration in the Biotechnology Industry. In D. C. Mowery, ed., *International Collaborative Ventures in U.S. Manufacturing.* Cambridge, MA: Ballinger.

Plosila, Walter. 2001. Universities, Entrepreneurs, and Regional Innovation Centers. Presentation to the Kennedy School-National Commission on Entrepreneurship Conference on Entrepreneurship and Public Policy, April 10.

Porter, M. E. 1985. *Competitive Advantage.* New York: Free Press.

Porter, Michael E. 1990. *The Competitive Advantage of Nations.* New York: Free Press.

Porter, Michael E. 1995. The Competitive Advantages of the Inner City. *Harvard Business Review*, May–June, 55–71.

Porter, Michael E. 1998. Clusters and the New Economics of Competition, *Harvard Business Review*, November–December, 77–90.

Porter, M. E. 2000a. Locations, Clusters, and Company Strategy. In G. L. Clark, M. P. Feldman, and M. S. Gertler, eds., *The Oxford Handbook of Economic Geography*. Oxford, U.K.: Oxford University Press.

Porter, Michael E. 2000b. Location, Competition and Economic Development: Local Clusters in a Global Economy. *Economic Development Quarterly* 14:15–34.

Porter, Michael E. 2000c. Clusters and Government Policy. *Wirtschaftspolitische Blaetter* 472:144–154.

Posner, Richard A. 1976. *The Robinson-Patman Act: Federal Regulation of Price Differences*. Washington, D.C.: American Enterprise Institute.

Powell, W. W., and J. Owen-Smith. 1998. Universities and the Market for Intellectual Property in the Life Sciences. *Journal of Policy Analysis and Management* 172:227–253.

Powell, Walter W., Kenneth W. Koput, and Laurel Smith-Doerr. 1996. Interorganizational Collaboration and the Locus of Innovation. *Administrative Science Quarterly* 41:116–145.

Pratt's Guide to Venture Capital Sources, 1995; 2000 Editions. NY: Securities Data Publishing Press.

President's Interagency Task Force on Women Business Owners. 1979. *The Bottom Line: Unequal Enterprise in America*. Washington, D.C.: Interagency Task Force on Women Business Owners.

Preston, John T. 1993. Testimony before the Subcommittee on Energy, Committee on Science, Space, and Technology, U.S. House of Representatives. In *Technology Transfer* (93–H701–32). Washington, D.C.: GPO.

Preston, John T. 1997. Technology Innovation and Environmental Progress. In M. Chertow and D. Esty, eds., *Thinking Ecologically: The Next Generation of Environmental Policy*. New Haven: Yale University Press.

Prevezer, M. 1997. The Dynamics of Industrial Clustering in Biotechnology. *Small Business Economics* 93:255–271.

Prevezer, Martha. 1998. Comparison and Interaction between Computing and Biotechnology. In G. M. Peter Swann, Martha Prevezer, and David Stout, eds., *The Dynamics of Industrial Clustering*. Oxford, U.K.: Oxford University Press.

Prevezer, Martha. 2001. Ingredients in the Early Development of the U.S. Biotechnology Industry. *Small Business Economics* 17:17–29.

Prodi, Romano. 2002. For a New European Entrepreneurship. Paper delivered to the Instituto de Empresa Madrid, February.

Progressive Policy Institute. 1999. *Metropolitan New Economy Index*. Washington, D.C.: PPI.

Putnam, Robert. 2001. *Bowling Alone*. New York: Touchstone Publishers.

Quigley, John M. 1998. Urban Diversity and Economic Growth. *Journal of Economic Perspectives* 12:127–138.

Rae, Andre. 1994. A National Study of Economic Development Organizations at the State Level: The Key Organizations, Their Industrial Constituencies, and Their Networks. *Economic Development Quarterly* 8:292–301.

Raider, H. 1998. Repeated Exchange and Evidence of Trust in the Substance Contract. Unpublished working paper. New York: Columbia University.

Reichert, Janice. 2000. New Biopharmaceuticals in the USA. *Trends in Biotechnology* 18:364–369.

Reinhold, Barbara. 2001. *Free to Succeed*. New York: Plume.

Reynolds, Paul D. 2000. National Panel Study of Business Startups: Background and Methodology. *Advances in Entrepreneurship, Firm Emergence and Growth* 4:153–227.

Reynolds, P. D., S. M. Camp, W. D. Bygrave, E. Autio, and M. Hay. 2001. *Global Entrepreneurship Monitor*. Kansas City, MO: Kauffman Center for Entrepreneurial Leadership.

Reynolds, Paul D., Michael Hay, and S. Michael Camp. 1999. *Global Entrepreneurship Monitor 1999*. Kansas City, MO: Kauffman Foundation.

Reynolds, P. D., M. Hay, W. D. Bygrave, S. M. Camp, and E. Autio. 2000. *Global Entrepreneurship Monitor*. Kansas City, MO: Kauffman Center for Entrepreneurial Leadership.

Reynolds, P. D., B. Miller, and W. R. Maki. 1995. Explaining Regional Variation in Business Births and Deaths: U.S. 1976–1988. *Small Business Economics* 7:389–407.

Riding, A., and C. Swift. 1990. Women Business Owners and Terms of Credit: Some Empirical Findings of the Canadian Experience. *Journal of Business Venturing* 5:327–340.

Riesman, David. 1950. *The Lonely Crowd*. New Haven: Yale University Press.

Rivette, Kevin G., and David Kline. 2000. *Rembrandts in the Attic*. Cambridge, MA: Harvard Business School Press.

Romer, Paul M. 1990. Endogenous Technological Change. *Journal of Political Economy* 98:S71–S102.

Romer, Paul. 1993. Economic Growth. In David R. Henderson, ed., *The Fortune Encyclopedia of Economics*. New York: Time Warner Books.

Romer, Paul. 2000. Should the Government Subsidize Supply or Demand in the Market for Scientists and Engineers? National Bureau of Economic Research (NBER) Working Paper 7723 (June).

Rosenberg, Nathan. 1994. *Exploring the Black Box*. New York: Cambridge University Press.

Rosenberg, Nathan, and L. E. Birdzell, Jr. 1986. *How the West Grew Rich*. New York: Basic Books.

Rosenberg, N., and R. R. Nelson. 1994. American Universities and Technical Advance in Industry. *Research Policy* 23:325–348.

Rosenfeld, Stuart A. 2001. Networks and Clusters. In *Exploring Policy Options for a New Rural America*. Kansas City, MO: Federal Reserve Bank of Kansas City.

Ross, Doug, and Robert E. Friedman. 1990. The Emerging Third Wave. *The Entrepreneurial Economy Review* 9:3–10.

Rowen, Henry. 2000. Serendipity or Strategy. In Chong-Moon Lee et al., eds., *Silicon Valley Edge*. Stanford: Stanford University Press.

Roy, William G. 1997. *Socializing Capital: The Rise of the Large Industrial Corporation in America*. Princeton: Princeton University Press.

Ruttan, Vernon W. 2001. *Technology, Growth, and Development*. Oxford, U.K.: Oxford University Press.

Samuelson, Pamela. 1996. The Copyright Grab. *Wired*, January, 134.

Saxenian, A. 1990. Regional Networks and the Resurgence of Silicon Valley. *California Management Review* 33:89–111.

Saxenian, Annalee. 1994. *Regional Advantage*. Cambridge, MA: Harvard University Press.

Saxenian, Annalee. 1999. *Silicon Valley's New Immigrant Entrepreneurs*. San Francisco, CA: Public Policy Institute of California.

Schachtel, M. R. B., and M. P. Feldman. 2000. Reinforcing Interactions Between the Advanced Technology Program and State Technology Programs. In *Volume I: A Guide to State Business Assistance Programs for New Technology Creation and Commercialization*. Report prepared for the Advanced Technology Program, National Institute of Standards and Technology, U.S. Department of Commerce. April.

Scherer, F. M. 1992. *International High-Technology Competition*. Cambridge, MA: Harvard University Press.

Scherer, F. M. 1999. *New Perspectives on Economic Growth and Technological Innovation*. Washington: Brookings Institution Press.

Scherer, F. M., and Dietmar Harhoff. 2000. Technology Policy For A World Of Skew-Distributed Outcomes. *Research Policy* 29:559–566.

Schipke, Alfred. 2001. *Why Do Governments Divest?* New York: Springer.

Schumpeter, Joseph A. 1942. *Capitalism, Socialism and Democracy*. New York: Harper Brothers.

Schumpeter, Joseph. 1947. The Creative Response in Economic History. *Journal of Economic History* 7:149–159.

Schweke, William. 1985. Why Local Governments Need an Entrepreneurial Policy. *Public Management* 67:3–6.

Science. 2001. The Human Genome. *Science* 291:1145–1434.

Scoles, Eugene, and Peter Hay. 1992. *Conflict of Laws*, 2nd edition. St. Paul: West Publishing Company.

Servan-Schreiber, J.-J. 1968. *The American Challenge*. London: Hamish Hamilton.

Servon, Lisa. 1999. *Bootstrap Capital*. Washington, D.C.: Brookings Institution Press.

Servon, Lisa, and Timothy Bates. 1998. Microenterprise as an Exit Route from Poverty. *Journal of Urban Affairs* 20:419–441.

Shane, Scott, and S. Venkataraman. 2000. The Promise of Entrepreneurship as a Field of Research. *Academy of Management Review* 25:217–226.

Shapero, Albert. 1981. Entrepreneurship. *Economic Development Commentary* 7:19–23.

Shapira, Philip. 1998. Manufacturing Extension. In Lewis M. Branscomb and James H. Keller, eds., *Investing in Innovation*. Cambridge, MA: MIT Press.

Shapira, Philip. 2000. Evaluating Manufacturing Extension Services in the U.S. Paper presented at U.S.-EU Workshop, Bad Herrenalb, Germany, September.

Shapiro, C., and H. R. Varian. 1998. *Information Rules: A Strategic Guide to the Network Economy*. Boston: Harvard Business School Press.

Shell, Karl. 1966. Toward a Theory of Inventive Activity and Capital Accumulation. *American Economic Review* 56:62–68.

Shell, Karl. 1967. A Model of Inventive Activity and Capital Accumulation. In K. Shell, ed., *Essays on the Theory of Optimal Economic Growth*. Cambridge, MA: MIT Press.

Shepherd, D. A., and E. J. Douglas. 1999. *Attracting Equity Investors: Positioning, Preparing and Presenting the Business Plan*. Thousand Oaks, CA: Sage Publications.

Shils, Edward. 1997. *The Order of Learning*. New Brunswick, NJ: Transaction Publishers.

Simon, Herbert A. 1957. *Administrative Behavior: A Study of Decision-Making Processes in Administrative Organizations*, 2nd ed. New York: Macmillan.

Sohl, Jeffrey E. 1999. The Early-Stage Equity Market in the USA. *Venture Capital* 1:101–120.

Solomon, George T., Susan Duffy, and Ayman Tarabishy. 2002. The State of Entrepreneurship Education in the United States: A Nationwide Survey and Analysis. *International Journal of Entrepreneurship Education* 1:65–86.

Spar, Debora L. 2001. *Ruling the Waves*. New York: Harcourt.

Spiller, Pablo T., and Carlo G. Cardilli. 1997. The Frontier of Telecommunications Deregulation. *Journal of Economic Perspectives* 11:127–138.

Spohn, Suzanne Giannini. 1996. The Making of Environmental Policy Decisions. In Frederick B. Rudolph and Larry V. McIntire, eds., *Biotechnology*. Washington, D.C.: Joseph Henry Press.

Springboard Enterprises. 2000. About Us. <http://www.springboard2000.org/p/l1.asp?PID=2andSID=2>.

State Science and Technology Institute. 1998. *Survey of State Research and Development Expenditures*. Westerville, OH: SSTI.

Stein, T. 1997. Innovative Late Entrants Outsell Pioneers. *Journal of Marketing* 35:54–81.

Stephan, Paula. 1996. The Economics of Science. *Journal of Economic Literature* 34:1199–1235.

Stern, Nancy. 1981. *From ENIAC to UNIVAC*. Bedford, MA: Digital Press.

Stern, Scott. 1995. Incentives and Focus in University and Industrial Research. In Nathan Rosenberg, Annetine C. Gelijns, and Holly Dawkins, eds., *Sources of Medical Technology*. Washington, D.C.: National Academy Press.

Stern, Scott, Michael E. Porter, and Jeffrey L. Furman. 2000. The Determinants of National Innovative Capacity. Working Paper #W7876. Cambridge, MA: National Bureau of Economic Research.

Sternberg, R. 1996. Technology Policies and the Growth of Regions. *Small Business Economics* 82:75–86.

Sternberg, Robert. 1999. *Handbook of Creativity*. New York: Cambridge University Press.

Stough, Roger R., Kingsley E. Haynes, and Harrison S. Campbell, Jr. 1998. Small Business Entrepreneurship in the High Technology Services Sector. *Small Business Economics* 10:61–74.

Stout, Hilary. 1997. This Investment Fund Pries Loose Some Cash for Female-Run Firms. *Wall Street Journal* November 28, B1.

Swann, Peter G. M., Martha Prevezer, and David Stout. 1998. *The Dynamics of Industrial Clustering*. Oxford, U.K.: Oxford University Press.

Swanson, Robert. 1986. Entrepreneurship and Innovation. In Ralph Landau and Nathan Rosenberg, eds., *The Positive Sum Strategy*. Washington, D.C.: National Academy Press.

Tapscott, D. 1995. *The Digital Economy: Promise and Peril in the Age of Networked Intelligence*. New York: McGraw-Hill.

Thompson Financial Services Data. 1999. Venture Investments Reach a Record. Available at: http://nvca.org/90299nr.html

Thompson, Wilbur. 1965. *A Preface to Urban Economics*. Baltimore: Johns Hopkins University Press.

Thornton, Patricia H. 1999. The Sociology of Entrepreneurship. *Annual Review of Sociology* 25:19–46.

Thursby, J., and M. Thursby. 2000a. Industry Perspectives on Licensing University Technologies: Sources and Problems. *The Journal of the Association of University Technology Managers* 12:9–23.

Thursby, J., and M. Thursby. 2000b. Who is Selling the Ivory Tower? Working Paper #W7718. Cambridge, MA: National Bureau of Economic Research.

Timmons, Jeffry A. 1998. America's Entrepreneurial Revolution. Unpublished working paper. Waltham, MA: Babson College.

Timmons, J. A., and W. D. Bygrave. 1997. Venture Capital: Reflections and Projections. In D. L. Sexton and R. Smilor, eds., *Entrepreneurship 2000*. Chicago, IL: Upstart Publishing, 29–46.

Timmons, J. A., and H. Sapienza. 1992. Venture Capital: The Decade Ahead. In D. L. Sexton and J. Kasarda, eds., *The State of the Art of Entrepreneurship*. Boston: PWS Kent.

Timmons, Jeffry A., Leonard E. Smollen, and Alexander L. M. Dingee, Jr. 1990. *New Venture Creation*. Boston: Irwin.

Toole, Andrew A. 2000. The Impact of Public Basic Research on Industrial Innovation. SIEPR Discussion Paper, No. 00-07. Stanford: Stanford Institute for Economic Policy Research.

Toole, Andrew A. 2001. Do Venture Capital and Public Biomedical R&D Stimulate the Formation of New Biotechnology Firms? A Regional Analysis. A Report Prepared for Conference on Between Invention and Innovation, Harvard University, Kennedy School of Government, May 1.

Triendl, Robert. 1999. France Acts to Spur Tech Entrepreneurship. *Research Technology Management*, March/April, 5–7.

Tufts Center for the Study of Drug Development. 2001. Press Packet. Available at: www.tufts.edu/med/csdd/.

Tushman, M. L., and C. A. O'Reilly, III. 1997. *Winning Through Innovation: Leading Organizational Change and Renewal*. Boston: Harvard Business School Press.

U.S. Bureau of the Census. 1991. *Survey of Minority-Owned Business Enterprises*. Washington, D.C.: U.S. Department of Commerce.

U.S. Bureau of the Census. 1996. *Survey of Minority-Owned Business Enterprises*. Washington, D.C.: U.S. Department of Commerce.

U.S. Bureau of the Census. 2001. *Survey of Minority-Owned Business Enterprises*. Washington, D.C.: U.S. Department of Commerce.

U.S. Commission on Minority Business Development. 1992. *Final Report*. Washington, D.C.: GPO.

U.S. Comptroller General. 1973. *Limited Success of Federally Financed Minority Business in Three Cities*. Washington, D.C.: GPO.

U.S. Congress, Office of Technology Assessment. 1988. *New Developments in Biotechnology*. Washington, D.C.: GPO.

U.S. Congress, Office of Technology Assessment. 1991. *Biotechnology in a Global Economy*. Washington, D.C.: GPO.

U.S. Small Business Administration. 1970. *SBA: What It Is . . . What It Does*. Washington, D.C.: GPO.

U.S. Small Business Administration. 1992. *Women Owned Business: The New Economic Force*. Washington, D.C.: GPO.

U.S. Small Business Administration. 1998. *Women in Business*. Washington, D.C.: SBA.

U.S. Small Business Administration. 2001. *Women in Business.* Washington, D.C.: GPO.

Utterback, James M. 1994. *Mastering the Dynamics of Innovation: How Companies Can Seize Opportunities in the Face of Technological Change.* Boston: Harvard Business School Press.

Van Brunt, Jennifer. 1999. Biotechnology Spin-offs Seek New Orbits. *Signals Magazine (online)*, June 25. Available at: http://www.signalsmag.com/signalsmag.nsf/0/CF05408F18ADDA9D8825679B0052D533>.

Venables, A. J. 1996. Localization of Industry and Trade Performance. *Oxford Review of Economic Policy* 12:52–60.

Vogel, Stephen K. 1996. *Freer Markets, More Rules.* Ithaca: Cornell University Press.

Von Hippel, E. 1994. Sticky Information and the Locus of Problem Solving. *Management Science* 40:429–439.

Von Mehren, Arthur, and Donald Trautman. 1965. *The Law of Multistate Problems.* Boston: Little, Brown.

Waits, Mary Jo. 2000. The Added Value of the Industry Cluster Approach to Economic Analysis, Strategy Development, and Service Delivery. *Economic Development Quarterly* 14:35–50.

Walker, Jack L., Jr. 1991. *Mobilizing Interest Groups in America: Patrons, Professions, and Social Movements.* Ann Arbor: University of Michigan Press.

Wallsten, Scott. 1998. Rethinking the Small Business Innovation Research Program. In Lewis M. Branscomb and James H. Keller, *Investing in Innovation.* Cambridge, MA: MIT Press.

Watson, Kirk. 2001. The Austin Experience. Presentation to the Kennedy School-National Commission on Entrepreneurship Conference on Entrepreneurship and Public Policy, April 10.

Weber, Steven. 2000. The Political Economy of Open Source Software. Working Paper #140. Berkeley: Berkeley Roundtable on the International Economy.

Weitzman, Martin L. 1998. Recombinant Growth. *Quarterly Journal of Economics* 113: 331–360.

Welbourne, T., and L. Cyr. 1999. The Human Resource Executive Effect in Initial Public Offering Firms. *Academy of Management Journal* 39:891–919.

Wells, Matthew G. 2001. Internet Business Method Patent Policy, 87 *Va. L. Rev.* 729.

Wessner, C., ed. 2000. *The Small Business Innovation Research Program.* Washington, D.C.: National Academy Press.

West, Robert, and Michael Ivie. 2001. A Hard Year at the Office. *Telephony*, June 4, 252–258.

White, M. A., S. Blaisdell, and M. Anderson-Rowland. 2000. Women in Engineering Scholars Programs. Available at: <http://www.foundationcoalition.org/home/keycomponents/minorities.html>.

Whyte, William H. 1960. *The Organization Man*. Hammondsworth, Middlesex, U.K.: Penguin.

Wildes, Karl, and Nilo Lindgren. 1985. *A Century of Electrical Engineering and Computer Science at MIT, 1882–1982*. Cambridge, MA: MIT Press.

Williamson, Oliver E. 1968. Economies as an Antitrust Defense. *American Economic Review* 58:18–36.

Women in Business. 2001. Washington, D.C.: GPO.

Wong, Andrew. 2002. Angel Finance: The Other Venture Capital. Unpublished manuscript. Chicago: University of Chicago, Graduate School of Business.

Wright, Gavin. 1999. Can a Nation Learn? In Naomi Lamoreaux et al., eds., *Learning by Doing in Markets, Firms, and Countries*. Chicago: University of Chicago Press.

Young, Robert. 1999. Giving It Away. In Chris DiBona, Sam Ockman, and Mark Stone, eds., *Open Sources*. Cambridge, MA: O'Reilly.

Zacharakis, Andrew, Paul D. Reynolds, and William D. Bygrave. 1999. *National Entrepreneurship Assessment: United States of America, 1999 Executive Report*. Washington, D.C.: National Commission on Entrepreneurship.

Zachary, G. Pascal. 2000. *The Global Me, New Cosmopolitans and the Competitive Edge: Picking Globalism's Winners and Losers*. New York: Public Affairs.

Zacks, Rebecca. 2000. The TR University Research Scorecard. *Technology Review*, July–August.

Zeckhauser, Richard. 1996. The Challenge Of Contracting For Technological Information. *Proceedings of the National Academy of Sciences* 93:12743–12748.

Zimbalist, Andrew. 1992. *Baseball and Billions: A Probing Look Inside the Big Business of Our National Pastime*. New York: Basic Books.

Zimbalist, Andrew, and Roger Noll. 1997. *Sports, Jobs, and Taxes: The Economic Impact of Sports Teams and Stadiums*. Washington, D.C.: Brookings Institution Press.

Zucker, L. G., and M. R. Darby. 1996. Star Scientists and Institutional Transformation. *Proceedings of the National Academy of Science* 93:12709–12716.

Zucker, Lynne G., and Michael R. Darby. 1997. The Economist's Case for Biomedical Research. In Claude E. Barfield and Bruce L. R. Smith, eds., *The Future of Biomedical Research*. Washington, D.C.: American Enterprise Institute and The Brookings Institution.

Zucker, L. G., M. R. Darby, and J. Armstrong. 1998. Geographically Localized Knowledge: Spillovers or Markets? *Economic Inquiry* 36: 65–86.

Zucker, L. G., M. R. Darby, and M. B. Brewer. 1998. Intellectual Human Capital and the Birth of U.S. Biotechnology Enterprises. *American Economic Review* 87:290–306.

Zweiger, Gary. 2001. *Transducing the Genome*. New York: McGraw-Hill.

Index

Lightning Source UK Ltd.
Milton Keynes UK
18 May 2010

154378UK00002B/10/P